P9-CDO-120

Athenæum Press Series

A BOOK OF SEVENTEENTH CENTURY LYRICS

SELECTED AND EDITED WITH AN INTRODUCTION

BY

FELIX E. SCHELLING

PROFESSOR OF ENGLISH LITERATURE IN THE UNIVERSITY OF PENNSYLVANIA

BOSTON, U.S.A.
GINN & COMPANY, PUBLISHERS
The Athenæum Press
1899

UNIVERSITY CLUB
OF PHILADELPHIA

PREFACE.

THIS book is made up of English lyrics which fall between the years 1625 and 1700. The first quarter of the seventeenth century is here unrepresented, because the lyrical poetry, like most other kinds of literature of that period, was produced under impulses and maintained by traditions almost wholly Elizabethan. The method pursued in the selection and arrangement of the poems constituting this book is much that of the editor's *Elizabethan Lyrics*. Some poems have been retained, the exclusion of which a standard of the highest literary and poetic worth might demand. This is justified by a recognition of the fact that a book such as this must be, to a certain extent, historically representative. The same requirement has prompted a rigid adherence to chronological order in the arrangement of material and to the rule that no poem shall appear except in its completeness and in that form in which it may reasonably be supposed to have had its author's maturest revision. The term *lyric* has necessarily been interpreted with some liberality in the consideration of a period which tended, towards its close, to the conscious exercise of artifice and wit in poetry rather than to the spontaneous expression of emotion. If Mr. Henley's recent enunciation of the essential antithesis between the lyric and the epigram is to be accepted in its rigor, many of the poems of this collection must fall under his ban.[1] And

[1] See the Introduction to Mr. Henley's collection of *English Lyrics*.

yet much might be said — were this the place for it — of the lyrical quality which frequently accompanies even the cynical gallantry and coxcombry of Suckling, Sedley, and Rochester. If poems such as many of theirs and of Dryden's be excluded from the category of the lyric on the score of artificiality or insincerity, they must assuredly be restored to their place for the power of music in them.

The poems in this book have been selected, not only from the works of the individual poets represented, but from contemporary poetical miscellanies and from the incidental lyrical verse contained in dramas, romances, and other works of the time. Care has been taken to make the text as correct as possible by a collation with authoritative sources; and, wherever necessary, the sources of preferred readings will be found mentioned in the Notes. In the Introduction an attempt has been made to trace the course of English lyrical poetry during the period, to explain its relations to the previous age, and to trace the influences which determined its development and its final change of character. It is hoped that the Notes and Indexes may furnish the reader with such help as he may reasonably demand, and encourage the student to a deeper study of a rich and interesting period in one of its most distinctive forms of artistic expression.

In conclusion, I wish to record my recognition of a few amongst many favors. My acknowledgments are due here, as ever, to Dr. Horace Howard Furness for the loan of books and for much kind encouragement; to Dr. Clarence G. Child, especially amongst my colleagues, for valuable suggestions and many services; and above all to Professor Kittredge, one of the general editors of this series, whose wide learning and untiring care have been generously bestowed to better this book.

FELIX E. SCHELLING.

JUNE 16, 1899.

CONTENTS.

INTRODUCTION.

THE ENGLISH LYRIC OF THE SEVENTEENTH CENTURY.[1]

I.

IN the Introduction to *A Book of Elizabethan Lyrics* I have said that "not the least merit of Elizabethan literature, defining both words strictly, is its soundness and its health; its very lapses from decorum are those of childhood, and its extravagances those of youth and heated blood, both as far as possible removed from the cold cynicism, the doubt of man and God, that crept into England in the train of King James, and came in time to chill and benumb the pulses of the nation."[2]

This statement I believe to be strictly and literally true, though it may here need some explanation. There was both crime and wickedness in Elizabeth's day; there was virtue and nobility of life in the days of James. But a cleavage between art and morals had come about early in the seventeenth century, if indeed not before; the Renaissance, now somewhat spent and losing in freshness and virility, threw off its former alliance with the rude but wholesome ethical spirit which animated the drama during the lifetime of

[1] The reader is referred to the earlier paragraphs of the Introduction to the editor's *A Book of Elizabethan Lyrics* for a general discussion of the nature and limitations of the term *lyric*.

[2] p. xxxvii.

Shakespeare, and contracted from a broad humanitarian love of art as an imitation of the whole range of human action and emotion into the narrower, if choicer, spirit of the dilettante, whose taste in trifles is perfect, whose joy is not a little in the skill and cleverness of the artist, whose range for art, in a word, is contracted within the limits of good society. On the other hand, the moral aspect of the world was not lost, although it seemed all but lost to literature for a time. Any statement that the complex of moral, religious, and political agencies which is loosely called Puritanism was an unmixed evil to literature is wide of the truth. The marvellously rich devotional poetry of the period, a poetry which knew no sect and existed the common possession of Romanist, Churchman, and Dissenter, is alone a sufficient refutation of such an opinion. Still that spirit which translated the joys of the world into vanities and denounced the most innocent show of human emotion as the lust of the flesh and the temptation of the devil withdrew itself apart and lived alone in later forms of Puritanism, which became stern and austere, unmollified by grace and unsweetened with charity.

Nothing could better illustrate the essential relation which exists in art between truth and that typical presentation of nature which we somewhat inaccurately call beauty, than the history of English poetry in the seventeenth century, especially the history of the lyric, always that form of poetry most sensitive to the subtler influences of an age. Moreover, whatever fastidious literary taste may prefer, the student of literature must beware of generalizations formed on anything short of a consideration of all the literary phenomena at hand. Perversions of art have their lesson for the historian of literature, and must be considered if the picture is to be true. Thus we must recognize, not only the rhetorical and "metaphysical" excesses of lesser and later Donnians, but the extraordinary stripping off of the gauds and ornaments of poetic diction which marks the work of Wither when he leaves the praises of *Fair Virtue* to sing hymns of diviner praise. No less must we take into account that one of the most remarkable and artistically perfect poems of Carew is unquotable to-day; whilst it was not a mere following of the bad example which his master, Jonson, had set him in translating some of the more objectionable epigrams of Martial, which has given us, in Herrick, a garden of the *Hesperides* foul in places with the filth of the kennel. These things are not wholly to be laid to the score of coarse or unrestrained manners. The root of the matter is in this separation of the ethical from the æsthetic principle, a separation which produced in the one case the moral, but for the most part unillumined, verses of Quarles and Wither, and, in the other (with much that was an aberration from both ethical and æsthetic ideals), the perfect Hedonistic lyrics of Carew and Herrick, which exist for their beauty and for their beauty alone.

To consider the cult of beauty as a new thing in the poetry of any period would be as absurd as to assume, by the extension of a doctrine attributed by Walter Bagehot to Ulrici, a concealed and deadly moral purpose for each and every poem of the earlier age.[1] But if we will turn to the poetry of Spenser, Jonson, Donne, and Shakespeare we shall find it informed with an element of truth, whether half concealed in allegory, didactically paraded, intellectually subtilized, or set forth in an unerring justness of conception as to the dramatic relations of men to men. This we do not find in nearly an equal degree in the poetry of the succeeding age, and the ideals of such a poet as Carew — to take the most successful of his class — become much the same as those of the school which in our own day has given rise to the phrase "art for art's sake," a school accompanying

[1] *Shakespeare, Literary Studies*, I, 169.

whose æsthetic posturings we sooner or later behold the cynical leer of satire. Take the following:

> If when the sun at noon displays
> His brighter rays,
> Thou but appear,
> He then, all pale with shame and fear,
> Quencheth his light,
> Hides his dark brow, flies from thy sight
> And grows more dim
> Compared to thee than stars to him.
> If thou but show thy face again
> When darkness doth at midnight reign,
> The darkness flies, and light is hurled
> Round about the silent world:
> So as alike thou driv'st away
> Both light and darkness, night and day.[1]

This is beautiful and fanciful poetry. It is hyperbolic to a degree, so much so that we feel it to be no more than a figure of gallantry, the charming and perfectly expressed compliment of a courtly gentleman to a high-born and radiant beauty. In a poem of this kind we are not concerned with the truth; indeed the truth might perhaps spoil the effect. There is nothing new in the idea, but the artist has daintily set it like a gem in the filigree of a carefully considered comparison. Romeo, under the quickening influence of a new and all-consuming passion, forged the same thought into a pregnant metaphor:

> What light through yonder window breaks?
> It is the east, and Juliet is the sun!
> Arise, fair sun, and kill the envious moon,
> Who is already sick and pale with grief,
> That thou her maid art far more fair than she.[2]

[1] *Poems of Thomas Carew*, reprint of ed. 1640, Edinburgh, 1824, p. 8.
[2] ii. 2. 2.

The hyperbole of Romeo is justified by the overwrought emotion of the moment; it stirs in the hearer a sympathy with the lover's passion. The hyperbole of Carew is no less justified, for it, too, arrives at its purpose, which is no more than to amuse. There is about it, from its very extravagance, a suspicion of delicate raillery, which becomes certain when the poet leaves us at the end with a charming paradox. She would have been but an unsophisticated maiden at court who could have taken such a fine compliment from the king's cupbearer to figure forth anything more than "How pretty you 're looking this morning, my dear!"

"The artifice and machinery of rhetoric," says De Quincey, "furnishes in its degree as legitimate a basis for intellectual pleasure as any other; that the pleasure is of an inferior order, can no more attaint the idea or model of the composition, than it can impeach the excellence of an epigram that it is not a tragedy. Every species of composition is to be tried by its own laws."[1] The much-vaunted test of comparison, by which Byron set beside Keats or Shelley appears tawdry or uninspired, is often preposterously misleading. There are reds that "kill" each other, though each may be beautiful apart; the mood in which to read Horace may not be precisely the mood for Catullus. In the seventeenth century lyric and its overflow into the occasional verse of the day we have neither the universality of Shakespeare, the scope and majesty of Milton, nor the consummate constructive, if conventionalized, art of Dryden and Pope; and yet there are some of us who feel that we could no more spare the dainty grace and beauty of *Corinna's Going A-Maying* than we could endure to lose a book of *Paradise Lost.* To critics of the nature of William Hazlitt, in those unlucid intervals in which his prejudices stood all on end, such poets as Carew or Suckling are "delicate court triflers" and noth-

[1] *Rhetoric, Historical Essays*, II, 229.

ing more; to those who love the art of an intaglio or the delicate curves of a Grecian urn, and can admire either without stricture that it is not the Capitoline Jupiter, the best of the poetry of the reign of Charles I seems to imply no decaying school, but a height of lyric excellence combined with an exquisite workmanship which only the greatest poets of our day or of Elizabeth's have surpassed.

In its general characteristics the poetry of the seventeenth century, extending onward from the accession of Charles I, is intensive rather than expansive, fanciful rather than imaginative, and increasingly restrictive in its range and appeal, until it comes at length to be the utterance of a single class of society.

The period in its earlier years was too close to that of Elizabeth and James not to feel the strong pulse and enthusiastic love of beauty which was theirs, and the great political events that made the seventeenth one of the most momentous centuries in the history of England kept men from falling too rapidly into the conventionalized conception of literature and life which came to prevail in the next century. It is precisely as we find a poet rising above these general qualities of narrow intensiveness, fantasticality of thought and expression, and class prejudice, that we recognize in him the special qualities that make him great. The æsthetic Milton, with the rich blood of the Renaissance tingling in his veins, bursts forth in the fine *Ode on the Morning of Christ's Nativity* and in the great poetry which followed it. In his later poetical period too, it is his lofty artistic purpose and his ethical nobility which lift Milton out of his own time and convert him into a world poet, despite a certain hardness of spirit which bitter partizanship had fostered and which could not but grow out of the warring elements of his age in a nature so grave and stern. Thus again, a genuine love of nature unites such diverse names as those of Vaughan, Marvell, and Cotton, the last especially delighting in the sensuous enjoyment of pleasant sight and soothing sound. In Marvell is added to an artistic touch a moral rectitude that at once dignifies his poetry and gives it a distinguished place in literature; whilst Vaughan, added to a religious fervor which he shares with Herbert and Crashaw, but in differing mode, displays, in his tenderness for natural objects, a spiritual contemplativeness which every now and then flashes a revealing light upon the relation of man to the universe. Herrick, in his humaneness, in his artless delight in those small things which go so far to make up our daily life, Carew, in the sincerity of his workmanship and in his artistic propriety, rise above the temporary conventions of a single age, and become, each in his own way, poets fraught with a message to following times.

II.

That the poets of the reigns of James and Charles I wrote under the combined influences of Ben Jonson and Donne, and that the older influence of Spenser continued to animate poet after poet, has been repeated again and again, and may be accepted as substantially true. It seems well, under the circumstances, briefly to consider wherein these influences really consisted, less in their abstract principles than in the manner in which the ideals of each great poet manifested themselves in his work, and especially in their subsequent effects on his followers. What may be called the manner of Spenser (i.e., Spenser's way of imitating and interpreting nature artistically by means of poetic expression) may be summarized as consisting of a sensuous love of beauty combined with a power of elaborated pictorial representation, a use of classical imagery for decorative effect, a fondness for melody, a flowing sweetness, naturalness and continuousness of diction amounting to diffuseness at times, the diffuseness of a fragrant, beautiful, flowering vine. We may say of the poets that employ this manner that they are worshippers of beauty rather than students of beauty's laws; ornate in their expression of the type, dwelling on detail in thought and image lovingly elaborated and sweetly prolonged. To such artists it is no matter if a play have five acts or twenty-five, if an epic ever come to an end, or if consistency of parts exist; rapt in the joy of gentle onward motion, in the elevation of pure poetic thought, even the subject ceases to be of much import, if it but furnish the channel in which the bright, limpid liquid continues musically to flow.

Besides his pastorals, Drayton Spenserized the enormous *Polyolbion*. The Fletchers followed with subjects theological and anatomical also allegorized after the manner of Spenser. But the poetry of none of these need concern us here: not even the beautiful later pastorals of Wither and Browne. For, Drayton aside, the last two poets are the only followers of Spenser who have achieved the unity and repression of a successful lyric; and by the accession of King Charles, Browne had ceased to write, and Wither had already straggled off into his innumerable devotional pamphlets, verse and prose, in which were much fibre and many tendrils, but little bloom. In the period with which this book is concerned the direct influence of Spenser is chiefly to be found in the earlier poetry of Milton, which, despite its remarkable originality and the traces of other influences than this, exhibits in the main the distinctive "notes" of Spenserianism, restrained by a chaster taste and by a spirit profoundly imbued with the classics.

As Milton is chief amongst the poets included in this book, it cannot be wide of our purpose to stop in our discussion to consider these Spenserian "notes" in his earlier poetry. Take the following;

> *Genius.* Stay, gentle swains, for, though in this disguise,
> I see bright honor sparkle through your eyes;
> Of famous Arcady ye are, and sprung
> Of that renownèd flood, so often sung,
> Divine Alpheus, who, by secret sluice,
> Stole under seas to meet his Arethuse;
> And ye, the breathing roses of the wood,
> Fair silver-buskined Nymphs, as great and good.
> I know this quest of yours and free intent
> Was all in honor and devotion meant
> To the great mistress of yon princely shrine,
> Whom with low reverence I adore as mine,
> And with all helpful service will comply
> To further this night's glad solemnity,
> And lead ye where ye may more near behold
> What shallow-searching Fame hath left untold;
> Which I full oft, amidst these shades alone,
> Have sat to wonder at, and gaze upon.

This is early work of Milton and exhibits nearly every one of the "notes" mentioned above, — sweetness, melody, naturalness, continuousness in metre and sense, personification: "What shallow-searching Fame hath left untold"; classical allusion: Arcady, Alpheus, Arethusa, "Fair silver-buskined Nymphs." A use of nature for decorative effect pervades the whole passage. For pictorial vividness, in which however Milton never surpassed his master, we must look to other passages. A more striking example of some of these qualities of Milton's earlier poetry will be found in the famous song from *Comus*, *Sabrina fair* (p. 38, below, vv. 9–32), wherein we have almost a complete list of the ancient deities of the sea from "great Oceanus" to "fair Ligea's golden comb." Some of the allusions of this song (e.g., "the Carpathian wizard's hook")[1] we may suspect were not altogether luminous to the casual reader of Milton's own day, despite his "greater

[1] See note on this passage, p. 243, below.

wont" in the classics. Milton's evident delight in passages such as this is made up of two elements: first, a sensuous love of musical sound, the mingled charm of sonorous classical words and their unusual effect in the contrast of their English setting; and, secondly, the scholar's satisfaction — pedantic in a lesser man — in lavishing his learning on his verse: for Milton possessed to the full the scholar's consciousness in the practice of his art. In view of the rhetorical finish of Milton's poetry, and the high sense of constructiveness which informs his work in even its apparently most unpremeditated flights, especially in view of the carefully wrought and subtly varied cadences of his blank verse, I do not feel certain that the customary classification of Milton with the poets of the past age, rather than with his actual contemporaries, is a classification wholly to be justified.

If now we turn to the poetry of Ben Jonson, more especially to his lyrical verse, the first thing that we note is a sense of form, not merely in detail and transition like the "links . . . bright and even" of *The Faery Queen*, but a sense of the entire poem in its relation to its parts. This sense involves brevity and condensity of expression, a feeling on the part of the poet that the effect may be spoiled by a word too much — a feeling which no true Spenserian ever knew. There is about this poetry a sense of finish rather than of elaboration; it is less continuous than complete; more concentrated, less diffuse; chaste rather than florid; controlled, and yet not always less spontaneous; reserved, and yet not always less natural. There are other things to note in the Jonsonian manner. It retained classical allusion less for the sake of embellishment than as an atmosphere — to borrow a term from the nomenclature of art. Its drafts upon ancient mythology become allusive, and the effects produced by Horace, Catullus, or Anacreon are essayed in reproduction under

English conditions. Not less eager in the pursuit of beauty than the Spenserian, the manner of Jonson seeks to realize her perfections by means of constructive excellence, not by entranced passion. It concerns itself with choiceness in diction, selectiveness in style, with the repression of wandering ideas and loosely conceived figures — in a word, the manner of Jonson involves classicality.

Into the nature of the poetry of Donne I need not enter at length here. It is sufficient for our purposes to remember that the tokens of the presence of Donne consist in an excessive subjectivity that involves at times all but a total oblivion to the forms of the outward, visible world; a disregard of the tried and conventional imagery and classical reference of the day, and the substitution for it of images of abstraction derived from contemporary philosophy and science; an habitual transmutation of emotion into terms of the intellect; and an analytic presentation and handling of theme, involving great rhetorical, and at times dialectic skill. To these qualities must be added a successful inventive ingenuity in the device of metrical effects, which despised tradition; and, most important of all, a power in dealing with the abstract relations of things which raises Donne, in his possession of the rare quality, poetic insight, at times to a poet of the first order.

Thus we find Spenser and Jonson standing as exponents, respectively, of the expansive or romantic movement and the repressive or classical spirit. In a different line of distinction Donne is equally in contrast with Spenser, as the intensive or subjective artist. Both are romanticists, in that each seeks to produce the effect demanded of art by means of an appeal to the sense of novelty; but Spenser's romanticism is that of selection, which chooses from the outer world the fitting and the pleasing and constructs it into a permanent artistic joy; Donne's is the romanticism of insight, which, looking inward, descries the subtle relations of things and transfigures them with a sudden and unexpected flood of light. Between Jonson and Donne there is the kinship of intellectuality; between Spenser and Donne the kinship of romanticism; between Spenser and Jonson the kinship of the poet's joy in beauty. Spenser is the most objective, and therefore allegorical and at times mystical; Jonson is the most artistic, and therefore the most logical; Donne is the most subjective and the most spiritual.

III.

In the year 1625 many traces of the poetry of the last century remained, especially in the lyric. The impetus which had been given by Lyly and Shakespeare to the writing of lyrical verse to be set to music in the incidental songs of the drama continued in the dramatists Dekker, Fletcher, Massinger, and Jonson himself. All carried on their own earlier practice, Ford and Shirley following. These last two poets have left lyrics scarcely less beautiful than the best of the earlier age; whilst not a few of the minor playwrights, Thomas May, Thomas Goffe, Richard Brome, Thomas Randolph, even Aurelian Townsend, have reached distinction in individual instances. The popularity of song books continued throughout the century, but we have no work in this field approaching the poetry of Campion. The general character of collections such as his, which offered original words with original music, was maintained in the various works of Wilson, Henry and William Lawes, Lanier, Playford, D'Urfey, and many others. The poetical miscellany held its popularity in collections of very mixed quality, from sacred or secular lyrical poetry to the satirical broadside or book of jests and coarse epigrams. Some of these books contain gleanings from the best poets of the day, but the general quality of the lyrical poetry therein is far inferior to similar productions in the preceding reigns, as the popular taste had turned from sentiment and poetry to the wit and ribaldry of the tavern.[1]

At the accession of Charles, Ben Jonson had twelve years yet to live; and, although his best work was now done, his position as the great literary dictator, with the added sanction of court patronage, produced a powerful effect upon the imaginations of scholarly and courtly young men. Poets and dramatists spoke of themselves as "sons of Ben," delighting in his society while he lived, and honoring his memory when he died. Six months after his death a volume appeared, entitled *Jonsonus Virbius*, in which peers and commons, bishops and laymen united to celebrate in verses English, Latin, and Greek, the greatness of the deceased laureate, and to express the esteem and veneration in which they held him as a man.[2] English literature knows no other such tribute; it is above many monuments. Let us glance at the contributors to *Jonsonus Virbius*, for among them are some of the most characteristic, if not the greatest, of the "sons of Ben." First is the amiable and accomplished Lucius Carey, Lord Falkland, in bravery, courtesy, loyalty, all but literature — although a graceful poet — the Sidney of his age; next, the genial and kindly Henry King, later Bishop of Chichester, author of the best lines of the volume; Thomas May, Shak-

[1] The quantity of this "literature" is very great, and much of it has little but an historical and social value. One of the most characteristic collections is *Wit's Recreations*, first published in 1641, and going through nearly a dozen editions before the close of the century. Other miscellanies were *Wit Restored*, *Wit and Drollery*, *The Loyal Garland*, *The Muses' Recreation*. The song books of the period begin with Hilton's *Book of Airs*, 1627, and extend through innumerable songs, airs, and dialogues to Dr. Purcell's *Collection of Airs*, 1697.

[2] *Jonsonus Virbius* is reprinted in the collected editions of Jonson by Whalley, Gifford, and Cunningham.

erley Marmion, Jasper Mayne, and William Cartwright, all dramatists of repute, some of them writing into Restoration times, the last a consummate master of panegyric and a lyric and elegiac poet after the manner of his other master, Donne. James Howell, the author of the charming *Epistolae Ho-Elianae*, long intimate with Jonson, contributes a few lines; as do John Clieveland, the trenchant loyalist satirist; Sir John Beaumont, cousin of the dramatist, a poet chiefly by kinship; Habington, author of *Castara;* and Buckhurst, descendant of the author of *Gorboduc*, and father of Charles Sackville, Earl of Dorset, the courtly poet of the next reign. John Ford, the great dramatist, writes as an equal, not as a "son"; and last comes Edmund Waller, whose contact with earlier poetry is generally forgotten in the fact that he is the historical link between the lyric of Jonson and that of the Restoration. Shirley, the last illustrious name of the old drama, does not appear; although a friend of Ford, he was probably without the charmed circle. Neither Herrick nor Carew contribute, though the former, certainly a veritable "son," as several of his poems attest, was now a recluse in "loathèd Devonshire"; whilst Carew, an older man, whose occasional verses show close intimacy with Jonson, was to survive but two years.[1]

If now we look into the contents of a volume of one of these "sons of Ben," we shall find that he has followed his master alike in the diversity and in the limitations of his art. He may give a greater preponderance to one species of verse, but he tries all — drama, the poetical epistle, epigram, lyric song and ode, commendatory verse, prologue and epilogue. The sonnets, pastorals, and madrigals of the past age have been superseded, despite the fact that Habington

[1] Cf. Herrick's two epigrams on Jonson, his *Prayer* to him, and his *Ode;* ed. Grosart, II, 78, 79, 185; III, 11. See also Carew's *To Ben Jonson*, ed. Hazlitt, p. 84.

may throw his verses into a kind of irregular sequence and limit some of his poems to fourteen lines, and although Herrick may invent a new and dainty pastoral mode of his own by a fresh return to nature.[1] It is notable that few of these writers of the days of Charles are men of both tongues like Greene, Dekker, or Heywood, who wrote verse and prose, and even mingled them at times in one work. Moreover, not one of these writers was a literary man in the sense which Jonson exemplified, unless we except Howell and Davenant. Falkland, Habington, Carew, Randolph, and Waller were courtiers; Cartwright, Herrick, and King clergymen; Herbert was successively both. Most of those who survived to the civil wars sided with the king or fought for him; not a few fell in his cause.

But if these writers are the professed "sons of Ben" and inherited his love of form, his fondness for learning well displayed, and at times his didacticism and heavy satirical hand, they inherited also, each after his capacity, many of the idiosyncrasies of Donne, their other master; and the idiosyncrasies of Donne are precisely those which are the most dangerous in the hands of mediocrity. It was thus that Donne's extraordinary originality in the invention and application of figure — a power which, it is frankly to be confessed, he often used tastelessly and irresponsibly — became the source of Cartwright's lapses from good taste, Crashaw's confusion, and Cowley's irregularity of thought, and the all but universal search after 'conceit' and far-fetched imagery. Thus it was that Donne's lordly contempt for mere form came to be made accountable for the slovenly and clumsy carelessness of metre and sense which mars the work of such poets as Suckling and makes the verse of Lovelace, except for some half-dozen lyrics, unreadable.

In the contemplation of such aberrations as these, and in

[1] Cf. *Corinna's Going A-Maying*, below, p. 10.

the midst of a complete triumph of principles diametrically opposed to the romantic ideals which had begot this freedom and excess, it was to be expected that the critics of the next century should do injustice to the past. Severe and condemnatory, flippantly patronizing or weakly apologetic — such is the attitude of these and even of later critics as to Donne and his imitators. Rarely has criticism passed beyond the lines so carefully and so perversely drawn by Dr. Samuel Johnson in his famous passage on the "metaphysical poets" in his life of Cowley. As this subject is of prime importance in any discussion of the poetry of the seventeenth century, no apology need be offered for quoting once more the familiar words of Dr. Johnson.

"The metaphysical poets were men of learning, and to show their learning was their whole endeavor: but, unluckily resolving to show it in rhyme, instead of writing poetry they only wrote verses, and very often such verses as stood the trial of the finger better than of the ear; for the modulation was so imperfect that they were only found to be verses by counting the syllables.

"If the father of criticism has rightly denominated poetry τέχνη μιμητικὴ, an imitative art, these writers will, without great wrong, lose their right to the name of poets; for they cannot be said to have imitated anything: they neither copied nature nor life; neither painted the forms of matter nor represented the operations of the intellect.

"Those however who deny them to be poets, allow them to be wits. Dryden confesses of himself and his contemporaries, that they fall below Donne in wit; but maintains, that they surpass him in poetry."[1]

This famous deliverance is a glaring instance of that species of criticism which is worked up out of the critical dicta of others, a mystery not wholly confined to Dr. Johnson

[1] *Lives of the English Poets*, *Cowley*, ed. Tauchnitz, I, 11.

nor to his age. If now we turn to Dryden's *Discourse concerning the Original and Progress of Satire*,[1] we shall find the following passage addressed to the Earl of Dorset and concerned mainly with a eulogy of the poetry of that noble author.

"There is more salt in all your verses, than I have seen in any of the moderns, or even of the ancients; but you have been sparing of the gall, by which means you have pleased all readers, and offended none. Donne alone, of all our countrymen, had your talent; but was not happy enough to arrive at your versification; and were he translated into numbers, and English, he would yet be wanting in the dignity of expression. . . . You equal Donne in the variety, multiplicity, and choice of thoughts; you excel him in the manner and the words. I read you both with the same admiration, but not with the same delight. He affects the *metaphysics*, not only in his satires, but in his amourous verses; and perplexes the minds of the fair sex with nice speculations of philosophy, when he should engage their hearts and entertain them with the softness of love. In this (if I may be pardoned for so bold a truth) Mr. Cowley has copied him to a fault."[2]

Several things are to be remarked on this passage: (1) that Donne is only mentioned incidentally, the main purpose being the encomium upon the satire of the noble and now forgotten lord; (2) that the discussion is confined to satire, although a side reference is made to Donne's amorous verse, and Cowley is charged with imitating these products of Donne; (3) that Donne is praised for "variety, multiplicity, and choiceness of thought"; (4) that he is said to be "wanting in dignity of expression" and "in manner and

[1] This essay was originally prefixed to the translation of Juvenal (ed. Scott-Saintsbury, XII, 1–123). See also Professor Hales' introductory note to Donne in Ward's *English Poets*, I, 558. [2] *Ibid.*, p. 6.

words"; (5) that he needs translation "into numbers and English"; and (6) that he affects the *metaphysics* in his amorous verse, where nature only should reign. Here it was then that Dr. Johnson obtained the suggestion of linking the names of Donne and Cowley and the specific dictum which he extended to all their work; here it was that he found the word "metaphysical," which he liberally enlarged by inference to include most of the poets of the reigns of James I and his son who differed in manner from Dryden and Waller. From the same passage Pope and Parnell derived the idea of translating "into numbers and English" the satires of Donne; and the only thing which the critics of the next age omitted was the "variety, multiplicity, and choice of thoughts," which even the master of the rival school, who had read though he had not studied Donne, could not deny him. This is not the place in which to follow subsequent criticism of "the metaphysical poets." It is based almost wholly on Dr. Johnson's dictum, and involves the same sweeping generalizations of undoubtedly salient defects into typical qualities and the same want of a reference of these defects to their real sources.[1]

Other terms have been used to express the obliquity of thought — if I may so employ the word — which is peculiar to Donne and his school. Such is the adjective 'fantastic,' from the excessive play of images of the fancy which these poets permit themselves. This is less happy than Dryden's 'metaphysical,' to which a real value attaches in that it singles out the unquestioned fondness of these writers for 'conceits' drawn from the sciences and from speculative

[1] In another place (the Dedication to *Eleonora*, ed. Scott-Saintsbury, XI, 123) Dryden designated Donne "the greatest wit, though not the best poet of our nation." Here again Johnson found a cue for his famous discussion of wit, which follows the last paragraph of the passage quoted above.

philosophy. De Quincey proposed the word 'rhetorical,' with a characteristic refinement restricting its meaning to the sense in which "rhetoric lays the principal stress on the management of thoughts and only a secondary one upon the ornaments of style."[1] This has the merit of recognizing the dialectical address and the constructive design and ingenuity which were Donne's and Carew's, though by no means equally Cowley's. When all has been said, we must recognize that none of these terms fully explains the complex conditions of the lyric of this age.

Special characteristics aside, there is no more distinctive mark of the poetry of this age than the all but universal practice of 'conceit.' By Jonson and Bacon this word was employed for the thing conceived, the thought, the image. It was likewise employed, however, in the significa-tion, more current later, of a thought far-fetched and ingen-ious rather than natural and obvious. That the 'conceit' in this latter sense was no stranger to the verse and prose of the reign of Elizabeth is attested by innumerable examples from the days of Sidney to those of Donne.[2]

Thus Gascoigne, with a more vivid consciousness of the persistence of hackneyed poetical figure than is usual amongst minor poets, declares: "If I should undertake to wryte in prayse of a gentlewoman, I would neither praise hir christal eye, nor hir cherrie lippe, etc. For these things are *trita et obvia.* But I would either find some supernatu-rall cause whereby my penne might walke in the superlative

[1] *Historical Essays*, American ed. 1856, II, 228, 229.

[2] Murray (*Dictionary*, *s.v.*) quotes Puttenham (ed. Arber, p. 20) for an early use of this word: "Others of a more fine and pleasaunt head . . . in short poemes uttered prettie merry conceits, and these men were called Epigrammatists." Sidney (according to Dr. C. G. Child) is the earliest English poet to exhibit the conceit as a distinctive feature of style.

degree, or else . . . I would . . . make a strange discourse of some intollerable passion, or finde occasion to pleade by the example of some historie, or discover my disquiet in shadows *per Allegoriam*, or use the covertest meane that I could to avoyde the uncomely customes of common writers."[1]

That this species of wit became more and more popular as the reign of James advanced is explained by the general decline from imagination to fancy which marks the trend of the whole age, and which came in time to ascribe a false dignity and importance to keenness and readiness in the discovery of accidental and even trivial similarities in things unlike. The gradations of the word 'wit' range from *ingenium*, insight, mental power, to the snap of the toy cracker denominated a pun. Wit may consist in the thought and the wisdom thereof or in the merest accident of sound or form. The genuine Caroline 'conceit' is mostly in the fibre of the thought, and, unlike the antithetical wit of the next age, is, as a rule, unaided by structural or rhetorical device. Thus Cowley says of those who carved the wooden images for the temple of Jerusalem:

> [They] carve the trunks and breathing shapes bestow,
> Giving the trees more life than when they grow[2];

and Clieveland asks, apropos of the possibility of a bee's stinging his mistress:

> What wasp would prove
> Ravaillac to my queen of love?[3]

[1] With the foreign sources of the Elizabethan and Jacobean conceit we cannot be here concerned. See on this subject the forthcoming monograph of Dr. Clarence G. Child on *The Seventeenth Century Conceit*, shortly to appear in the *Publications of the Modern Language Association of America*.

[2] *The Davideis*, ii. 528, 529.

[3] *Clievelandi Vindiciae*, ed. 1677, p. 4.

On the other hand, the balanced form of wit appears in Dryden's words of Doeg:

> A double noose thou on thy neck dost pull
> For writing treason and for writing dull.[1]

Of like nature is the diamond cross on the bosom of Pope's Belinda,

> Which Jews might kiss, and infidels adore.[2]

Even where epigrammatic point is not demanded, ideas so shape themselves:

> By music minds an equal temper know
> Nor swell too high nor sink too low.[3]

Either form of wit may flash a revealing light and rise from the range of fancy, which plays with similitudes because they are pleasing, to the domain of the imagination, which adds the sanction and dignity of truth. That form of wit which depends more on thought and less on the accident of expression is more likely to become imaginative and revealing. To deny, however, that form enters essentially into all successful art is to fall into vagary. The illustrations above are all dependent upon fancy; Cowley's is ingenious, Clieveland's forced, Dryden's and Pope's epigrammatic, Pope's last commonplace, unnecessary, and redundant. Vaughan's famed figure of the first stanza of *The World*, which can never be too often quoted, is an

[1] *Absalom and Achitophel*, Part II, 496.
[2] *Rape of the Lock*, canto ii.
[3] Pope, *Ode on Saint Cecilia's Day*.

instance of a 'conceit' dilated by its dignity to imaginative sublimity and power:

> I saw Eternity the other night
> Like a ring of pure and endless light,
>   All calm as it was bright;
> And round beneath it, Time in hours, days, years
>   Driven by the spheres,
> Like a vast shadow moved, in which the world
>   And all her train were hurled.[1]

It is an error to regard the Caroline conceit as wholly referable to Donne's irresponsible use of figure. It is neither so limited and abstract in the range of phenomena chosen for figurative illustration, so unconcerned with the recognition of the outward world, nor so completely referable to the intellectualization of emotion. Let us take a typical passage of Donne:

> But, O, alas! so long, so far
>   Our bodies why do we forbear?
> They are ours, though not we; we are
>   The intelligences, they the spheres;
> We owe them thanks, because they thus
>   Did us to us at first convey,
> Yielded their senses' force to us,
>   Nor are dross to us but alloy.
> On man heaven's influence works not so,
>   But that it first imprints the air;
> For soul into the soul may flow
>   Though it to body first repair.[2]

This passage is subtle, almost dialectic. A keen, sinuous, reasoning mind is playing with its powers. Except for the implied personification of the body regarded apart from the soul, the language is free from figure; there is no confusion

[1] See the whole poem, below, p. 145.
[2] *The Ecstasy*, ed. 1650, p. 43.

of thought. There is the distinctively Donnian employment of ideas derived from physical and speculative science: the body is the 'sphere' or superficies which includes within it the soul, a term of the old astro-philosophy; the body is not 'dross' but an 'alloy,' alchemical terms; the 'influence' of heaven is the use of that word in an astrological sense, meaning "the radiation of power from the stars in certain positions or collections affecting human actions and destinies"; and lastly, the phrase "imprints the air" involves an idea of the old philosophy, by which "sensuous perception is explained by effluxes of atoms from the things perceived whereby images are produced ('imprinted') which strike our senses." Donne subtly transfers this purely physical conception to the transference of divine influences.[1]

On the other hand, take this, the one flagging stanza of Crashaw's otherwise noble *Hymn of the Nativity*. The Virgin is spoken of, and represented with the Child, who is addressed by the poet:

> She sings thy tears asleep, and dips
>   Her kisses in thy weeping eye;
> She spreads the red leaves of thy lips,
>   That in their buds yet blushing lie.
> She 'gainst those mother diamonds tries
> The points of her young eagle's eyes.[2]

This difficult passage may perhaps be thus explained: the Virgin sings to her babe until, falling asleep, his tears cease to flow. "And dips her kisses in thy weeping eye," she kisses lightly his eyes, suffused with tears. Here the lightness of the kiss and the over-brimming fullness of the eyes suggest the hyperbole and the implied metaphor, which likens the kiss to something lightly dipped into a stream.

[1] See Ueberweg's *History of Philosophy*, I, 71.

[2] See below, p. 113.

"She spreads the red leaves of thy lips," i.e., kisses the child's lips, which lie lightly apart in infantile sleep, and which are like *rosebuds* in their color and in their childish undevelopment. "Mother diamonds" are the eyes of the Virgin, bright as diamonds and resembling those of the child. "Points" are the rays or beams of the eye, which, according to the old physics, passed, in vision, from one eye to another. Lastly, the eyes of the child are likened to those of a young eagle, and the Virgin tests them against her own as the mother eagle is supposed to test her nestling's eyes against the sun.

Leaving out the figure involved in 'points,' which is Donnian and probably wholly due to the fashion set by him, this passage of Crashaw is inspired, not by the intellect, which clears and distinguishes objects, but by passion, which blends and confuses them. The language is one mass of involved and tangled figure, in which similarity suggests similarity in objects contemplated and intensely visualized — not in abstractions incapable of visualization. Donne fetches his images from the byways of mediæval science and metaphysic and intellectualizes them in the process. Crashaw derives his imagery from the impetus of his feelings and from an intense visualization of the outer world, which causes him to revel in light, color, motion, and space. He at times confuses his images in a pregnancy of thought that involves a partial obscuration of the thing to be figured. These two methods are at the very poles from each other, and incapable of derivation, the one from the other. But if the difficulties of Donne are largely due to subtlety of thought, and those of Crashaw to impetus of feeling, the figures of the lesser poets may often be referred to a striving after original effect, an ingenious pursuit of similitudes in things repugnant, that amounts to a notorious vice of style. The books are full of illustrations of this false taste, and it is easy to find them in the verse of Quarles, Cartwright, Crashaw, Lovelace, and Davenant; even in Carew, Herbert, and Vaughan. Cowley, who has been much abused on this score, but who is often a true poet, gives us this typical instance of the hunted conceit, on that eternal quibble of the amorists, "My true love hath my heart and I have his":

> So much thyself does in me live,
> That when it for thyself I give,
> 'T is but to change that piece of gold for this,
> Whose stamp and value equal is.
> Yet, lest the weight be counted bad,
> My soul and body, two grains more, I 'll add.[1]

With all the lapses into bad taste and extravagance to which the passion for 'conceit' led, and notwithstanding a frank confession that the verse of amateur poets like Lovelace and Suckling is often so wantonly careless and slovenly that it becomes not only unpoetical and unliterary but, in places, all but absolutely unintelligible, a sense of constructiveness none the less distinguishes much of the poetry of this age. It is this that De Quincey recognizes in the term 'rhetorical' noticed above. From its source in the absorption of classical theories and ideas, whether consciously and directly, as with Jonson himself, or indirectly, as with many of his followers, I have ventured to call this quality of the seventeenth century poetry its assimilative classicism. This term may be more clearly apprehended in the contrast which exists between it and the empirical classicism of Spenser and Sidney, which consisted almost entirely in imitation and experiment with the superficialities of classic allusion and versification. Not less distinguishable is the assimilative classicism of Jonson and his followers from the restrictive and, in some respects, pseudo-classicism of the age of Anne,

[1] *The Bargain*, from *The Mistress*, *Cowley*, ed. Grosart, I, 112.

although the former led the way to those restraints of form in design and in expression that came ultimately to work a revolution in English poetry. If we will examine a successful lyric of Carew, Herrick, or Waller, we shall often find its success to consist in an orderly and skilful presentation of material, in a minute attention to the weight and value of words and the proper placing of them, whilst controlling all is an ever-present and wholesome sense of design.

IV.

Thomas Carew and Robert Herrick are so important in themselves, and, though in many respects strikingly in contrast, so typical of the secular lyric of the seventeenth century at its best, that this subject cannot be better treated than in a brief consideration of these two poets. The following are some of the qualities which Carew and Herrick possess in common. With natures versatile, but neither deep nor passionate, both are equally devoid of the didactic fibre of Jonson and of the spiritual depth of Donne. The sincere and beautiful religious lyrics of Herrick form but a fraction of his poetical work and not the part for which he is most distinguished. As to Carew, he thus expresses his relation to "sacred verses" in his *Epistle to George Sandys*[1]:

> I press not to the choir, nor dare I greet
> The holy place with my unhallowed feet;
> My unwashed Muse pollutes not things divine,
> Nor mingles her profaner notes with thine;
> Here humbly at the porch she stays,
> And with glad ears sucks in thy sacred lays.

Both of these poets are artists, the eye faithfully on the subject, with a sense of design before them and a genuine

[1] *On his Translation of the Psalms*, ed. Carew, 1825, p. 116.

fidelity to that 'nature' which serves them for theme. This all will grant Herrick, for his flowers and fair maids are 'nature' in the sense employed by every one. But Carew also can compass 'nature' in this narrower sense and sing charmingly of the quickening approach of spring, which

> wakes in hollow tree
> The drowsy cuckoo and the humble bee.[1]

Nor is he less true to nature when he gives us — as he does often in his wise and graceful occasional verses — a glimpse of loftier ideals.[2] These poets are English, like their masters, Jonson and Donne, and entirely free from Italianism. Their classicism sits easily upon them, especially that of Carew, and is the classicism of men of the world, informing their style and illuminating their thoughts, not cumbering them with unnecessary learning. Carew is more prone to the use of 'conceit' than Herrick; but in both good taste, artistically speaking, prevents an excessive use of intellectualized imagery. Both poets are, for the same reason, remarkably equal, rarely allowing inferior work to see the light. In neither poet is there the slightest use of allegory or anything in the nature of mysticism. Each lives on the earth, content to enjoy the good things thereof, to regret the fleetness of time and the fragility of beauty, but ready to seize the day and revel in its pleasures. Lastly, both are consummate stylists in construction, ordering of thought, choice and placing of words, and nicety of versification.

If we turn to the points of difference, a great contrast at once appears in the lives of these two poets. Carew was from early manhood one of the accepted wits of the court,

[1] See p. 63, below.

[2] See Carew's ideal man, *To the Countess of Anglesy*, ed. Carew, 1825, p. 87, vv. 41 ff., and contrast with Herrick's *His Cavalier*, ed. Grosart, I, 51.

living in the heart of the best society, in daily attendance upon the king. He had but to open his lips to be appreciated and applauded, and his poetry was produced, not for the world, but for the inner circle of the best society of England. His occasional verses are few, and well chosen as to dedicatees: to majesty, to the Lord Chief Justice of England, to peers and peeresses; of poets, to Donne, to Jonson, Sandys, and the contemporary laureate, Davenant; to some few courtly friends; to many fair ladies, whose anonymity is becomingly preserved from the prying scrutiny of the outside world in initials and pseudonymes. Herrick, on the other hand, banished from the society of the wits which he loved, forced into retirement for the sake of a livelihood, enjoyed the compensation of a closer association with nature. His poetry was written for his own pleasure and that of a few friends who loved the work for the man's sake. Herrick was nearly sixty before *The Hesperides* was printed, and the volume made no great stir, nor is likely to have done so even had it appeared in more propitious times. His occasional verse contains lines to royalty, addressed from afar, but exhibits no familiarity with 'great ones.' His dedicatees are the small country gentry, that sound, wholesome stock which maintained the honesty and purity of English blood when the court had become a veritable plague spot and threatened the life of the nation.

With such contrasted environments as these acting upon temperaments susceptible in each case, we must expect contrasted results even within the well-defined limits of this species of lyric. In Herrick we have the elasticity and freedom that come with the breath of open air, a greater openness and geniality of disposition. His range of subject, so charmingly set forth in *The Argument to his Book*, begins with "brooks and blossoms, birds and bowers," and ends with heaven. Between lie many things — the seasons, country mirth, "cleanly wantonness," "the court of Queen Mab and the Fairy King." Considering only Carew's most characteristic lyrics, we may say that his range is contained in a corner of this spacious garden of Herrick. In Carew the view of life is narrower, more conventional; there is greater repression, but more civility, more elegance and polish. Despite occasional touches of truth in the observation of nature, we find a use of natural objects for decorative effect and a frequent employment of metaphor which applies the work of man to illustrate nature.[1] Carew knows nothing of "country glee" or fairyland, and better appreciates the cold brilliancy of diamonds than the blush of "July-flowers," the odors of spicery than the "essences of jessamine." Yet, granting this limitation, which is the more apparent if we consider Herrick's charming folklore or "paganism of the country side," his prevailing eroticism draws him near to Carew; whilst the touches of a wider experience in his occasional poetry disclose unrealized possibilities in Carew.

In nothing is the difference between these poets so plainly set forth as in what may be called their temper. Herrick is genial, *naïf*, playful at times; there is a spontaneousness about him, a sincerity that disarms criticism. Take this characteristic little poem, *To his Conscience:*

> Can I not sin, but thou wilt be
> My private prothonotary?
> Can I not woo thee to pass by
> A short and sweet iniquity?
> I'll cast a mist, a cloud upon
> My delicate transgression,
> So utter dark, as that no eye
> Shall see the hugged impiety:
> Gifts blind the wise, and bribes do please,

[1] Cf. *The Spring*, p. 63 of this volume, vv. 2, 3. See also Herrick's *The Primrose*, and Carew's *To the New Year*.

And wind all other witnesses;
And wilt not thou with gold be tied
To lay thy pen and ink aside?
That in the mirk and tongueless night,
Wanton I may, and thou not write?
It will not be: and therefore, now,
For times to come, I'll make this vow,
From aberrations to live free;
So I'll not fear the Judge and thee.[1]

There is no lack of clear vision here; yet who believes in the seriousness of this pretty repentance? This 'vow' is of the same nature as his vows to Apollo, Bacchus, or Venus:

Make her this day smile on me
And I'll roses give to thee.[2]

In a word, the engaging temper of a man not wholly impeccable, nor seeking to have you believe that he is, shines forth — a man of kindly heart, much beloved by his parishioners, charitable, simple, unostentatious, loving mirth and playful gallantry, not a stranger to the cup or to full-blooded life, hating the unlovely, and writing horrid epigrams on what he detested, measured by his detestation; shrinking somewhat from deeper thoughts, from an omnipresent dread of death, the mortal antipathy of every true Hedonist.

The temper of Carew was greatly in contrast with this. Evidently a man of few friends, of much reserve, there was in him more inward fire than might have been supposed under his perfect control. Carew was a man altogether sophisticate, never to be carried away into portrayal of self; of pointed and polished wit, and a gentleman in the use of it; a master in the arch and wilfully perverse hyperbole of compliment; but neither satirist nor cynic, from the feeling

[1] *Noble Numbers*, ed. Grosart, III, 147.
[2] *Hesperides*, *ibid.* 52.

that satire and cynicism withdraw a man from that easy contact with his fellows in which good society consists, a contact the essence of which is a graceful waiving of the distinctions of rank in the midst of an ever-present sense of their existence.

If we consider what are the characteristics which mark the variety of poetry called *vers de société*, we shall find them to consist largely in the following: the recognition of man living in a highly organized state of society as a fitting theme for poetry, the making of the conventions of social life into a subject for art which may involve as faithful realism as the imitation of any other phase of nature. It is only the man who knows this phase of life from within who can truly depict it; not because it is superior to other life, but because it is broken up into a greater number of facets, each reflecting its own little picture. Defining *vers de société*, then, as an attempt to produce the effect demanded of poetry from the materials existing in the highly organized status of cultivated life, we may expect to find this species of poetry wherever such life exists, and in England it came to exist in its perfection in the reign of King James. The earlier age was too much engrossed with great ideas; it was too expansive, and hence too little intent on what was near. *Vers de société* demands self-control, at times daring, ease and elegance of manner, delicacy of touch, wit, an entire absence of pedantry, perfection of form and of finish. Carew has all this. He has even much of the French *gaiété* and *esprit*, while preserving with his English spirit a remarkable originality on an instrument of such limited scale.

Herrick, too, wrote verse of this class, but he wrote more and better on other themes. It is not strange, considering the environment of each of these poets and their differing success in reaching their contemporary public, that Herrick should have affected his successors far less than Carew.

Carew was in the direct line of development from the assimilative classicism of Ben Jonson to the restrictive classicism of Edmund Waller; Herrick was without the range of that course of development, territorially and artistically. He was really above it. And yet Herrick was not without his later kindred, less by direct influence than by the common bond that unites all true poets in the love of nature and of man. Andrew Marvell and Charles Cotton both breathe the fresh country air that Herrick so loved. But it is doubtful if either owes much directly to Herrick; it is certain that Cotton owes much to Carew.

The complex poetical relations of Waller must be deferred to a later consideration. It is sufficient to notice here that while he owes most to Carew in the thought and manner of his lyrics, as Pope long since pointed out,[1] Waller did not disdain to borrow an occasional thought from the less-known vicar of Dean Prior. In a late edition of *Wit's Recreations*, a miscellany made up of an indiscriminate garnering of fragments, some good, some very bad, from poets of past and contemporary repute, three poems on the rose appear side by side. Two of them are by Waller, one the famed *Go, lovely Rose*, the other, probably the original, is by Herrick.[2] The idea of another of Waller's most highly praised lyrics, *On a Girdle*, will also be found paralleled in Herrick's *Upon Julia's Ribband*. Here is the same familiar thought as treated in the manner of three differing schools. Herrick says in simple affirmation:

> Nay 't is the zonulet of love,
> Wherein all pleasures of the world are wove.[3]

[1] Cf. a rough draft of a *Discourse on the Rise and Progress of English Poetry*, Riverside ed., *Pope*, I, clv.

[2] See p. 125 and the note thereon.

[3] Ed. Hale, p. 20.

The language is direct, the idea fancifully but tastefully treated; the poet employs an unusual and musical word, 'zonulet,' and his versification is free but artistic.

> Give me but what this ribband bound,
> Take all the rest the world goes round![1]

cries Waller in rhetorical exclamation, reducing fancy to sense, avoiding unusual poetical words, but practising a verse of perfect regularity. Lastly Clieveland contorts the thought into a conceit, far-fetched and unpoetical, and asks:

> Is not the universe strait-laced
> When I can clasp it in a waist?[2]

Returning to Herrick and Carew, both of these poets habitually form their poems into a completed organism, and both possess a diction simple, pure, and of limpid clearness. To say a thing directly is apparently so easy a matter that poets like these are sometimes treated with contempt as men who have done trifling things within the power of any one. In truth, simplicity of style, as illuminating and intangible as the light of day, is the latest grace vouchsafed to the conscientious artist. Take this of Herrick:

> A funeral stone
> Or verse, I covet none;
> But only crave
> Of you that I may have
> A sacred laurel springing from my grave;
> Which being seen
> Blest with perpetual green
> May grow to be
> Not so much called a tree
> As the eternal monument of me.

[1] Below, p. 124.

[2] *Clievelandi Vindiciae*, 1677, *The Senses' Festival*, p. 6.

Aside from the beautiful and becoming sentiment, notice the direct flow of the words, each in its natural place and order. The only inversion is in the first clause, where it becomes organic and adds to the effect. Notice the beauty of the phrasing, which, with a recurrence of rhyme not always at the phrase's end, gives us a dainty variety in unity. 'None,' an emphatic word from its position at the end of the clause, becomes doubly so by the rhyme and the weight attaching to an end-stopped line. The same is true of 'grave,' which is still further reinforced in emphasis by the fact that it is the third rhyme on the same sound. Note, too, how the difference in the grammatical relations of the rhyme-words adds to the elements making for variety. The whole poem is one sentence, and there is no other collocation of the clauses which is at once so natural and so artistic as this.

Carew is the latest poet, until the coming of Keats, to preserve the Elizabethan secret of handling English trochaic octosyllabics; whilst the fertility and inventiveness of Herrick in lyrical form are rivalled only by Lodge, Shakespeare, and Campion in the preceding age. Very few of Herrick's metrical experiments fall short of perfect success, and his management of the more usual metres of his time is always masterly and often supremely original.

V.

Since the days of the venerable Bede and his beautiful story of the divine call to a poetic mission given to Cædmon, English poets have paid their tithe and more to the celebration of religious subjects, whether in translation, paraphrase, or in the expression of their own religious emotions. By the unerring instinct that makes the artist of one age the kin of all artists to come, poets have been especially attracted to that union of genuine devotion with the highest form of lyrical expression, the *Psalms* of David.[1] If we leave paraphrase, which extended to nearly all the noble stories of the Old Testament and to many of the New, reaching its climax in the divine epic of *Paradise Lost*, we shall find this religious spirit often communicated, even in otherwise original poetry, in the very terms of Biblical style and phrase; but, despite this, preserving in the product a tone and sanction above mediocrity of thought or unoriginality of diction. "It would not be easy to find a sonnet in any language," says the late Mark Pattison, "of equal power to vibrate through all the fibres of feeling with sonnet xix, *Avenge, O Lord, thy slaughtered innocents.* The new and nobler purpose to which Milton puts the sonnet is here in its splendor: 'In his hand the thing became a trumpet whence he blew soul-animating strains.' Yet with what homely material is the effect produced! Not only is there not a single purple patch in the wording, but of thought, or image, all that there is is a borrowed thought, and one repeatedly borrowed, viz., Tertullian's saying, 'The blood of the martyrs is the seed of the Church.' It would not be impossible, but it would be sacrilege to point to distinct faults in this famous piece; yet we may say that with a familiar quotation for its only thought and with diction almost below the ordinary, its thoughtful flood of suppressed passion sweeps along the hackneyed Biblical phrases of which it is composed, just as a swollen river rolls before it the worn pebbles long ago brought down from the mountain-side. From this sonnet we may learn that the poetry of a poem is lodged somewhere else than in its matter or its thoughts, or its imagery, or its words. Our heart is here taken by storm, but not by any of these things.

[1] Wyatt, Surry, Sternhold, Hopkins, and Parker all paraphrased some of the Psalms before Elizabeth's accession; Gascoigne, Sidney, and Bacon — to mention only the chief names — in her reign; Milton, Bishop King, and Sandys later.

The poet hath breathed on us, and we have received his inspiration. In this sonnet is realized Wordsworth's definition of Poetry: 'The spontaneous overflow of powerful feeling.'"[1]

We have here the secret of the greater diversity of opinion which exists in critical estimates of certain "divine poets" as compared with our current estimates of their profaner brethren. It is not granted to every one to be at all times in the mood in which the sincerity of the devotional poet can awaken a responsive chord. The greatest of poets can compel this response most generally, and therein lies much of their power; those less great often fail, not so much because of their own defects as because the music which they offer falls upon deaf ears, or upon ears deadened and ringing with the din of things wherein is neither poetry nor life.

It might be hard to find two devotional poets whose artistic ideals were more widely at variance with those of to-day than Francis Quarles and George Wither. Their ethical purpose, though worthy of praise as an ethical purpose, is paraded in a manner so foreign to our pretence of concealment in such matters that it is difficult for us fairly to appreciate their achievement. Yet to have given solace and moral support to thousands of their fellow-countrymen — for these men were read and reread, Quarles in innumerable editions, like Tupper in the days of our fathers — to have given this solace with that modicum of literary buoyancy which was sufficient to float the moralizing, the didacticism, and other heavy matters in the somewhat dense medium for which it was intended — all this is surely no trifle. The flippancy of thought into which a figure may betray one cannot diminish the historical importance of such writers, although it may well remain a question how far the applica-

[1] *The Sonnets of Milton*, Introduction, pp. 58–60; and see the sonnet, below, p. 167.

tion of poetry of any species to specific needs and occasions may take it out of the category of fine art.

If the reader will consider the practice of devotional poetry in the sixteenth century as contrasted with the practice of it in the age under consideration, he will discover several points of interest. If we except such an enthusiastic devotee as Father Southwell,[1] few poets of the earlier age were so undividedly devotional in their themes as were Quarles, Herbert, Sandys, Crashaw, and Vaughan. Nor is this unexplainable: the earlier age had been much taken up with the world and its beauties; the new age was taken up with the world and its vanities. It was no part of Anglican Catholicism to quarrel with what was beautiful in the world. It was regarded as in the spirit of worship to use and enjoy what has been granted us for use and enjoyment. Far different is it in an age in which the deep self-questionings of Puritanism have discovered, or thought that they have discovered, deception, vanity, and idleness in the shows of the world. The cleavage between the æsthetic and the ethical view of the purpose of literature is complete, and the poets no longer write, as did Spenser, hymns to earthly and to heavenly love and beauty, bound together in one volume, but devote themselves solely to the celebration of one or the other, as did Carew and Herbert, or poignantly regret the earthly leanings of their earlier Muses, as did Wither and Vaughan.

The earlier poets, too, seemed at times to write devotional verse as a sort of duty, like going to church, the proper thing to do. This continued, and we feel that Herrick — poor pagan that he was — hardly wrote some of his prayers to God with the same naturalness and abandon with which he addressed Juno, Venus, or Apollo. The latter was a

[1] *Saint Peter's Complaint* and *Maeoniae* were both published in the year of Southwell's death, 1595.

thing to sport with and no danger; on the best authority there were no such personages as these statuesque, delightful old pagan gods, — would that there were! The former was a very different affair; like the wearing of Sunday clothes, a serious matter, and not to be done lightly or altogether comfortably, except for a sustaining sense of decorum. Greatly in contrast is the beautiful and spiritually devoted feeling of Herbert, a man who humbly and devoutly held his poetical gift in trust that he might therewith do the will of God. Izaak Walton's touching account of Herbert's delivery of the manuscript of his book of poetry, *The Temple*, almost upon his death bed cannot be too often quoted: "He did with so sweet a humility as seemed to exalt him, bow down to Mr. Duncan, and with a thoughtful and contented look, say to him: 'Sir, O pray deliver this little book to my dear brother, Farrar, and tell him he shall find in it a picture of the many spiritual conflicts that have passed twixt God and my soul, before I could subject mine to the will of Jesus, my Master, in whose service I have now found perfect freedom; desire him to read it, and then, if he can think it may turn to the advantage of any dejected poor soul, let it be made public; if not, let him burn it, for I and it are the least of God's mercies.'"[1]

Notwithstanding the richness and variety of the religious and moral poetry that dignifies the age of Elizabeth, the devotional poetry of the reign of Charles gained in fervor and depth of thought. We cannot say that it retained that finish and sense of artistic design which continued longer to pervade secular poetry. The devotional poet has his eye almost wholly upon the subject, and the very spontaneity of his emotions hurries him on — if he be less than the greatest — to the facile verbosity of Wither, the metrical lapses of Quarles, or the ruggedness and defective execution of

[1] Walton's *Lives*, Herbert, ed. Morley, p. 277.

Vaughan. In a man like Milton the artistic instinct on the other hand is so strong that sincerity of workmanship becomes the feature of his very worship. To praise God with less than the perfection of man's power is impiety, and even the fervor of passion must fall within the controlling regulations of all human activity. Thus it is that in the self-contained and at times to us somewhat cold and austere Miltonic poetry, we have really a higher form of worship in art than we get from didactic Wither, saintlike Herbert, or rapturous Crashaw. In Milton we have the adoration of a great and sincere soul, a man who had known the chastening of adversity, a man who had risked all, and indeed lost much, that he might do the duty nearest him.

Let us now consider these products of the devotional poets of the reign of Charles. Quarles and Wither both began writing in the reign of James. If we except the several devotional verse-pamphlets of Nicholas Breton and some others of earlier times, Quarles was one of the first as he long remained by far the most popular of what may be termed the devotional pamphleteers. As early as 1621 he had published his *Hadessa, The History of Queen Esther*, followed by *Sion's Elegies*, 1624, *Sion's Sonnets*, 1625, *The Feast for Worms* and *Job Militant*, both in 1626, *The History of Samson*, 1631, and *Divine Fancies* in 1632. Many of these works, as their titles indicate, are paraphrases of Biblical story, but in *Sion's Elegies* and *Sion's Sonnets* we have the devotional lyric. The idea of the collection of such poems in a sequence Quarles probably derived from Wither's *Hymns and Songs of the Church*, 1623. Sequences of "divine sonnets," as they were called, had been well known among the writings of men like Constable and Breton before the close of the last century.[1] Wither's book "comprehends

[1] Cf. Barnes' *Divine Century of Spiritual Sonnets*, 1595, Constable's *Spiritual Sonnets*, of doubtful date, Breton's *The Soul's Harmony*,

the canonical hymns, and such parcels of Holy Scripture as may properly be sung, with some other ancient songs . . . appropriated to the several tunes and occasions observable in the church of England." There are hymns in the companion volume, *Haleluiah*, 1641, "When oppressors and wicked men flourish," "for one legally censured, whether justly or unjustly," "for one that is promoted," a "thanksgiving after drought." The fatherly solicitude of this worthy versifier provided for every sort and condition of man, and for every contingency of life. The poet of *Fair Virtue*, Wither's immortal volume of secular verse, has almost disappeared, except for a certain naïveté and fluency in verse which marks everything that this facile writer touched. All ornament, figure, and epithet have been ruthlessly destroyed, until the verse is as direct and unadorned as the baldest prose, and scarcely more inspired. The following is a fair specimen of this devotional commonplace :

> O hear us though we still offend,
> Augment our wasted store ;
> Into this land that plenty send
> Which filled it heretofore ;
> Then give us grace to use it so
> That thou may'st pleasèd be,
> And that when fuller we shall grow
> We think not less on thee.[1]

In most respects no two poets could present more opposite methods than Wither and Quarles. There may be some figures of speech in the devotional verse of Wither — I have

Donne's *Coronet*, and Davies of Herford's *Wit's Pilgrimage*, 1610, 1611.

[1] *Haleluiah*, Part II, Hymn lxix, ed. Spenser Soc., p. 129. There is some entertaining reading on the function of sacred poetry in Wither's preface to this work.

not found them; Quarles is nothing if not abundantly and grotesquely figurative, allegorical, and enigmatic. Wither is direct in construction if garrulous, and of easy flapping, onward flight; Quarles is at times much twisted and contorted, and soars after his kind with absurd intermittent flops and downfalls. Quarles, too, is garrulous; but while Wither is apt to say the same thing about many things, Quarles says a great many things about the same thing. There is a homely sincerity of speech about Wither which is as far above the strained ingenuity of Quarles as it is below the revealing poetical insight of Vaughan.

The most famous book of Quarles is his *Emblems*, 1635. It is probable that this was the most popular book of verse published during the century. It is still reprinted for religious edification with a reproduction of the hideous allegorical wood-cuts of the original edition. Although his verse is much overgrown with conceits, repetition, and verbiage, and impaired by slovenly versification (a fault which he shares with contemporaries far greater than he), there is much real poetry in Quarles. In moments of fervid religious excitement the gauds and baubles of his ordinary poetic diction drop away and he writes with manly directness:

> O whither shall I fly? what path untrod
> Shall I seek out to scape the flaming rod
> Of my offended, of my angry God?
>
> Where shall I sojourn? what kind sea will hide
> My head from thunder? where shall I abide,
> Until his flames be quenched or laid aside?
>
> What if my feet should take their hasty flight,
> And seek protection in the shades of night?
> Alas, no shades can blind the God of Light.[1]

[1] *Emblems*, ed. London, 1823, p. 124, and p. 53, below.

Two years earlier Herbert's *Temple* had appeared and at once taken hold upon the hearts of the readers. George Herbert was a gentleman by birth and a rare scholar; he had been a courtier and a man of the world, so far as that pure and modest spirit could be of the world. Like Quarles, Herbert reached the serious readers of his age with his sincerity, his piety, his rhetorical if somewhat artificial and 'conceited' style, and his originality of figure. He went much further, for Herbert, whatever be his rank amongst others, is a true poet who, alike in form and spirit, often raises the particular idea into the sphere of the universal and makes it a thing of new beauty and potency.

We may pass over the *Fourth Part of Castara*, 1639–1640, the devotional poetry of which is not without considerable merit, although bookish and imitative, like most of Habington's work. Of greater interest are the scriptural paraphrases of George Sandys the traveller, including a complete and excellent version of the *Psalms*, *Job*, and *Ecclesiastes*. The dignified original poem *Deo Optimo Maximo* is a good specimen of the devotional eloquence of Sandys, who appears to have been a man of fine fibre and delicacy of feeling. To Sandys has been assigned the place amongst devotional poets that Waller holds among the amorists: that of a man whose somewhat formal and restrained nature lent itself readily to the reaction in rhetoric and versification which was setting in. Sandys has even been considered "the first of all Englishmen [to make] a uniform practice of writing in heroic couplets which are, on the whole, in accord with the French rule, and which, for exactness of construction, and for harmonious versification, go far towards satisfying the demands of the later 'classical' school in England."[1] Of the absolute incorrectness of this opinion, despite its long entrenchment,

[1] See Professor Wood's paper mentioned below, p. lx.

and of its accidental origin in a scribbled note of Pope, I shall write below.

In 1646 appeared *Steps to the Temple*, with a few secular poems under the sub-title, *The Delights of the Muses*, by Richard Crashaw. The *Steps* was so named in modest reference and relation to Herbert's *Temple*, which was Crashaw's immediate inspiration. Crashaw while a student at Cambridge came under influences which, considering the difference in the two ages, are not incomparable to the Oxford or Tractarian Movement of our own century. In the fervent and pious life of Nicholas Ferrar, into whose hands we have already seen the dying Herbert confiding his poetry, Crashaw found much to emulate and admire. Ferrar, notable in science, and a successful man of affairs, forsook the world and formed, with his kinfolk about him, a small religious community at Little Giddings in Huntingdonshire, where he sought to lead a spiritual life in accord with the principles of the Anglican Church. Predisposed as was Crashaw to that intense and sensuous visualization of spiritual emotion which has characterized the saints and fathers of the Roman Church in many ages, in the life of Saint Theresa the poet found his ideal and his hope. His artistic temperament had led him early "to denounce those who disassociate art from religious worship"; the charity and benignity of his temper caused him equally to oppose those who made an attack upon the papacy an article of faith. It is easy to see how this attitude, under the spiritual influence of such men as Herbert, Robert Shelford, and Ferrar, should gradually have led Crashaw, with the help of some added political impetus, over to the old faith. This impetus came in the form of the parliamentary act by which it was provided that all monuments of superstition be removed from the churches and that the fellows of the universities be required to take the oath of the Solemn League and Covenant. On the enforcement of this act against Peterhouse, Crashaw's own college, and the consequent desecration of its beautiful chapel, Crashaw indignantly refused the League and Covenant, and was expelled from his fellowship. Before long he withdrew to Paris, where he met Cowley. Crashaw died in Italy a few years later, a priest of the Church of Rome. The picture of Cowley, the fair-minded, meditative Epicurean, befriending the young enthusiast, when both were in exile, is pleasant to dwell upon.

The relation of Crashaw to Herbert, save for his discipleship, which changed very little Crashaw's distinctive traits, is much that of Herrick and Carew. Herbert and Crashaw were both good scholars; Herbert knew the world and put it aside as vanity; Crashaw could never have been of the world; his was a nature alien to it, and yet there is a greater warmth in Crashaw than in Herbert. Crashaw turns the passions of earth to worship and identifies the spiritual and the material in his devotion; Herbert has the Puritan spirit within him, which is troubled in the contemplation of earthly vanities, and struggles to rise above and beyond them. It is the antithesis of Protestantism and Roman Catholicism, an antithesis which we can understand better if we can bring ourselves to sympathize with each than if we seek to throw ourselves into an attitude of attack or defense of either.

In matter of poetic style, too, despite his quips and conceits, and despite the fact that with him, as with many devotional poets, execution waits upon the thought and often comes limpingly after, Herbert is far more self-restrained, and his poetry of more uniform workmanship and excellence. But if Herbert has never fallen into Crashaw's extravagances, he is equally incapable of his inspired, rhapsodic flights. Herbert felt the beauties of this visible world and has some delicate touches of appreciation, as where he says:

> I wish I were a tree
> For sure then I should grow
> To fruit or shade; at least some bird would trust
> Her household to me, and I should be just.[1]

Crashaw knows less of the concrete objects of the world, but is a creature of light and atmosphere, and revels in color and the gorgeousness thereof. Crashaw often rhapsodizes without bridle, and is open at times to grave criticism on the score of taste. It is for these shortcomings that he has been, time out of mind, the stock example of the dreadful things into which the ill-regulated poetical fancy may fall. The "sister baths" and "portable oceans" of *Magdalene* are easily ridiculed, but it is almost as easy, while ridiculing these distortions of fancy, to forget the luminousness and radiance, the uncommon imaginative power and volatility of mind — if I may venture the term — of this devout Shelley of the reign of Charles I.

Two years after the first edition of Crashaw's poems, appeared Herrick's *Noble Numbers*, bearing date 1647, but bound in after the *Hesperides*, 1648. Herrick was too good a poet not to write well on any theme, and some of these devotional and moral poems have the same artless and dainty charm that is possessed in fuller measure by their more worldly sisters. The stately and gracious forms of Anglican worship must have been dear to such a man as Herrick, but it is unlikely that any deep spiritual yearnings disturbed the pastoral serenity of Dean Prior. Herrick is best when his devotional poetry touches the picturesque details of his own life in poems like the *Grange*, *A Thanksgiving for his House*, or when the subject grows out of a touching Biblical situation which may be elaborated with art, as in the fine *Dirge for Jephthah's Daughter*.[2] But even these sincere and beautiful religious lyrics are as ripples on a shallow lake in

[1] Herbert, ed. Grosart, p. 40. [2] Pp. 109, 143, and 147 of Hale's ed.

comparison with the crested waves of Crashaw or the deep-sea stirrings of Vaughan.

If we look forward we shall find the practice of the sustained religious narrative poem, first popularized by Quarles, continuing down to very late times. Thus Cowley wrote an epic, the *Davideis*, and Prior esteemed his *Solomon* the best of his work. Parnell wrote on *Moses*, *Deborah*, *Hezekiah*, and others, Blackmore on all *Creation*,[1] whilst the seemly and graceful turning out of a hymn, meditation, or short Biblical paraphrase became one of the ordinary accomplishments of a gentleman. No less a celebrity than the eminent Mr. Waller wrote cantos of *Divine Love*, of the *Fear of God*, and of *Divine Poesy*, with poetical reflections on the Lord's Prayer[2]; and his great successors, Dryden and Pope, did not disdain to follow his example in the decorous if occasional practice of a like art.

The gracious and musical lyrics of Andrew Marvell were written in all probability before he took service under the Commonwealth in 1652. Like Milton, Marvell laid aside the companionship of the Muses to fight worldly battles for what he believed to be the right; but, unlike Milton, he never returned to poetry again, but remained in the toil and sweat of battle to the last. Marvell's devotional poems are only a few, but there is about them, as about all the lyrical verse which this rare poet has left us, a moral wholesomeness, a genuine joy in external nature, and withal so well-contained a grace of expression, that Marvell must be assigned no mean place among the lyrists of his century.[3] Curiously enough, Marvell has extended the pastoral to embrace religious poetry in one or two not unsuccessful

[1] *Davideis* is in Anderson's *British Poets*, V, 389–426; Prior's, Parnell's and Blackmore's works are in the same collection, VII, 473–492; 25 f., 596–642.

[2] Anderson's *English Poets*, V, 498–506.

[3] See Grosart's ed. of Marvell.

efforts. The ode celebrating the nativity, which from its theme always partook of the pastoral nature, was to be sure, no new thing; and Herrick, with others before him, had applied the pastoral to occasional verse.[1] Marvell's poems are different, and while didactic in intent, are yet distinctly artistic. Such poems are *Clorinda and Damon*, and *A Dialogue between Thyrsis and Dorinda*.[2]

There remains one great name, that of Henry Vaughan, the Silurist, whose secular verse, published as early as 1646, was succeeded by long years of religious study and contemplation, and the production of many books in verse and prose, all devotional in cast.[3] Vaughan knew Randolph and Cartwright and venerated the memory of Jonson, who died when Vaughan was a youth at Oxford; under this influence he translated Juvenal and wrote some erotic poetry not above that of Randolph or Stanley. From the little we know of his life, it seems that Vaughan, like Herbert, had been of the world in his younger days, and that the chastening hand of adversity had fallen heavily upon him and led him away from earthly themes to the contemplative and devout life of a recluse. Without violence to the probable facts, we may conceive of Vaughan in his beautiful home in South Wales as we think of Wordsworth in later times in his beloved Lake Country, a lover of woods and hills and the life that makes them melodious, but a lover of them not merely for their beauty, but for the divine message which they bear to man, their revelation and ethical import. Vaughan's nature, like that of Wordsworth, is alike expansive and narrow. The expansiveness of the two poets is not unlike, and consists in a large-souled interpretation of the goodness of God

[1] Cf. *A Pastoral upon the Birth of Prince Charles*, ed. Hale, p. 35.

[2] Ed. Aitken, 1892, pp. 41 and 77; and below, pp. 152 and 154.

[3] Grosart has collected the secular and devotional poetry of Vaughan in four volumes, 1868–1870.

as revealed to man in his works, in a loving appreciation of the beauties of nature, in a revealing ethical insight, and in a "high seriousness" intent on worthy themes. On the other hand, both poets were narrow, though differing in their limitations. To Wordsworth doubts, fears, and the complexities of modern life were naught; they did not exist for him. Vaughan had put the world from him, although he had known it and still heard it from afar, like the hum of a great and wicked city, out of which his soul had been delivered. Wordsworth, with all his greatness, was narrowed by egotism, by didacticism, by pride; Vaughan, far less — if at all — by any of these, than by his theology, which is often hard and formal, and at times unlovely. Vaughan was also limited — and here the like is true of Wordsworth — by an imperfect artistic sense and a halting execution.

Vaughan's "realism in detail," which is based not only upon a close observance of nature, but upon a sympathy and love extending to all living creatures, seems a heritage from a nobler age than his. In no one of his immediate contemporaries do we find it in the same strength and imbued with the same tenderness; not in the grand descriptive eloquence of Milton, in the homeliness of Marvell, nor in the sensuous delight of Herrick. It is thus that Vaughan addresses a bird:

> Hither thou com'st. The busy wind all night
> Blew through thy lodging, where thy own warm wing
> Thy pillow was. Many a sullen storm,
> For which coarse man seems much the fitter born,
> Rained in thy bed
> And harmless head;
> And now as fresh and cheerful as the light
> Thy little heart in early hymns doth sing
> Unto that Providence, whose unseen arm
> Curbed them, and clothed thee well and warm.[1]

[1] *The Bird, Sacred Poems of Vaughan*, ed. Lyte, 1891, p. 174.

In Vaughan's mysticism we have a more general trait of the religious poet, a trait not more peculiar in this age to Vaughan than to Crashaw. Mysticism of symbol, whether it manifest itself in poetry or in philosophy and religion, is one of the most difficult subjects with which the critic has to deal, for it demands an ability to take the momentary subjective position of the author, and a complete reconstruction of his mood. The religious mysticism of Vaughan is distinguishable from that of Crashaw chiefly in the fact that Vaughan is less ecstatic and more musingly meditative; less purely emotional, although, when roused, stirred to the inner deeps of his nature. Not the least interesting quality of the poetry of Vaughan is its intellectuality, a quality which we are apt to think opposed to the spontaneity of emotion which inspires the highest forms of art and that naturalness or inevitability of expression in which the highest art is ever clothed. Yet intellectuality is alike the glory of Donne and of our own great contemporary, the late Robert Browning. Art is not to be regarded as a thing into which the rational processes enter very little as compared with the emotions; but rather as a production in which such a proportion of the impelling emotion and the regulative reason is preserved as neither to degrade the product into mere sensuousness nor to change its nature from art, which is the presentation of the typified image, to philosophy, which is the rational distinction of its actual properties. A wanton confusion of images which neither reveal and figure forth nor distinguish and make clear, is neither art nor philosophy, but a base product that fails utterly of the purposes of either.

We have thus traversed a period of scarcely sixty years and found in it, alongside of a large amount of poetry distinctly secular and often flippant in the worldliness of its tone, a body of devotional poetry of a quantity and a quality for which we may look in vain in any other half-century of English literature. A superficial consideration of this century is apt to divide all England into the hostile camps of Roundhead and Cavalier; to consider all the former as hypocrites, and all the latter as good loyal men; or — as is more usual in our country — to believe all supporters of the king utterly misguided and to assume that the virtues flourished in the Puritan party alone. In the face of these vulgar prejudices, it is interesting to note that among the devotional poets of that age, Habington and Crashaw were Romanists, Wither, Milton, Marvell (though "no Roundhead," as his most recent editor puts it) were Puritans, and all the others were members of the Established Church. The spirit of devotion which sought utterance in verse rose superior to the narrowness of mere dogma, and the inspiration of poetry waited not on a favored sect alone. Indeed, nothing could better prove the strong religious feeling which continued to animate the average Englishman of the seventeenth century than the great popularity of books like those of Quarles and Herbert among the communicants of the Church of England. The Non-Conformists had their imaginative literature, too, and produced in this century a man who, if not a poet, is almost everything else that literature can demand. *Pilgrim's Progress* is not much later than the latest work of Vaughan and marks a long step forward when compared with the contorted and mystical allegory of Quarles. In devotional literature, as in secular, the coming age was the age of prose, and in this immortal work the change was already complete.

With the return of Charles and the exiles, the popularity of religious verse decreased, controversial prose coming more and more to take its place with devout readers. However, some few lesser poets of conservative tastes, like John Norris of Bemerton, continued to cultivate 'divine poetry' far into the last quarter of the century. *Samson Agonistes* and the great epics of Milton do not concern us directly here, although they are the loftiest poetical utterances which the English Muse has devoted to religion. It is well known that contemporary influences contributed little to them, and that they were written upon a long-formed determination, and come as the late and crowning glory of a rich poetical past. The poems of Milton have lost somewhat in our day of rational thinking; criticism shudders at a cosmogony in which Christian legend and pagan mythology are mingled in Titanic confusion. It is with *Paradise Lost* much as it is with the stately fugues of John Sebastian Bach, the father of modern music. We prefer something very different, fountains with a thousand jets, artificial cataracts lit up with electricity. But the great ocean of the immortal music of Bach and of the no less immortal poetry of Milton will roll in sonorous waves and unfathomable depths, when all the little tuneful waterworks of poetical and musical mimicry are dumb.

VI.

Poetry drooped with the death of King Charles I. Milton had already thrown himself heart and soul into the political struggle; Marvell was soon to follow. Many of the Cavalier poets were dead; those that survived were either silent in the miseries of poverty with Lovelace, boisterously carolling drinking songs with Alexander Brome and Charles Cotton, or keeping up the unequal struggle in satire, ribald and hoarse with abuse, like Clieveland's. Stanley had turned to the consolations of philosophical study. Montrose, the last of that goodly line of English noblemen whose highly tempered mettle expressed itself unaffectedly in lyrical song, survived his sovereign but one year. If we except Vaughan, a few belated publications like those of Stanley, Sherburne, and King, and the posthumous volumes of Cartwright and

Crashaw, the fifth decade of the century is singularly barren of poetry. The younger men, who were shortly to evolve new ideals, were as yet unknown, although it must not be forgotten that at the Restoration Cowley had been before the public as a poet for nearly thirty years, and Waller rather longer.[1]

There are few subjects in the history of English literature attended with greater difficulty than the attempt to explain how the lapse of a century in time should have transformed the literature of England from the traits which characterized it in the reign of Queen Elizabeth to those which came to prevail under the rule of Queen Anne. The salient characteristics of the two ages are much too well known to call for a word here. Few readers, moreover, are unfamiliar with the more usual theories on this subject: how one critic believes that Edmund Waller invented the new poetry by a spontaneous exercise of his own cleverness[2]; how another demands that this responsibility be fixed upon George Sandys[3]; how some think that "classicism" was an importation from France, which came into England in the luggage of the fascinating Frenchwoman who afterwards became the Duchess of Portsmouth; and how still others suppose that the whole thing was really in the air to be caught by infection by any one who did not draw apart and live out of this literary miasma, as did Milton.[4] The conservative reaction in literature which triumphed at the Restoration has been so hardly treated and so bitterly scorned that there is much temptation to attempt a justification. Imaginative literature did lose in the change, and enormously; and as we are

[1] See the poem of the text, p. 5.

[2] Gosse, *Eighteenth Century Literature*, p. 2.

[3] Professor Henry Wood, *American Journal of Philology*, XI, 73, and see p. l, above.

[4] Gosse, *From Shakespeare to Pope*, p. 19.

engaged to a large extent in a consideration of imaginative products in treating of the lyric, it is to be expected that we shall find many things to deplore. But if the imagination, and with it the power which produces poetry, became for a time all but extinct, the understanding, or power which arranges, correlates, expounds, and explains, went through a course of development which has brought with it in the end nothing but gain to the literature considered as a whole.

If the reader will consider the three great names, Ben Jonson, finishing his work about 1635, John Dryden, at the height of his fame fifty years later, and Alexander Pope, with nearly ten years of literary activity before him a century after Jonson's death, he will notice certain marked differences in a general resemblance in the range, subject-matter, and diction of the works of these three. The plays of Jonson, despite the restrictive character of his genius, exemplify nearly the whole spacious field of Elizabethan drama, with an added success in the development of the masque which is Jonson's own. Jonson is the first poet that gave to occasional verse that variety of subject, that power and finish which made it for nearly two centuries the most important form of poetical expression. The works of Jonson are pervaded with satire, criticism, and translation, though all appear less in set form than as applied to original work. Finally, Jonson's lyrics maintain the diversity, beauty, and originality which distinguish this species of poetry in his favored age.

If we turn to Dryden, we still find a wide range in subject, although limitations are discoverable in the character of his dramas and of his lyrics. If we except his operas and those pseudo-dramatic aberrations in which he adapted the work of Shakespeare and Milton, Dryden writes only two kinds of plays, the heroic drama and the comedy of manners, whilst his lyrics, excepting the two odes for Saint Cecilia's Day and some perfunctory religious poems, are wholly amatory in the narrow and vitiated sense in which that term was employed in the time of Charles II. The strongest element of Dryden's work is occasional verse; and he makes a new departure, showing the tendency of the time in the development of what may be called occasional prose: the preface and dedicatory epistle. Satire takes form in the translation of Juvenal and in the author's own brilliant original satires; translation becomes Dryden's most lucrative literary employment; and criticism is the very element in which he lives. Lastly, we turn to Pope. Here are no plays and very few lyrics, scarcely one which is not an applied poem. Occasional verse, satire, criticism, and translation have usurped the whole field. There was no need that Pope should write his criticism in prose, as did Dryden, for verse had become in his hands essentially a medium for the expression of that species of thought which we in this century associate with the prose form. The verse of Pope was a medium more happily fitted for the expression of the thought of Pope, where rhetorical brilliancy and telling antithesis, rather than precision of thought, were demanded, than any prose that could possibly have been devised.

It has often been affirmed that England has the greater poetry, whilst France possesses the superior prose, and in the confusion or distinction of the two species of literature this difference has been explained.[1] Poetry must be governed by the imagination; it must not only see and imitate nature, it must transform what it sees, converting the actual into the terms of the ideal; if it does much beside, it is less poetry. On the other hand, prose is a matter of the understanding; it may call to its aid whatever other faculty you will, but it must be ruled by the intelligence alone, to the end that the object may be realized as it actually *is*. With this dis-

[1] See, in general, Matthew Arnold's essay *On the Literary Influence of Academies*.

tinction before us, when passion, real or simulated, when imagination, genuine or forced, takes the reins from the understanding, the product may become poetry, or enthusiasm, or rhapsody; it certainly ceases to be prose, good, bad, or indifferent. So, likewise, when the understanding supplants imagination we have also a product, which, whatever its form or the wealth of rhetoric bestowed upon it, is alien to poetry. This is to be interpreted into no criticism of the many English literary products which have the power to run and to fly; we could not spare one of the great pages of Carlyle or of Mr. Ruskin, and yet it may well be doubted if, on the whole, the French have not been the gainers from the care with which they have customarily, until lately, kept their prose and their poetry sundered.

The real value of the age of repression consisted in its recognition of the place that the understanding must ever hold, not only in the production of prose, but in the production of every form of enduring art. It endeavored to establish a standard by which to judge, and failed, less because of the inherent weakness of the restrictive ideal than because the very excesses of the imaginative age preceding drove the classicists to a greater recoil, and made them content with the correction of abuse instead of solicitous to found their reaction upon a sound basis. The essential cause of this great change in literature, above all mere questions of foreign origin, precocious inventiveness of individual poets, artificiality and "classical heroic couplets," lies in the gradual increase of the understanding as a regulative force in the newer literature, the consequent rise of a well-ordered prose, and the equally consequent suppression for several decades of that free play of the imagination which is the vitalizing atmosphere of poetry.

Whilst the larger number of poets between 1640 and 1670, according to temperament or circumstances, held either to the old manner, as did Milton and Marvell, or went over wholly to the new, as did Waller and Denham, a few were caught, so to speak, between the conflicting waves of the two movements and are of unusual historical interest on this account. Such was Davenant, whom Mr. Gosse has happily described as the Southey of the Restoration,[1] a man of strenuous endeavor, but, whatever value is attached to his epic and dramatic labors, far from a successful lyrist. Such, too, was Charles Cotton, who touches Izaak Walton on one side with his love of peaceful rural landscape and homely country life, and continues into the last quarter of the century the erotic lyrical vein of Carew, with native originality, but with inferior technical execution. Above either stands Abraham Cowley, the poet who, with Waller, enjoyed the greatest contemporary reputation in the interval between Jonson and Dryden, and who, take it all in all, fully deserved it. Much has been written on Cowley from the days of Sprat and Dr. Johnson to those of William Cullen Bryant and Mr. Gosse. It might be difficult, too, to find a poet of Cowley's rank who has been more variously estimated, a circumstance for which the eclecticism of his art may in a measure account.[2] Historically considered, Cowley is a son of Donne, in thought at times fantastic, in his wit often over-ingenious. He has an exasperating habit of dwelling on small matters, which deflect the stream of his thought and break it up into petty channels. None the less the lyrics of Cowley are estimable for their sincerity, for the genuine poetic worth of many whole poems and far more numerous passages, for their moral purity, for their honesty,

[1] *Shakespeare to Pope*, p. 132.

[2] Cf. the regularity of Cowley's couplets, especially in the *Davideis*, with the metrical and rhetorical looseness of the *Pindarique Odes*, Cowley's most lasting legacy to posterity, and traceable in their influence down to Wordsworth and Lowell.

humor, and originality, and for the pleasant cadence of their verse.

George Sandys has already been mentioned amongst devotional poets and as one of those to whom the "improved versification" of the next period has been confidently attributed.[1] I have endeavored elsewhere to show that as a matter of fact Sandys conforms more nearly to the type of this verse as used by Spenser and his school than to that of the eighteenth century, and that in versification, rhetoric, and general spirit the prototype of Dryden and Pope is Ben Jonson, and neither Sandys nor Waller.[2] Sandys was only one of many who contributed to the coming age of repression. His contribution was in the self-control and reserve of his style and in the regularity of his verse. But neither of these qualities is peculiar to him even in his own age, and the more distinctive qualities of the Popean manner in style, rhetoric, and versification — its balance, antithesis, epigrammatic wit, rhetorical emphasis, split of the verse into two halves — are none of them Sandys'. It is of interest to note that the notion, still widely current, that Waller through Sandys is responsible for the restrictive form of the decasyllabic couplet as employed by the poets of the eighteenth century, is traceable to a manuscript outline plan for a history of English poetry which was found amongst the papers of Pope, scribbled on a scrap, as was his wont. Therein Cowley, Drayton, Overbury, Randolph, Cartwright, Crashaw, and some others appear under the heading "School of Donne"; whilst "Carew and T. Carey" are noted as "models to Waller in matter, G. Sandys in his *Par*[*aphrase*] *of Job* and Fairfax" as Waller's models "in versification."[3] This is the

[1] *American Journal of Philology*, XI, 73.

[2] *Ben Jonson and the Classical School*, *Publications of the Modern Language Association*, XIII, No. 2.

[3] This note was first printed by Owen Ruffhead in his *Life of Pope*,

source of the notion which, losing sight of his unquestionable worth as a poet and a translator, has assigned to Sandys an undue prominence in the history of English versification.

Although we do Waller wrong to consider him the conscious originator of that revolution in poetry which substituted for the ideals of Spenser, Jonson or Donne those of Dryden and Pope, his age was right in declaring him the true exponent of the new "classicism," for it was in Waller, above all others, that the tendencies of conservatism in thought, diction, and versification at length became confirmed into a system which gave laws to English poetry for a hundred and fifty years. Waller had practised the old manner with a greater freedom than was ever that of Sandys; but the earlier part of Waller's career as a poet is difficult to make out, for when he had achieved success in the new and fashionable style, he became solicitous, like Malherbe, to have the world believe that his classicism began in his cradle.[1] In Waller we have a man the essence of whose character was time-serving, a man to whom ideals were nothing, but to whom immediate worldly success, whether in politics or letters, was much; a man whose very unoriginality and easy adaptability made him precisely the person to fill what Mr. Gosse deftly calls the post of "coryphæus of the long procession of the commonplace." The instinct of his followers was right in singling him out for that position of historical eminence; not because, as a boy, he sat down and deliberately resolved on a new species of poetry, but because

1769. It has recently been used by Mr. Courthope in the preface of his *History of English Poetry* as a point of departure for the discussion of that interesting question, How should a history of English poetry be written?

[1] Cf. *Ode à Louis XIII, partant pour la Rochelle*, ed. Malherbe, Paris, 1823, p. 75:

> Les puissantes faveurs, dont Parnasse m'honore
> Non loin de mon berceau commencèrent leur cours.

he chose out with unerring precision just those qualities of thought, form, and diction which appealed to the people of his age, and wrote and rewrote his poetry in conformity therewith. In Carew, Waller found the quintessence of *vers de société* and "reformed" it of its excessive laces and falling bands to congruity with the greater formality which governed the costume of the succeeding century. In Sandys, Fairfax, Drummond, and some others he found an increasing love of that regularity of rhythm which results from a general correspondence of length of phrase with length of measure, and he found, as well, a smoothness and sweetness of diction, in which these poets departed measurably from their immediate contemporaries and preserved something of the mellifluousness of the Spenserians. Lastly, in Jonson and the Elizabethan satirists he found, amongst much with which he was in little sympathy, a minute attention to the niceties of expression, a kind of spruce antithetical diction, and a versification of a constructiveness suited to the epigrammatic form in which the thought was often cast. With almost feminine tact Waller applied these things to his unoriginal but cleverly chosen subject-matter, and in the union of the two he wrought his success.

As we approach the end of the seventeenth century, the lyrists become fewer. The Elizabethan lyric, whose province was the whole world, which dignified great or petty themes alike with its fervid sincerity, has given place to a product more and more restricted to a conventional treatment of subjects within an ever-narrowing range. An occasional poet, absorbed in another art, like Thomas Flatman, a man of genuine poetic spirit, might neglect to learn the mannerisms of contemporary poetic craft; or, living without the popular literary current, might sing, as did Norris of Bemerton, a slender, independent strain. But in the main the lyric had ceased to be an instrument for the expression of literary thought, although it remained a plaything for the idle hours of writers whose business was with occasional verse, social satire, heroic drama, or the comedy of a "Utopia of gallantry." To Dorset, Sedley, Rochester, and Aphara Behn, a dissolute, cynical, godless rout of Comus — even to Dryden himself — a lyric is a love-song and nothing more. It may be languishing or disdainful, passionate or satirical; whether frank or indirect in its animalism, the subject is ever love, or what went by that much-abused name in the reign of the Merry Monarch. Although the true note recurs occasionally in the faltering quavers of Anne, Marchioness of Wharton, or the stronger tones of Katherine Philips, John Wilson the dramatist, or John Oldmixon, it is not too much to say that the lyric had all but disappeared from English literature before the year 1700. A style the essence of which is surprise, which demands the snap of the cracker of wit in every couplet and yet maintains a rigid adherence to conventions in metre, phrase, and manner, is precisely the style to destroy the lyric, the soul of which is its simplicity, artistic freedom, and inevitability. Aside from an occasional instance in which the poetry which was in the heart of John Dryden asserted itself, despite his sophistication and venal following of the lower tastes of his age, and aside from a few sincere and dainty little lyrics that Matthew Prior threw off in the intervals of his supposedly more valuable labors in epic and occasional verse, there is scarcely a lyric of the last quarter of the seventeenth century, from the hand of those poets who were in the prevailing mode, which rings unmistakably true. When Congreve, after repeating the hackneyed comparison of the rise of the sun with the rising of Sabrina, distinguishes the effects of these two luminaries upon mankind by exclaiming

> How many by his warmth will live!
> How many will her coldness kill!

we are tickled with his wit, if we have not neard the thing too often. To be moved by the simple and beautiful expression of an emotion which we are fain to repeat again and again because of the pleasure it gives us, is to be moved as poetry can move. To witness the pyrotechnics of the most consummate wit and ingenuity once is enough; the fuse and powder are consumed, and nothing but the dead design, sullied with smoke, is left. What is worse, we have not always the pyrotechnics of wit, but too commonly, in the lyric of this age, a false product written with the rhetorician's condescension to what he feels an inferior species of literature, a condescension like to nothing but the contemporary attitude towards the inferior capacity and understanding of "females," with its mingled air of flattery and gallantry, itself an affront. Thus after a sojourn with the Elizabethan and seventeenth-century lyrists it becomes difficult to support the insipidity of this later literature of Chloe, Celia, and Dorinda, unless it be seasoned with the salt of cynicism, and then the product turns out to be something else, a something, whatever its merit, forever untranslatable into the terms of true poetry.

SEVENTEENTH CENTURY LYRICS.

BEN JONSON, *Pan's Anniversary*,
1631; acted before 1625.

THE SHEPHERDS' HOLIDAY.

THUS, thus begin the yearly rites
Are due to Pan on these bright nights;
His morn now riseth and invites
To sports, to dances, and delights:
  All envious and profane, away, 5
  This is the shepherds' holiday.

Strew, strew the glad and smiling ground
With every flower, yet not confound;
The primrose-drop, the spring's own spouse,
Bright day's-eyes and the lips of cows, 10
  The garden-star, the queen of May,
  The rose, to crown the holiday.

Drop, drop, you violets; change your hues,
Now red, now pale, as lovers use;
And in your death go out as well 15
As when you lived unto the smell,
  That from your odor all may say,
  This is the shepherds' holiday.

HYMN

TO PAN.

Of Pan we sing, the best of singers, Pan,
  That taught us swains how first to tune our lays,
And on the pipe more airs than Phœbus can.
  Hear, O you groves, and hills resound his praise.

Of Pan we sing, the best of leaders, Pan, 5
  That leads the Naiads and the Dryads forth;
And to their dances more than Hermes can.
  Hear, O you groves, and hills resound his worth.

Of Pan we sing, the best of hunters, Pan,
  That drives the hart to seek unusèd ways, 10
And in the chase more than Silvanus can.
  Hear, O you groves, and hills resound his praise.

Of Pan we sing, the best of shepherds, Pan,
  That keeps our flocks and us, and both leads forth
To better pastures than great Pales can. 15
  Hear, O you groves, and hills resound his worth;
    And, while his powers and praises thus we sing,
    The valleys let rebound and all the rivers ring.

Thomas Dekker, *The Sun's Darling*, 1656; written before 1625.

COUNTRY GLEE.

Haymakers, rakers, reapers, and mowers,
  Wait on your summer-queen;
Dress up with musk-rose her eglantine bowers,
  Daffodils strew the green;

Sing, dance, and play, 5
'T is holiday;
The sun does bravely shine
On our ears of corn.
Rich as a pearl
Comes every girl: 10
This is mine! this is mine! this is mine!
Let us die, ere away they be borne.

Bow to the sun, to our queen, and that fair one
Come to behold our sports:
Each bonny lass here is counted a rare one, 15
As those in princes' courts.
These and we
With country glee,
Will teach the woods to resound,
And the hills with echo's holloa: 20
Skipping lambs
Their bleating dams,
'Mongst kids shall trip it round;
For joy thus our wenches we follow.

Wind, jolly huntsmen, your neat bugles shrilly, 25
Hounds make a lusty cry;
Spring up, you falconers, the partridges freely,
Then let your brave hawks fly.
Horses amain,
Over ridge, over plain, 30
The dogs have the stag in chase:
'T is a sport to content a king.
So ho ho! through the skies
How the proud bird flies,
And sousing kills with a grace! 35
Now the deer falls; hark, how they ring!

CAST AWAY CARE.

Cast away care, he that loves sorrow
Lengthens not a day, nor can buy to-morrow;
Money is trash; and he that will spend it,
Let him drink merrily, Fortune will send it.
    Merrily, merrily, merrily, O ho! 5
    Play it off stiffly, we may not part so.

Wine is a charm, it heats the blood too,
Cowards it will arm, if the wine be good too;
Quickens the wit, and makes the back able,
Scorns to submit to the watch or constable. 10
    Merrily, merrily, merrily, O ho!
    Play it off stiffly, we may not part so.

Pots fly about, give us more liquor,
Brothers of a rout, our brains will flow quicker;
Empty the cask; score up, we care not; 15
Fill all the pots again; drink on and spare not.
    Merrily, merrily, merrily, O ho!
    Play it off stiffly, we may not part so.

From *Christ Church MS.* I. 4. 78;
date uncertain.

TO TIME.

Victorious Time, whose wingèd feet do fly
More swift than eagles in the azure sky,
Haste to thy prey, why art thou tardy now
When all things to thy powerful fate do bow?
O give an end to cares and killing fears, 5
Shake thy dull sand, unravel those few years

Are yet untold, since nought but discontents
Clouds all our earthly joys with sad laments,
That, when thy nimble hours shall cease to be,
We may be crowned with blest eternity. 10

THOMAS MAY, *The Old Couple*,
1658; acted 1625.

LOVE'S PRIME.

DEAR, do not your fair beauty wrong
In thinking still you are too young;
The rose and lily in your cheek
Flourish, and no more ripening seek;
Those flaming beams shot from your eye 5
Do show love's midsummer is nigh;
Your cherry-lip, red, soft, and sweet,
Proclaims such fruit for taste is meet;
Love is still young, a buxom boy,
And younglings are allowed to toy; 10
Then lose no time, for Love hath wings
And flies away from agèd things.

EDMUND WALLER, *Poems*, 1645;
written 1627.

SONG.

STAY, Phoebus, stay!
The world to which you fly so fast,
Conveying day
From us to them, can pay your haste
With no such object, nor salute your rise 5
With no such wonder as De Mornay's eyes.

Well does this prove
The error of those antique books
Which made you move
About the world: her charming looks 10
Would fix your beams, and make it ever day,
Did not the rolling earth snatch her away.

JAMES SHIRLEY, *The Witty Fair One*, 1633; acted 1628.

LOVE'S HUE AND CRY.

In Love's name you are charged hereby
To make a speedy hue and cry
After a face, who t' other day,
Came and stole my heart away.
For your directions in brief 5
These are best marks to know the thief:
Her hair a net of beams would prove
Strong enough to captive Jove
Playing the eagle; her clear brow
Is a comely field of snow; 10
A sparkling eye, so pure a gray
As when it shines it needs no day;
Ivory dwelleth on her nose;
Lilies, married to the rose,
Have made her cheek the nuptial bed; 15
[Her] lips betray their virgin's weed,
As they only blushed for this,
That they one another kiss.
But observe, beside the rest,
You shall know this felon best 20

By her tongue; for if your ear
Shall once a heavenly music hear,
Such as neither gods nor men
But from that voice shall hear again,
That, that is she, O take her t' ye, 25
None can rock heaven asleep but she.

JOHN FORD, *The Lover's Melancholy*, 1629; acted 1628.

FLY HENCE, SHADOWS.

FLY hence, shadows, that do keep
Watchful sorrows charmed in sleep.
Though the eyes be overtaken,
Yet the heart doth ever waken
Thoughts, chained up in busy snares 5
Of continual woes and cares:
Love and griefs are so exprest
As they rather sigh than rest.
Fly hence, shadows, that do keep
Watchful sorrows charmed in sleep. 10

JOHN FORD, *The Broken Heart*, 1633; acted about 1629.

A BRIDAL SONG.

COMFORTS lasting, loves increasing,
Like soft hours never ceasing;
Plenty's pleasure, peace complying,
Without jars, or tongues envying;
Hearts by holy union wedded, 5
More than theirs by custom bedded;

Fruitful issues; life so graced,
Not by age to be defaced;
Budding as the year ensu'th,
Every spring another youth: 10
All what thought can add beside,
Crown this bridegroom and this bride.

SONG.

O, NO more, no more, too late
  Sighs are spent; the burning tapers
Of a life as chaste as Fate,
  Pure as are unwritten papers,
Are burnt out; no heat, no light 5
Now remains; 't is ever night.

Love is dead; let lovers' eyes,
  Locked in endless dreams,
  Th' extremes of all extremes,
Ope no more, for now Love dies. 10
  Now Love dies — implying
Love's martyrs must be ever, ever dying.

DIRGE.

GLORIES, pleasures, pomps, delights, and ease
    Can but please
Outward senses, when the mind
Is untroubled or by peace refined.
Crowns may flourish and decay, 5
Beauties shine, but fade away.
Youth may revel, yet it must
Lie down in a bed of dust.
Earthly honors flow and waste,
Time alone doth change and last. 10

Sorrows mingled with contents prepare
Rest for care;
Love only reigns in death; though art
Can find no comfort for a broken heart.

THOMAS GOFFE, *The Careless Shepherdess*, 1656; written before 1629.

SYLVIA'S BOWER.

COME, shepherds, come, impale your brows
With garlands of the choicest flowers
The time allows;
Come, nymphs, decked in your dangling hair,
And unto Sylvia's shady bower 5
With haste repair;
Where you shall see chaste turtles play,
And nightingales make lasting May,
As if old Time his useful mind
To one delighted season had confined. 10

ROBERT HERRICK, *Hesperides*, 1648; written before 1629.

TO DIANEME.

SWEET, be not proud of those two eyes,
Which, star-like, sparkle in their skies;
Nor be you proud that you can see
All hearts your captives, yours yet free;

Be you not proud of that rich hair, 5
Which wantons with the love-sick air;
Whenas that ruby which you wear,
Sunk from the tip of your soft ear,
Will last to be a precious stone,
When all your world of beauty 's gone. 10

CORINNA'S GOING A-MAYING.

GET up, get up for shame, the blooming morn
Upon her wings presents the god unshorn.
See how Aurora throws her fair
Fresh-quilted colors through the air!
Get up, sweet slug-a-bed, and see 5
The dew bespangling herb and tree.
Each flower has wept, and bowed toward the east,
Above an hour since; yet you not drest,
Nay! not so much as out of bed?
When all the birds have matins said, 10
And sung their thankful hymns; 't is sin,
Nay, profanation to keep in,
Whenas a thousand virgins on this day
Spring, sooner than the lark, to fetch in May.

Rise, and put on your foliage, and be seen 15
To come forth, like the spring-time, fresh and green
And sweet as Flora. Take no care
For jewels for your gown or hair;
Fear not, the leaves will strew
Gems in abundance upon you; 20
Besides, the childhood of the day has kept,
Against you come, some orient pearls unwept;
Come, and receive them while the light
Hangs on the dew-locks of the night,

And Titan on the eastern hill 25
Retires himself, or else stands still
Till you come forth. Wash, dress, be brief in praying:
Few beads are best, when once we go a-Maying.

Come, my Corinna, come; and coming mark
How each field turns a street, each street a park 30
Made green, and trimmed with trees; see how
Devotion gives each house a bough
Or branch; each porch, each door, ere this
An ark, a tabernacle is,
Made up of white-thorn neatly enterwove, 35
As if here were those cooler shades of love.
Can such delights be in the street
And open fields, and we not see 't?
Come, we 'll abroad, and let 's obey
The proclamation made for May, 40
And sin no more, as we have done, by staying;
But, my Corinna, come, let 's go a-Maying.

There 's not a budding boy or girl, this day,
But is got up and gone to bring in May.
A deal of youth, ere this, is come 45
Back, and with white-thorn laden home.
Some have dispatched their cakes and cream,
Before that we have left to dream;
And some have wept, and woo'd, and plighted troth,
And chose their priest, ere we can cast off sloth. 50
Many a green-gown has been given;
Many a kiss, both odd and even;
Many a glance too has been sent
From out the eye, love's firmament;
Many a jest told of the key's betraying 55
This night, and locks picked, yet w' are not a-Maying.

Come, let us go, while we are in our prime,
And take the harmless folly of the time.
  We shall grow old apace and die
  Before we know our liberty. 60
  Our life is short, and our days run
  As fast away as does the sun,
And as a vapor, or a drop of rain,
Once lost can ne'er be found again;
  So when or you or I are made 65
  A fable, song, or fleeting shade,
  All love, all liking, all delight,
  Lies drown'd with us in endless night.
Then while time serves, and we are but decaying;
Come, my Corinna, come, let 's go a-Maying. 70

NIGHT PIECE, TO JULIA.

HER eyes the glow-worm lend thee,
The shooting stars attend thee,
    And the elves also,
    Whose little eyes glow
Like the sparks of fire, befriend thee. 5

No will-o'-th'-wisp mislight thee;
Nor snake or slow-worm bite thee;
    But on, on thy way,
    Not making a stay,
Since ghost there 's none to affright thee. 10

Let not the dark thee cumber;
What though the moon does slumber;
    The stars of the night
    Will lend thee their light,
Like tapers clear without number. 15

Then Julia, let me woo thee,
Thus, thus to come unto me:
And when I shall meet
Thy silv'ry feet,
My soul I'll pour into thee. 20

TO ELECTRA.

I DARE not ask a kiss,
I dare not beg a smile,
Lest having that, or this,
I might grow proud the while.

No, no, the utmost share 5
Of my desire shall be
Only to kiss that air,
That lately kissèd thee.

ROBERT HERRICK, in *Wit's Recreations*, ed. 1641; written before 1629.

A HYMN TO LOVE.

I WILL confess
With cheerfulness,
Love is a thing so likes me,
That, let her lay
On me all day, 5
I'll kiss the hand that strikes me.

I will not, I,
Now blubb'ring cry:

'It, ah! too late repents me
That I did fall 10
To love at all,
Since love so much contents me.'

No, no, I 'll be
In fetters free;
While others they sit wringing 15
Their hands for pain,
I 'll entertain
The wounds of love with singing.

With flowers and wine,
And cakes divine, 20
To strike me I will tempt thee;
Which done, no more
I 'll come before
Thee and thine altars empty.

THOMAS DEKKER, *London's Tempe*, 1629.

SONG OF THE CYCLOPS.

BRAVE iron, brave hammer, from your sound
The art of music has her ground;
On the anvil thou keep'st time,
Thy knick-a-knock is a smith's best chime.
Yet thwick-a-thwack, thwick, thwack-a-thwack, thwack, 5
Make our brawny sinews crack:
Then pit-a-pat, pat, pit-a-pat, pat,
Till thickest bars be beaten flat.

We shoe the horses of the sun,
Harness the dragons of the moon ; 10
Forge Cupid's quiver, bow, and arrows,
And our dame's coach that 's drawn with sparrows.
  Till thwick-a-thwack, etc.

Jove's roaring cannons and his rammers
We beat out with our Lemnian hammers ; 15
Mars his gauntlet, helm, and spear,
And Gorgon shield are all made here.
  Till thwick-a-thwack, etc.

The grate which, shut, the day outbars,
Those golden studs which nail the stars, 20
The globe's case and the axle-tree,
Who can hammer these but we ?
  Till thwick-a-thwack, etc.

A warming-pan to heat earth's bed,
Lying i' th' frozen zone half-dead ; 25
Hob-nails to serve the man i' th' moon,
And sparrowbills to clout Pan's shoon,
  Whose work but ours ?
  Till thwick-a-thwack, etc.

Venus' kettles, pots, and pans 30
We make, or else she brawls and bans ;
Tongs, shovels, andirons have their places,
Else she scratches all our faces.
  Till thwick-a-thwack, thwick, thwack-a-thwack, thwack,
  Make our brawny sinews crack : 35
  Then pit-a-pat, pat, pit-a-pat, pat,
  Till thickest bars be beaten flat.

BEN JONSON, *The New Inn*, 1631; acted 1629.

PERFECT BEAUTY.

IT was a beauty that I saw
So pure, so perfect, as the frame
Of all the universe was lame
To that one figure, could I draw,
Or give least line of it a law. 5
A skein of silk without a knot,
A fair march made without a halt,
A curious form without a fault,
A printed book without a blot,
All beauty, and without a spot. 10

From DR. JOHN WILSON'S *Cheerful Airs or Ballads*, 1660; written before 1630.

THE EXPOSTULATION.

GREEDY lover, pause awhile,
And remember that a smile
Heretofore
Would have made thy hopes a feast;
Which is more 5
Since thy diet was increased,
Than both looks and language too,
Or the face itself, can do.

Such a province is my hand
As, if it thou couldst command 10
Heretofore,
There thy lips would seem to dwell;

Which is more,
Ever since they sped so well,
Than they can be brought to do 15
By my neck and bosom too.

If the centre of my breast,
A dominion unpossessed
Heretofore,
May thy wandering thoughts suffice, 20
Seek no more,
And my heart shall be thy prize :
So thou keep above the line,
All the hemisphere is thine.

If the flames of love were pure 25
Which by oath thou didst assure
Heretofore,
Gold that goes into the clear
Shines the more
When it leaves again the fire : 30
Let not then those looks of thine
Blemish what they should refine.

I have cast into the fire
Almost all thou couldst desire
Heretofore; 35
But I see thou art to crave
More and more.
Should I cast in all I have,
So that I were ne'er so free,
Thou wouldst burn, though not for me. 40

LOVE'S IDOLATRY.

WHEN I behold my mistress' face,
Where beauty hath her dwelling-place,
And see those seeing stars her eyes,
In whom love's fire for ever lies,
And hear her witty, charming words 5
Her sweet tongue to mine ear affords,
Methinks he wants wit, ears, and eyes
Whom love makes not idolatrise.

LOVE WITH EYES AND HEART.

WHEN on mine eyes her eyes first shone,
I all amazèd
Steadily gazèd,
And she to make me more amazèd,
So caught, so wove, four eyes in one 5
As who had with advisement seen us
Would have admired love's equal force between us.

But treason in those friend-like eyes,
My heart first charming
And then disarming, 10
So maimed it, e'er it dreamed of harming,
As at her mercy now it lies,
And shews me, to my endless smart,
She loved but with her eyes, I with my heart.

From *Egerton MS.*, 2013; author
and date unknown.

WE MUST NOT PART AS OTHERS DO.

We must not part as others do,
With sighs and tears as we were two.
Though with these outward forms we part,
We keep each other in our heart.
What search hath found a being, where 5
I am not, if that thou be there?

True Love hath wings, and can as soon
Survey the world, as sun and moon;
And everywhere our triumphs keep
Over absence, which makes others weep: 10
By which alone a power is given
To live on earth, as they in heaven.

STAY, STAY, OLD TIME.

Stay, stay, old Time! repose thy restless wings,
Pity thyself, though thou obdurate be,
And wilfully wear'st out all other things.
Stay, and behold a face, which, but to see,
Will make thee shake off half a world of days, 5
And wearied pinions feather with new plumes.
Lay down thy sandy glass, that never stays,
And cruel crooked scythe, that all consumes,
To gaze on her, more lovely than Apollo.
Renew thyself, continue still her youth, 10
O, stay with her, (and him no longer follow)
That is as beauteous as thy darling Truth.

ROBERT HERRICK, in *Wit's Recreation*, ed. 1641; written before 1630.

UPON A MAID.

HERE she lies, in bed of spice,
Fair as Eve in Paradise;
For her beauty, it was such
Poets could not praise too much.
Virgins, come, and in a ring
Her supremest requiem sing;
Then depart, but see ye tread
Lightly, lightly o'er the dead.

JOHN MILTON, *Poems both English and Latin*, 1645; written 1629–31.

ON TIME.

TO BE SET ON A CLOCK-CASE.

FLY, envious Time, till thou run out thy race!
Call on the lazy leaden-stepping Hours,
Whose speed is but the heavy plummet's pace,
And glut thyself with what thy womb devours,
Which is no more than what is false and vain 5
And merely mortal dross;
So little is our loss,
So little is thy gain!
For whenas each thing bad thou hast entombed,
And, last of all, thy greedy self consumed, 10
Then long Eternity shall greet our bliss
With an individual kiss.

And joy shall overtake us as a flood,
When everything that is sincerely good
And perfectly divine, 15
With Truth, and Peace, and Love, shall ever shine
About the supreme throne
Of him, t' whose happy-making sight alone
When once our heavenly-guided soul shall climb
Then, all this earthly grossness quit, 20
Attired with stars we shall for ever sit,
Triumphing over Death, and Chance, and thee, O Time!

SONG ON MAY MORNING.

Now the bright morning star, day's harbinger,
Comes dancing from the east, and leads with her
The flowery May, who from her green lap throws
The yellow cowslip and the pale primrose.
Hail, bounteous May, that dost inspire 5
Mirth, and youth, and warm desire;
Woods and groves are of thy dressing,
Hill and dale both boast thy blessing.
Thus we salute thee with our early song,
And welcome thee, and wish thee long. 10

JOHN MILTON, in *Mr. William Shakespeare's Comedies, Histories, and Tragedies*, ed. 1632; written 1630.

AN EPITAPH ON THE ADMIRABLE DRAMATIC POET, WILLIAM SHAKESPEARE.

WHAT need my Shakespeare for his honored bones
The labor of an age in pilèd stones?
Or that his hallowed relics should be hid
Under a star-ypointing pyramid?

Dear son of memory, great heir of fame, 5
What need'st thou such weak witness of thy name?
Thou in our wonder and astonishment,
Hast built thyself a livelong monument.
For whilst to the shame of slow-endeavoring art
Thy easy numbers flow, and that each heart 10
Hath from the leaves of thy unvalued book
Those Delphic lines with deep impression took;
Then thou, our fancy of itself bereaving,
Dost make us marble with too much conceiving;
And, so sepulchred, in such pomp dost lie, 15
That kings for such a tomb would wish to die.

JOHN MILTON, *Poems both English and Latin*, 1645; written 1630–31.

SONNETS.

I.

TO THE NIGHTINGALE.

O NIGHTINGALE, that on yon bloomy spray
Warblest at eve, when all the woods are still;
Thou with fresh hope the lover's heart dost fill,
While the jolly Hours lead on propitious May.
Thy liquid notes that close the eye of day, 5
First heard before the shallow cuckoo's bill,
Portend success in love; O, if Jove's will
Have linked that amorous power to thy soft lay,
Now timely sing, ere the rude bird of hate
Foretell my hopeless doom in some grove nigh; 10
As thou from year to year hast sung too late
For my relief, yet hadst no reason why:
Whether the Muse, or Love, call thee his mate,
Both them I serve, and of their train am I.

II.

ON HIS BEING ARRIVED TO THE AGE OF TWENTY-THREE.

How soon hath Time, the subtle thief of youth,
Stolen on his wing my three and twentieth year!
My hasting days fly on with full career,
But my late spring no bud or blossom shew'th.
Perhaps my semblance might deceive the truth, 5
That I to manhood am arrived so near;
And inward ripeness doth much less appear,
That some more timely-happy spirits endu'th.
Yet be it less or more, or soon or slow,
It shall be still in strictest measure even 10
To that same lot, however mean or high,
Toward which Time leads me, and the will of heaven:
All is, if I have grace to use it so,
As ever in my great Taskmaster's eye.

PHILIP MASSINGER, *The Emperor of the East*, 1632; acted 1631.

DEATH INVOKED.

WHY art thou slow, thou rest of trouble, Death,
To stop a wretch's breath,
That calls on thee, and offers her sad heart
A prey unto thy dart?
I am nor young nor fair; be, therefore, bold: 5
Sorrow hath made me old,
Deformed, and wrinkled; all that I can crave
Is quiet in my grave.

Such as live happy, hold long life a jewel;
But to me thou art cruel 10
If thou end not my tedious misery
And I soon cease to be.
Strike, and strike home, then! pity unto me,
In one short hour's delay, is tyranny.

RICHARD BROME, *The Northern Lass*, 1632; written 1631.

HUMILITY.

NOR Love nor Fate dare I accuse
For that my love did me refuse,
But O! mine own unworthiness
That durst presume so mickle bliss.
It was too much for me to love 5
A man so like the gods above:
An angel's shape, a saint-like voice,
Are too divine for human choice.

O had I wisely given my heart
For to have loved him but in part; 10
Sought only to enjoy his face,
Or any one peculiar grace
Of foot, of hand, of lip, or eye, —
I might have lived where now I die:
But I, presuming all to choose, 15
Am now condemnèd all to lose.

RICHARD BRATHWAITE, *The English Gentlewoman*, 1631.

MOUNTING HYPERBOLES.

SKIN more pure than Ida's snow,
Whiter far than Moorish milk,
Sweeter than ambrosia too,
Softer than the Paphian silk,
Indian plumes or thistle-down, 5
Or May-blossoms newly blown,
Is my mistress rosy-pale,
Adding beauty to her veil.

JAMES MABBE, *Celestina*, 1631.

NOW SLEEP, AND TAKE THY REST.

Now sleep, and take thy rest,
  Once grieved and painèd wight,
Since she now loves thee best
  Who is thy heart's delight.
Let joy be thy soul's guest, 5
  And care be banished quite,
Since she hath thee expressed
  To be her favourite.

WAITING.

YOU birds whose warblings prove
  Aurora draweth near,
Go fly and tell my love
  That I expect him here.

The night doth posting move, 5
  Yet comes he not again:
God grant some other love
  Do not my love detain.

AURELIAN TOWNSEND, *Albion's Triumph*, 1631–32.

MERCURY COMPLAINING.

Mercury.

WHAT makes me so unnimbly rise,
  That did descend so fleet?
There is no uphill in the skies,
  Clouds stay not feathered feet.

Chorus.

Thy wings are singed, and thou canst fly 5
But slowly now, swift Mercury.

Mercury.

Some lady here is sure to blame,
  That from Love's starry skies
Hath shot some beam or sent some flame
  Like lightning from her eyes. 10

Chorus.

Tax not the stars with what the sun,
Too near approached, incensed, hath done.

Mercury.

I 'll roll me in Aurora's dew
  Or lie in Tethys' bed,

Or from cool Iris beg a few 15
Pure opal showers new shed.

Chorus.

Nor dew, nor showers, nor sea can slake
Thy quenchless heat, but Lethe's lake.

From WALTER PORTER'S *Madrigals and Airs*, 1632.

LOVE IN THY YOUTH.

LOVE in thy youth, fair maid; be wise,
Old Time will make thee colder,
And though each morning new arise
Yet we each day grow older.
Thou as heaven art fair and young, 5
Thine eyes like twin stars shining:
But ere another day be sprung,
All these will be declining;
Then winter comes with all his fears,
And all thy sweets shall borrow; 10
Too late then wilt thou shower thy tears,
And I too late shall sorrow.

DISDAIN RETURNED.

HE that loves a rosy cheek,
Or a coral lip admires,
Or from starlike eyes doth seek
Fuel to maintain his fires;
As old Time makes these decay, 5
So his flames must waste away.

But a smooth and steadfast mind,
  Gentle thoughts and calm desires,
Hearts with equal love combined,
  Kindle never-dying fires. 10
Where these are not, I despise
Lovely cheeks or lips or eyes.

No tears, Celia, now shall win
  My resolved heart to return;
I have searched thy soul within, 15
  And find naught but pride and scorn;
I have learned thy arts, and now
  Can disdain as much as thou.
Some power, in my revenge, convey
That love to her I cast away. 20

PETER HAUSTED, *The Rival Friends*, 1632.

HAVE PITY, GRIEF.

HAVE pity, Grief; I cannot pay
  The tribute which I owe thee, tears;
    Alas those fountains are grown dry,
    And 't is in vain to hope supply
  From others' eyes; for each man bears 5
    Enough about him of his own
    To spend his stock of tears upon.

Woo then the heavens, gentle Love,
  To melt a cloud for my relief,
    Or woo the deep, or woo the grave; 10
    Woo what thou wilt, so I may have

Wherewith to pay my debt, for Grief
Has vowed, unless I quickly pay,
To take both life and love away.

WILLIAM HABINGTON, *Castara, Part I*, ed. 1634; written about 1632.

TO ROSES

IN THE BOSOM OF CASTARA.

YE blushing virgins happy are
In the chaste nunn'ry of her breasts,
For he 'd prophane so chaste a fair
Who e'er should call them Cupid's nests.

Transplanted thus, how bright ye grow, 5
How rich a perfûme do ye yield!
In some close garden, cowslips so
Are sweeter than i' th' open field.

In those white cloisters live secure
From the rude blasts of wanton breath, 10
Each hour more innocent and pure,
Till you shall wither into death.

Then that which living gave you room
Your glorious sepulchre shall be.
There wants no marble for a tomb, 15
Whose breast hath marble been to me.

UPON CASTARA'S DEPARTURE.

Vows are vain; no suppliant breath
Stays the speed of swift-heeled Death.
Life with her is gone and I
Learn but a new way to die.
See the flowers condole, and all 5
Wither in my funeral.
The bright lily, as if day,
Parted with her, fades away;
Violets hang their heads and lose
All their beauty; that the rose 10
A sad part in sorrow bears,
Witness all those dewy tears,
Which as pearl, or diamond like,
Swell upon her blushing cheek.
All things mourn; but O behold 15
How the withered marigold
Closeth up now she is gone,
Judging her the setting sun.

Castara, *Part II*, ed. 1634.

TO CASTARA IN A TRANCE.

Forsake me not so soon; Castara stay,
And as I break the prison of my clay,
I'll fill the canvas with m' expiring breath
And with thee sail o'er the vast main of death.
Some cherubim thus as we pass shall play: 5
'Go happy twins of love'; the courteous sea
Shall smooth her wrinkled brow; the winds shall sleep
Or only whisper music to the deep.
Every ungentle rock shall melt away,
The sirens sing to please, not to betray, 10

Th' indulgent sky shall smile; each starry choir
Contend which shall afford the brighter fire;
While Love, the pilot, steers his course so even,
Ne'er to cast anchor till we reach at heaven.

AGAINST THEM THAT LAY UNCHASTITY TO THE SEX OF WOMAN.

THEY meet with but unwholesome springs
  And summers which infectious are,
They hear but when the mermaid sings,
  And only see the falling star,
      Who ever dare 5
  Affirm no woman chaste and fair.

Go cure your fevers, and you 'll say
  The dog-days scorch not all the year;
In copper mines no longer stay
  But travel to the west and there 10
      The right ones see,
  And grant all gold 's not alchemy.

What madman 'cause the glow-worm's flame
  Is cold, swears there 's no warmth in fire?
'Cause some make forfeit of their name 15
  And slave themselves to man's desire,
      Shall the sex, free
  From guilt, damnèd to bondage be?

Nor grieve, Castara, though 't were frail,
  Thy virtue then would brighter shine, 20
When thy example should prevail
  And every woman's faith be thine:
      And were there none,
  'T is majesty to rule alone.

GEORGE HERBERT, *The Temple*, 1633; written between 1630 and 1633.

THE ALTAR.

A BROKEN altar, Lord, thy servant rears,
Made of a heart, and cemented with tears,
Whose parts are as thy hand did frame;
No workman's tool hath touched the same.
A heart alone 5
Is such a stone,
As nothing but
Thy power doth cut.
Wherefore each part
Of my hard heart 10
Meets in this frame,
To praise thy name:
That if I chance to hold my peace
These stones to praise thee may not cease.
O, let thy blessed sacrifice be mine, 15
And sanctify this altar to be thine!

EASTER WINGS.

LORD, who createdst man in wealth and store,
Though foolishly he lost the same,
Decaying more and more,
Till he became
Most poor: 5

With thee
O let me rise,
As larks, harmoniously,
And sing this day thy victories:
Then shall the fall further the flight in me. 10

My tender age in sorrow did begin;
And still with sicknesses and shame
Thou didst so punish sin,
That I became
Most thin. 15

With thee
Let me combine,
And feel this day thy victory;
For if I imp my wing on thine,
Affliction shall advance the flight in me. 20

EMPLOYMENT.

If as a flower doth spread and die,
Thou wouldst extend me to some good,
Before I were by frost's extremity
Nipt in the bud;

The sweetness and the praise were thine; 5
But the extension and the room
Which in thy garland I should fill, were mine
At thy great doom.

For as thou dost impart thy grace
The greater shall our glory be. 10
The measure of our joys is in this place,
The stuff with thee.

Let me not languish then, and spend
A life as barren to thy praise
As is the dust, to which that life doth tend, 15
But with delays.

All things are busy; only I
Neither bring honey with the bees,
Nor flowers to make that, nor the husbandry
To water these. 20

I am no link of thy great chain,
But all my company is a weed.
Lord, place me in thy consort; give one strain
To my poor reed.

VIRTUE.

SWEET day, so cool, so calm, so bright,
The bridal of the earth and sky;
The dew shall weep thy fall to-night;
For thou must die.

Sweet rose, whose hue, angry and brave, 5
Bids the rash gazer wipe his eye;
Thy root is ever in its grave,
And thou must die.

Sweet spring, full of sweet days and roses,
A box where sweets compacted lie; 10
My music shows ye have your closes,
And all must die.

Only a sweet and virtuous soul,
Like seasoned timber, never gives;
But, though the whole world turn to coal, 15
Then chiefly lives.

THE QUIP.

THE merry World did on a day
With his train-bands and mates agree

To meet together where I lay,
And all in sport to jeer at me.

First, Beauty crept into a rose, 5
Which when I pluckt not, 'Sir,' said she,
'Tell me, I pray, whose hands are those?'
But thou shalt answer, Lord, for me.

Then Money came, and chinking still,
'What tune is this, poor man?' said he; 10
'I heard in music you had skill:'
But thou shalt answer, Lord, for me.

Then came brave Glory, puffing by
In silks that whistled, who but he?
He scarce allowed me half an eye: 15
But thou shalt answer, Lord, for me.

Then came quick Wit and Conversation,
And he would needs a comfort be,
And, to be short, make an oration:
But thou shalt answer, Lord, for me. 20

Yet when the hour of thy design
To answer these fine things shall come,
Speak not at large, say, I am thine,
And then they have their answer home.

FRAILTY.

LORD, in my silence how do I despise
What upon trust
Is stylèd honor, riches, or fair eyes,
But is fair dust!

I surname them gilded clay, 5
Dear earth, fine grass or hay;
In all, I think my foot doth ever tread
Upon their head.

But when I view abroad both regiments,
The world's and thine, 10
Thine clad with simpleness and sad events,
The other fine,
Full of glory and gay weeds,
Brave language, braver deeds,
That which was dust before doth quickly rise, 15
And prick mine eyes.

O, brook not this, lest if what even now
My foot did tread
Affront those joys wherewith thou didst endow
And long since wed 20
My poor soul, even sick of love, —
It may a Babel prove,
Commodious to conquer heaven and thee,
Planted in me.

WILLIAM HABINGTON, *Castara, Part I*, ed. 1635; written about 1633.

TO THE WORLD.

THE PERFECTION OF LOVE.

You who are earth and cannot rise
Above your sense,
Boasting the envied wealth which lies
Bright in your mistress' lips or eyes,
Betray a pitied eloquence. 5

That which doth join our souls, so light
And quick doth move,
That like the eagle in his flight
It doth transcend all human sight,
Lost in the element of love. 10

You poets reach not this, who sing
The praise of dust
But kneaded, when by theft you bring
The rose and lily from the spring
T' adorn the wrinkled face of Lust. 15

When we speak love, nor art nor wit
We gloss upon;
Our souls engender, and beget
Ideas which you counterfeit
In your dull propagation. 20

While Time seven ages shall disperse
We 'll talk of love,
And when our tongues hold no commérce
Our thoughts shall mutually converse,
And yet the blood no rebel prove. 25

And though we be of several kind,
Fit for offence,
Yet are we so by love refined
From impure dross we are all mind:
Death could not more have conquered sense. 30

How suddenly those flames expire
Which scorch our clay!
Prometheus-like when we steal fire
From heaven, 't is endless and entire,
It may know age, but not decay. 35

JOHN MILTON, *Arcades, or the Arcadians*, 1645; written 1634.

SONG II.

O'ER the smooth enamelled green,
Where no print of step hath been,
Follow me, as I sing
And touch the warbled string,
Under the shady roof 5
Of branching elm, star-proof,
Follow me:
I will bring you where she sits
Clad in splendor as befits
Her deity. 10
Such a rural queen
All Arcadia hath not seen.

SONG III.

NYMPHS and shepherds, dance no more
By sandy Ladon's lilied banks;
On old Lycæus, or Cyllene hoar,
Trip no more in twilight ranks;
Though Erymanth your loss deplore, 5
A better soil shall give ye thanks.
From the stony Mænalus
Bring your flocks, and live with us;
Here ye shall have greater grace,
To serve the Lady of this place. 10
Though Syrinx your Pan's mistress were,
Yet Syrinx well might wait on her.
Such a rural queen
All Arcadia hath not seen.

A Masque Presented at Ludlow Castle, 1634.

SONG.

SWEET Echo, sweetest nymph, that liv'st unseen
Within thy airy shell,
By slow Meander's margent green,
And in the violet-embroidered vale
Where the love-lorn nightingale 5
Nightly to thee her sad song mourneth well:
Canst thou not tell me of a gentle pair
That likest thy Narcissus are?
O, if thou have
Hid them in some flowery cave, 10
Tell me but where,
Sweet queen of parley, daughter of the sphere!
So mayst thou be translated to the skies,
And give resounding grace to all heaven's harmonies.

SONG.

Spirit. Sabrina fair,
Listen where thou art sitting
Under the glassy, cool, translucent wave,
In twisted braids of lilies knitting
The loose train of thy amber-dropping hair; 5
Listen, for dear honor's sake,
Goddess of the silver lake,
Listen, and save.

Listen, and appear to us,
In name of great Oceanus; 10
By the earth-shaking Neptune's mace,
And Tethys' grave majestic pace;
By hoary Nereus' wrinkled look,

And the Carpathian wizard's hook;
By scaly Triton's winding shell, 15
And old soothsaying Glaucus' spell;
By Leucothea's lovely hands,
And her son that rules the strands;
By Thetis' tinsel-slippered feet,
And the songs of Sirens sweet; 20
By dead Parthenope's dear tomb,
And fair Ligea's golden comb,
Wherewith she sits on diamond rocks,
Sleeking her soft alluring locks;
By all the nymphs that nightly dance 25
Upon thy streams with wily glance:
Rise, rise, and heave thy rosy head
From thy coral-paven bed,
And bridle in thy headlong wave,
Till thou our summons answered have. 30
Listen and save.

Sabrina rises, attended by Water-Nymphs, and sings.

By the rushy-fringèd bank,
Where grows the willow and the osier dank,
My sliding chariot stays,
Thick set with agate, and the azurn sheen 35
Of turkis blue, and emerald green,
That in the channel strays;
Whilst from off the waters fleet
Thus I set my printless feet
O'er the cowslip's velvet head, 40
That bends not as I tread.
Gentle swain, at thy request
I am here!

Spirit. Gŏddess dear,
We implore thy powerful hand 45
To undo the charmèd band

Of true virgin here distressed
Through the force, and through the wile
Of unblest enchanter vile.

Sabrina. Shepherd, 't is my office best 50
To help ensnarèd chastity.
Brightest Lady, look on me:
Thus I sprinkle on thy breast
Drops that from my fountain pure
I have kept of precious cure; 55
Thrice upon thy finger's tip,
Thrice upon thy rubied lip:
Next this marbled venomed seat,
Smeared with gums of glutinous heat,
I touch with chaste palms moist and cold. 60
Now the spell hath lost his hold;
And I must haste ere morning hour
To wait in Amphitrite's bower.

Sabrina descends, and the Lady rises out of her seat.

Spirit. Virgin, daughter of Locrine,
Sprung of old Anchises' line, 65
May thy brimmèd waves for this
Their full tribute never miss
From a thousand petty rills
That tumble down the snowy hills:
Summer drouth or singèd air 70
Never scorch thy tresses fair,
Nor wet October's torrent flood
Thy molten crystal fill with mud;
May thy billows roll ashore
The beryl and the golden ore; 75
May thy lofty head be crowned
With many a tower and terrace round,
And here and there thy banks upon
With groves of myrrh and cinnamon.

THE SPIRIT'S EPILOGUE.

To the ocean now I fly,
And those happy climes that lie
Where day never shuts his eye,
Up in the broad fields of the sky.
There I suck the liquid air, 5
All amidst the gardens fair
Of Hesperus, and his daughters three
That sing about the golden tree.
Along the crispèd shades and bowers
Revels the spruce and jocund Spring; 10
The Graces and the rosy-bosomed Hours
Thither all their bounties bring.
There eternal summer dwells,
And west-winds with musky wing
About the cedarn alleys fling 15
Nard and cassia's balmy smells.
Iris there with humid bow
Waters the odorous banks, that blow
Flowers of more mingled hue
Than her purfled scarf can shew, 20
And drenches with Elysian dew
(List, mortals, if your ears be true)
Beds of hyacinth and roses,
Where young Adonis oft reposes,
Waxing well of his deep wound, 25
In slumber soft, and on the ground
Sadly sits th' Assyrian queen.
But far above in spangled sheen,
Celestial Cupid, her famed son, advanced,
Holds his dear Psyche, sweet entranced 30
After her wandering labors long,
Till free consent the gods among

Make her his eternal bride,
And from her fair unspotted side
Two blissful twins are to be born, 35
Youth and Joy: so Jove hath sworn.
But now my task is smoothly done:
I can fly, or I can run
Quickly to the green earth's end,
Where the bowed welkin slow doth bend, 40
And from thence can soar as soon
To the corners of the moon.
Mortals, that would follow me,
Love Virtue: she alone is free;
She can teach ye how to climb 45
Higher than the sphery chime;
Or, if Virtue feeble were,
Heaven itself would stoop to her.

THOMAS CAREW, *Poems*, 1640; written 1634.

THE MARIGOLD.

MARK how the bashful morn, in vain,
Courts the amorous marigold,
With sighing blasts, and weeping rain;
Yet she refuses to unfold.
But when the planet of the day 5
Approacheth with his powerful ray,
Then she spreads, then she receives
His warmer beams into her virgin leaves.

So shalt thou thrive in love, fond boy;
If thy tears and sighs discover 10

Thy grief, thou never shalt enjoy
The just reward of a bold lover.
But when, with moving accents, thou
Shalt constant faith and service vow,
Thy Celia shall receive those charms 15
With open ears and with unfolded arms.

THOMAS RANDOLPH, *Poems, with the Muses' Looking Glass*, 1638; written before 1634-35.

AN ODE

TO MASTER ANTHONY STAFFORD TO HASTEN HIM INTO THE COUNTRY.

COME, spur away,
I have no patience for a longer stay,
But must go down,
And leave the charge'ble noise of this great town.
I will the country see, 5
Where old simplicity,
Though hid in gray,
Doth look more gay
Than foppery in plush and scarlet clad.
Farewell, you city wits, that are 10
Almost at civil war;
'Tis time that I grow wise, when all the world grows mad.

More of my days
I will not spend to gain an idiot's praise;
Or to make sport 15
For some slight puisne of the Inns-of-Court.

Then, worthy Stafford, say,
How shall we spend the day?
With what delights
Shorten the nights? 20
When from this tumult we are got secure,
Where mirth with all her freedom goes,
Yet shall no finger lose;
Where every word is thought, and every thought is pure.

There from the tree 25
We 'll cherries pluck, and pick the strawberry.
And every day
Go see the wholesome country girls make hay,
Whose brown hath lovelier grace
Than any painted face, 30
That I do know
Hyde Park can show.
Where I had rather gain a kiss than meet
(Though some of them in greater state
Might court my love with plate) 35
The beauties of the Cheap, and wives of Lombard Street.

But think upon
Some other pleasures: these to me are none.
Why do I prate
Of women, that are things against my fate? 40
I never mean to wed
That torture to my bed;
My Muse is she
My love shall be.
Let clowns get wealth and heirs; when I am gone, 45
And the great bugbear, grisly Death,
Shall take this idle breath,
If I a poem leave, that poem is my son.

Of this no more ;
We 'll rather taste the bright Pomona's store. 50
No fruit shall 'scape
Our palates, from the damson to the grape.
Then, full, we 'll seek a shade,
And hear what music 's made;
How Philomel 55
Her tale doth tell,
And how the other birds do fill the choir :
The thrush and blackbird lend their throats,
Warbling melodious notes;
We will all sports enjoy which others but desire. 60

Ours is the sky,
Where at what fowl we please our hawk shall fly;
Nor will we spare
To hunt the crafty fox or timorous hare ;
But let our hounds run loose 65
In any ground they 'll choose,
The buck shall fall,
The stag, and all:
Our pleasures must from their own warrants be,
For to my Muse, if not to me, 70
I 'm sure all game is free:
Heaven, earth, are all but parts of her great royalty.

And when we mean
To taste of Bacchus' blessings now and then,
And drink by stealth 75
A cup or two to noble Barkley's health,
I 'll take my pipe and try
The Phrygian melody;
Which he that hears,
Lets through his ears 80

A madness to distemper all the brain.
Then I another pipe will take
And Doric music make,
To civilise with graver notes our wits again.

TO ONE ADMIRING HERSELF IN A LOOKING-GLASS.

Fair lady, when you see the grace
Of beauty in your looking-glass:
A stately forehead, smooth and high,
And full of princely majesty:
A sparkling eye, no gem so fair, 5
Whose lustre dims the Cyprian star:
A glorious cheek divinely sweet,
Wherein both roses kindly meet:
A cherry lip that would entice
Even gods to kiss at any price: 10
You think no beauty is so rare
That with your shadow might compare;
That your reflection is alone
The thing that men most dote upon.
Madam, alas! your glass doth lie, 15
And you are much deceived; for I
A beauty know of richer grace
(Sweet, be not angry) — 't is your face.
Hence then, O, learn more mild to be,
And leave to lay your blame on me; 20
If me your real substance move,
When you so much your shadow love,
Wise Nature would not let your eye
Look on her own bright majesty,
Which had you once but gazed upon, 25
You could, except yourself, love none:

What then you cannot love, let me:
That face I can, you cannot, see.
Now you have what to love, you 'll say,
What then is left for me, I pray? 30
My face, sweetheart, if it please thee:
That which you can, I cannot, see.
So either love shall gain his due,
Yours, sweet, in me, and mine in you.

RICHARD BRATHWAITE, *The Arcadian Princess*, 1635.

THEMISTA'S REPROOF.

LIKE a top which runneth round
And never winneth any ground;
Or th' dying scion of a vine
That rather breaks than it will twine;
Or th' sightless mole whose life is spent 5
Divided from her element;
Or plants removed from Tagus' shore
Who never bloom nor blossom more;
Or dark Cimmerians who delight
In shady shroud of pitchy night; 10
Or mopping apes who are possessed
Their cubs are ever prettiest:
So he who makes his own opinion
To be his one and only minion,
Nor will incline in any season 15
To th' weight of proof or strength of reason,
But prefers will precipitate
'Fore judgment that 's deliberate;

He ne'er shall lodge within my roof
Till, rectified by due reproof, 20
He labor to reform this ill
By giving way to others' will.

EDMUND WALLER, *Poems*, 1645;
written about 1635.

TO MY YOUNG LADY LUCY SIDNEY.

WHY came I so untimely forth
Into a world which, wanting thee,
Could entertain us with no worth,
Or shadow of felicity,
That time should me so far remove 5
From that which I was born to love?

Yet, fairest blossom, do not slight
That age which you may know too soon;
The rosy morn resigns her light
And milder glory to the noon; 10
And then what wonders shall you do,
Whose dawning beauty warms us so!

Hope waits upon the flowery prime;
And summer, though it be less gay
Yet is not looked on as a time 15
Of declination and decay;
For with a full hand that does bring
All that was promised by the spring.

ON THE FRIENDSHIP BETWIXT SACCHARISSA AND AMORET.

TELL me, lovely, loving pair,
Why so kind and so severe?
Why so careless of our care,
Only to yourselves so dear?

By this cunning change of hearts, 5
You the power of Love control;
While the boy's deluded darts
Can arrive at neither soul.

For in vain to either breast
Still beguilèd Love does come, 10
Where he finds a foreign guest:
Neither of your hearts at home.

Debtors thus with like design,
When they never mean to pay,
That they may the law decline, 15
To some friend make all away.

Not the silver doves that fly,
Yoked to Cytherea's car,
Not the wings that lift so high
And convey her son so far, 20

Are so lovely, sweet, and fair,
Or do more ennoble love,
Are so choicely matched a pair,
Or with more consent do move.

TO AMORET.

Fair! that you may truly know,
What you unto Thyrsis owe;
I will tell you how I do
Sacharissa love, and you.
Joy salutes me when I set 5
My blest eyes on Amoret:
But with wonder I am strook,
While I on the other look.
If sweet Amoret complains,
I have sense of all her pains: 10
But for Sacharissa I
Do not only grieve, but die.
All that of myself is mine
Lovely Amoret! is thine.
Sacharissa's captive fain 15
Would untie his iron chain;
And, those scorching beams to shun,
To thy gentle shadow run.
If the soul had free election
To dispose of her affection; 20
I would not thus long have borne
Haughty Sacharissa's scorn;
But 't is sure some power above
Which controls our will in love!
If not a love, a strong desire 25
To create and spread that fire
In my breast, solicits me,
Beauteous Amoret! for thee.
'T is amazement, more than love,
Which her radiant eyes do move: 30
If less splendor wait on thine,
Yet they so benignly shine,

I would turn my dazzled sight
To behold their milder light.
But as hard 't is to destroy 35
That high flame, as to enjoy:
Which how eas'ly I may do,
Heaven (as eas'ly scaled) does know!
  Amoret as sweet and good
As the most delicious food, 40
Which, but tasted, does impart
Life and gladness to the heart;
  Sacharissa's beauty 's wine,
Which to madness doth incline:
Such a liquor, as no brain 45
That is mortal can sustain.
  Scarce can I to heaven excuse
The devotion which I use
Unto that adorèd dame:
For 't is not unlike the same 50
Which I thither ought to send,
So that if it could take end,
'T would to heaven itself be due,
To succeed her, and not you,
Who already have of me 55
All that 's not idolatry;
Which, though not so fierce a flame,
Is longer like to be the same.
  Then smile on me, and I will prove
Wonder is shorter-lived than love. 60

FRANCIS QUARLES, *Emblems, Divine and Moral*, 1635.

O WHITHER SHALL I FLY?

O WHITHER shall I fly? what path untrod
Shall I seek out to scape the flaming rod
Of my offended, of my angry God?

Where shall I sojourn? what kind sea will hide
My head from thunder? where shall I abide, 5
Until his flames be quenched or laid aside?

What if my feet should take their hasty flight,
And seek protection in the shades of night?
Alas, no shades can blind the God of Light.

What if my soul should take the wings of day, 10
And find some desert. If she spring away,
The wings of vengeance clip as fast as they.

What if some solid rock should entertain
My frighted soul? Can solid rocks restrain
The stroke of Justice, and not cleave in twain? 15

Nor sea, nor shade, nor shield, nor rock, nor cave,
Nor silent deserts, nor the sullen grave,
Where flame-eyed Fury means to smite, can save.

The seas will part, graves open, rocks will split,
The shield will cleave, the frighted shadows flit; 20
Where Justice aims, her fiery darts must hit.

No, no, if stern-browed Vengeance means to thunder,
There is no place above, beneath, nor under,
So close but will unlock or rive in sunder.

'T is vain to flee ; 't is neither here nor there 25
Can scape that hand until that hand forbear.
Ah me ! where is he not that 's everywhere ?

'T is vain to flee ; till gentle Mercy show
Her better eye, the further off we go,
The swing of Justice deals the mightier blow. 30

Th' ingenuous child, corrected, doth not fly
His angry mother's hand, but clings more nigh,
And quenches with his tears her flaming eye.

Shadows are faithless, and the rocks are false ;
No trust in brass, no trust in marble walls ; 35
Poor cots are even as safe as princes' halls.

Great God, there is no safety here below ;
Thou art my fortress, though thou seemst my foe ;
'T is thou that strik'st must guard the blow.

Thou art my God ; by thee I fall or stand, 40
Thy grace hath given me courage to withstand
All tortures, but my conscience and thy hand.

I know thy justice is thyself ; I know,
Just God, thy very self is mercy too ;
If not to thee, where ? whither should I go ? 45

Then work thy will ; if passion bid me flee,
My reason shall obey ; my wings shall be
Stretched out no further than from thee to thee.

MY BELOVED IS MINE AND I AM HIS.

Ev'n like two little bank-dividing brooks,
  That wash the pebbles with their wanton streams,
And having ranged and searched a thousand nooks,
  Meet both at length in silver-breasted Thames,
Where in a greater current they conjoin: 5
So I my best beloved's am, so he is mine.

Ev'n so we met, and, after long pursuit,
  Ev'n so we joined, we both became entire;
No need for either to renew a suit,
  For I was flax and he was flames of fire: 10
Our firm united souls did more than twine,
So I my best beloved's am, so he is mine.

If all those glitt'ring monarchs that command
  The servile quarters of this earthly ball,
Should tender in exchange their shares of land, 15
  I would not change my fortunes for them all:
Their wealth is but a counter to my coin,
The world 's but theirs; but my beloved 's mine.

Nay more, if the fair Thespian ladies all
  Should heap together their diviner treasure, 20
That treasure should be deemed a price too small
  To buy a minute's lease of half my pleasure:
'T is not the sacred wealth of all the mine
Can buy my heart from his or his from being mine.

Nor time, nor place, nor chance, nor death can bow 25
  My least desires unto the least remove;
He 's firmly mine by oath, I his by vow;
  He 's mine by faith, and I am his by love;
He 's mine by water, I am his by wine:
Thus I my best beloved's am, thus he is mine. 30

He is mine altar, I his holy place;
I am his guest, and he my living food;
I 'm his by penitence, he mine by grace;
I 'm his by purchase, he is mine by blood;
He 's my supporting elm and I his vine: 35
Thus I my best beloved's am; thus he is mine.

He gives me wealth, I give him all my vows;
I give him songs, he gives me length of days;
With wreaths of grace he crowns my conquering brows,
And I his temples with a crown of praise; 40
Which he accepts as an everlasting sign
That I my best beloved's am, that he is mine.

GEORGE SANDYS, *Paraphrase upon the Psalms of David*, 1636.

DEO OPTIMO MAXIMO.

O THOU who all things hast of nothing made,
Whose hand the radiant firmament displayed,
With such an undiscernèd swiftness hurled
About the steadfast centre of the world;
Against whose rapid course the restless sun 5
And wandering flames in varied motions run,
Which heat, life, light infuse; time, night, and day
Distinguish; in our human bodies sway:
That hung'st the solid earth in fleeting air,
Veined with clear springs, which ambient seas repair. 10
In clouds the mountains wrap their hoary heads;
Luxurious valleys clothed with flowery meads;
Her trees yield fruit and shade; with liberal breasts
All creatures she, their common mother, feasts.

Then man thy image mad'st; in dignity, 15
In knowledge, and in beauty like to thee;
Placed in a heaven on earth; without his toil
The ever-flourishing and fruitful soil
Unpurchased food produced; all creatures were
His subjects, serving more for love than fear. 20
He knew no lord but thee; but when he fell
From his obedience, all at once rebel,
And in his ruin exercise their might;
Concurring elements against him fight;
Troops of unknown diseases, sorrow, age, 25
And death assail him with successive rage.
Hell let forth all her furies; none so great
As man to man: — ambition, pride, deceit,
Wrong armed with power, lust, rapine, slaughter reigned,
And flattered vice the name of virtue gained. 30
Then hills beneath the swelling waters stood
And all the globe of earth was but one flood,
Yet could not cleanse their guilt. The following race
Worse than their fathers, and their sons more base,
Their god-like beauty lost; sin's wretched thrall 35
No spark of their divine original
Left unextinguished; all envelopèd
With darkness, in their bold transgressions dead:
When thou didst from the east a light display,
Which rendered to the world a clearer day; 40
Whose precepts from hell's jaws our steps withdraw,
And whose example was a living law;
Who purged us with his blood, the way prepared
To heaven, and these long chained-up doors unbarred.
How infinite thy mercy! which exceeds 45
The world thou mad'st, as well as our misdeeds;
Which greater reverence than thy justice wins,
And still augments thy honor by our sins.

O who hath tasted of thy clemency
In greater measure or more oft than I! 50
My grateful verse thy goodness shall display,
O thou who went'st along in all my way,
To where the morning with perfumèd wings
From the high mountains of Panchæa springs,
To that new found-out world, where sober Night 55
Takes from the antipodes her silent flight;
To those dark seas where horrid Winter reigns,
And binds the stubborn floods in icy chains;
To Libyan wastes, whose thirst no showers assuage,
And where the swollen Nilus cools the lion's rage. 60
Thy wonders in the deep I have beheld;
Yet all by those on Judah's hill excelled,
There, where the Virgin's son his doctrine taught,
His miracles and our redemption wrought;
Where I, by thee inspired, his praises sung, 65
And on his sepulchre my offering hung.
Which way soe'er I turn my face or feet,
I see thy glory, and thy mercy meet;
Met on the Thracian shores, where in the strife
Of frantic Simoans thou preservedst my life; 70
So, when Arabian thieves belaid us round,
And when, by all abandoned, thee I found.
That false Sidonian wolf, whose craft put on
A sheep's soft fleece, and me, Bellerophon,
To ruin by his cruel letter sent, 75
Thou didst by thy protecting hand prevent.
Thou savedst me from the bloody massacres
Of faithless Indians; from their treacherous wars;
From raging fevers, from the sultry breath
Of tainted air, which cloyed the jaws of death; 80
Preserved from swallowing seas, when towering waves
Mixed with the clouds and opened their deep graves;

From barbarous pirates ransomed, by those taught,
Successfully with Salian Moors we fought;
Then brought'st me home in safety, that this earth 85
Might bury me, which fed me from my birth;
Blest with a healthful age, a quiet mind,
Content with little, to this work designed,
Which I at length have finished by thy aid,
And now my vows have at thy altar paid. 90

ABRAHAM COWLEY, *Sylva*, 1636.

A VOTE.

THIS only grant me, that my means may lie
Too low for envy, for contempt too high.
  Some honor I would have,
Not from great deeds, but good alone:
Th' unknown are better than ill-known; 5
  Rumor can ope the grave.
Acquaintance I would have, but when 't depends
Not on the number, but the choice of friends.

Books should, not business, entertain the light;
And sleep, as undisturbed as death, the night. 10
  My house a cottage, more
Than palace, and should fitting be
For all my use, no luxury.
  My garden painted o'er
With Nature's hand, not Art's; and pleasures yield 15
Horace might envy in his Sabine field.

Thus would I double my life's fading space,
For he that runs it well, twice runs his race.

And in this true delight,
These unbought sports, this happy state, 20
I would not fear nor wish my fate,
But boldly say each night:
To-morrow let my sun his beams display,
Or in clouds hide them: I have lived to-day.

ODE VI.

UPON THE SHORTNESS OF MAN'S LIFE.

MARK that swift arrow how it cuts the air,
How it outruns thy hunting eye.
Use all persuasions now and try
If thou canst call it back or stay it there.
That way it went, but thou shalt find 5
No track of 't left behind.

Fool, 't is thy life, and the fond archer, thou!
Of all the time thou 'st shot away,
I 'll bid thee fetch but yesterday,
And it shall be too hard a task to do. 10
Besides repentance, what canst find
That it hath left behind?

Our life is carried with too strong a tide,
A doubtful cloud our substance bears
And is the horse of all our years; 15
Each day doth on a wingèd whirlwind ride.
We and our glass run out, and must
Both render up our dust.

But his past life who without grief can see,
Who never thinks his end too near 20
But says to fame 'Thou art mine heir,'

That man extends life's natural brevity:
This is, this is the only way
To outlive Nestor in a day.

SIR JOHN SUCKLING, *Aglaura*, 1638; acted 1637.

WHY SO PALE AND WAN, FOND LOVER?

WHY so pale and wan, fond lover?
Prithee why so pale?
Will, when looking well can't move her,
Looking ill prevail?
Prithee why so pale? 5

Why so dull and mute, young sinner?
Prithee why so mute?
Will, when speaking well can't win her,
Saying nothing do 't?
Prithee why so mute? 10

Quit, quit, for shame! this will not move,
This cannot take her;
If of herself she will not love,
Nothing can make her:
The devil take her! 15

TRUE LOVE.

No, no, fair heretic, it needs must be
But an ill love in me,
And worse for thee;
For were it in my power
To love thee now this hour 5

More than I did the last;
'T would then so fall,
I might not love at all;
Love that can flow, and can admit increase,
Admits as well an ebb, and may grow less. 10

True love is still the same; the torrid zones
And those more frigid ones,
It must not know:
For love grown cold or hot
Is lust or friendship, not 15
The thing we have.
For that 's a flame would die,
Held down or up too high:
Then think I love more than I can express,
And would love more, could I but love thee less. 20

ROBERT HERRICK, *Hesperides*, 1648; written after 1637.

AN ODE FOR BEN JONSON.

AH, Ben!
Say how, or when
Shall we thy guests
Meet at those lyric feasts,
Made at the Sun, 5
The Dog, the Triple Tun?
Where we such clusters had,
As made us nobly wild, not mad;
And yet each verse of thine
Out-did the meat, out-did the frolic wine. 10

My Ben!
Or come again:
Or send to us,
Thy wit's great over-plus;
But teach us yet 15
Wisely to husband it;
Lest we that talent spend:
And having once brought to an end
That precious stock, the store
Of such a wit the world should have no more. 20

THOMAS CAREW, *Poems*, 1640;
written between 1630 and 1638.

THE SPRING.

Now that winter 's gone, the earth hath lost
Her snow-white robes, and now no more the frost
Candies the grass, or casts an icy cream
Upon the silver lake and crystal stream.
But the warm sun thaws the benumbèd earth, 5
And makes it tender, gives a sacred birth
To the dead swallow, wakes in hollow tree
The drowsy cuckoo and the humble-bee.
Now do a choir of chirping minstrels bring,
In triumph to the world, the youthful spring; 10
The vallies, hills and woods, in rich array,
Welcome the coming of the longed-for May.
Now all things smile, only my love doth lower;
Nor hath the scalding noon-day sun the power
To melt that marble ice which still doth hold 15
Her heart congealed, and makes her pity cold.

The ox, which lately did for shelter fly
Into the stall, doth now securely lie
In open fields ; and love no more is made
By the fire side ; but, in the cooler shade, 20
Amyntas now doth with his Chloris sleep
Under a sycamore ; and all things keep
Time with the season — only she doth carry
June in her eyes, in her heart January.

PERSUASIONS TO LOVE.

THINK not 'cause men flatt'ring say,
Y' are fresh as April, sweet as May,
Bright as is the morning star,
That you are so ; or, though you are,
Be not therefore proud, and deem 5
All men unworthy your esteem :
For, being so, you lose the pleasure
Of being fair, since that rich treasure
Of rare beauty and sweet feature,
Was bestowed on you by nature 10
To be enjoyed ; and 't were a sin
There to be scarce, where she hath bin
So prodigal of her best graces.
Thus common beauties and mean faces
Shall have more pastime, and enjoy 15
The sport you lose by being coy.
Did the thing for which I sue
Only concern myself, not you —
Were men so framed, as they alone
Reaped all the pleasure, women none — 20
Then had you reason to be scant ;
But 't were madness not to grant
That which affords (if you consent)

To you the giver, more content
Than me the beggar. O then be 25
Kind to yourself if not to me;
Starve not yourself, because you may
Thereby make me pine away;
Nor let brittle beauty make
You your wiser thoughts forsake. 30
For that lovely face will fail,
Beauty 's sweet, but beauty 's frail;
'T is sooner past, 't is sooner done
Than summer's rain or winter's sun;
Most fleeting when it is most dear — 35
'T is gone while we but say 't is here.
These curious locks, so aptly twined,
Whose every hair my soul doth bind,
Will change their abron hue and grow
White and cold as winter's snow. 40
That eye, which now is Cupid's nest,
Will prove his grave, and all the rest
Will follow; in the cheek, chin, nose,
Nor lily shall be found, nor rose:
And what will then become of all 45
Those whom now you servants call?
Like swallows when your summer 's done,
They 'll fly and seek some warmer sun.
Then wisely choose one to your friend,
Whose love may, when your beauties end, 50
Remain still firm; be provident
And think, before the summer 's spent,
Of following winter; like the ant
In plenty hoard for time is scant.
Cull out amongst the multitude 55
Of lovers, that seek to intrude
Into your favor, one that may

Love for an age, not for a day;
One that will quench your youthful fires,
And feed in age your hot desires. 60
For when the storms of time have moved
Waves on that cheek that was beloved,
When a fair lady's face is pined,
And yellow spread where red once shined,
When beauty, youth, and all sweets leave her, 65
Love may return, but lover never:
And old folks say there are no pains
Like itch of love in agèd veins.
O love me then, and now begin it,
Let us not lose the present minute; 70
For time and age will work that wrack
Which time or age shall ne'er call back.
The snake each year fresh skin resumes,
And eagles change their agèd plumes;
The faded rose each spring receives 75
A fresh red tincture on her leaves:
But if your beauty once decay,
You never know a second May.
O then be wise, and whilst your season
Affords you days for sport, do reason; 80
Spend not in vain your life's short hour,
But crop in time your beauties' flower,
Which will away, and doth together
Both bud and fade, both blow and wither.

A CRUEL MISTRESS.

We read of kings and gods that kindly took
A pitcher filled with water from the brook;
But I have daily tendered without thanks
Rivers of tears that overflow their banks.

A slaughtered bull will appease angry Jove, 5
A horse the sun, a lamb the god of love ;
But she disdains the spotless sacrifice
Of a pure heart that at her altar lies.
Vesta is not displeased if her chaste urn
Do with repairèd fuel ever burn, 10
But my saint frowns, though to her honored name
I consecrate a never-dying flame.
The Assyrian king did none i' the furnace throw
But those that to his image did not bow;
With bended knees I daily worship her, 15
Yet she consumes her own idolater.
Of such a goddess no times leave record,
That burned the temple where she was adored.

MEDIOCRITY IN LOVE REJECTED.

Give me more love, or more disdain:
  The torrid, or the frozen zone
Bring equal ease unto my pain;
  The temperate affords me none:
Either extreme, of love or hate, 5
Is sweeter than a calm estate.

Give me a storm; if it be love,
  Like Danaë in that golden shower
I swim in pleasure; if it prove
  Disdain, that torrent will devour 10
My vulture-hopes; and he 's possessed
Of heaven that 's but from hell released.

Then crown my joys, or cure my pain;
Give me more love, or more disdain.

TO MY INCONSTANT MISTRESS.

When thou, poor excommunicate
From all the joys of love, shalt see
The full reward and glorious fate
Which my strong faith shall purchase me,
Then curse thine own inconstancy. 5

A fairer hand than thine shall cure
That heart which thy false oaths did wound;
And to my soul, a soul more pure
Than thine shall by love's hand be bound,
And both with equal glory crowned. 10

Then shalt thou weep, entreat, complain
To Love, as I did once to thee;
When all thy tears shall be as vain
As mine were then, for thou shalt be
Damned for thy false apostasy. 15

PERSUASIONS TO JOY.

If the quick spirits in your eye
Now languish, and anon must die;
If every sweet and every grace
Must fly from that forsaken face:
Then, Celia, let us reap our joys 5
Ere time such goodly fruit destroys.

Or, if that golden fleece must grow
For ever, free from agèd snow;
If those bright suns must know no shade,
Nor your fresh beauties ever fade; 10

Then fear not, Celia, to bestow
What still being gathered still must grow:
Thus, either Time his sickle brings
In vain, or else in vain his wings.

A DEPOSITION FROM LOVE.

I WAS foretold, your rebel sex
Nor love nor pity knew,
And with what scorn you use to vex
Poor hearts that humbly sue;
Yet I believed to crown our pain, 5
Could we the fortress win,
The happy lover sure should gain
A paradise within.
I thought love's plagues like dragons sate,
Only to fright us at the gate. 10

But I did enter, and enjoy
What happy lovers prove,
For I could kiss, and sport, and toy,
And taste those sweets of love
Which, had they but a lasting state, 15
Or if in Celia's breast
The force of love might not abate,
Jove were too mean a guest.
But now her breach of faith far more
Afflicts than did her scorn before. 20

Hard fate! to have been once possest,
As victor, of a heart
Achieved with labor and unrest,
And then forced to depart!
If the stout foe will not resign 25

When I besiege a town,
I lose but what was never mine;
But he that is cast down
From enjoyed beauty, feels a woe
Only deposèd kings can know. 30

CELIA SINGING.

You that think love can convey
No other way
But through the eyes, into the heart
His fatal dart,
Close up those casements, and but hear 5
This siren sing;
And on the wing
Of her sweet voice it shall appear
That love can enter at the ear.

Then unveil your eyes, behold 10
The curious mould
Where that voice dwells; and as we know
When the cocks crow
We freely may
Gaze on the day; 15
So may you, when the music 's done
Awake, and see the rising sun.

TO T. H.,

A LADY RESEMBLING HIS MISTRESS.

Fair copy of my Celia's face,
Twin of my soul, thy perfect grace
Claims in my love an equal place.

Disdain not a divided heart,
Though all be hers, you shall have part; 5
Love is not tied to rules of art.

For as my soul first to her flew,
It stayed with me; so now 't is true
It dwells with her, though fled to you.

Then entertain this wand'ring guest, 10
And if not love, allow it rest;
It left not, but mistook the nest.

Nor think my love, or your fair eyes
Cheaper 'cause from the sympathies
You hold with her, these flames arise. 15

To lead, or brass, or some such bad
Metal, a prince's stamp may add
That value which it never had.

But to pure refinèd ore,
The stamp of kings imparts no more 20
Worth than the metal held before;

Only the image gives the rate
To subjects, in a foreign state
'T is prized as much for its own weight.

So though all other hearts resign 25
To your pure worth, yet you have mine
Only because you are her coin.

IN THE PERSON OF A LADY TO HER INCONSTANT SERVANT.

When on the altar of my hand,
  (Bedewed with many a kiss and tear),
Thy now revolted heart did stand
  An humble martyr, thou didst swear
  Thus (and the god of love did hear): 5
'By those bright glances of thine eye,
Unless thou pity me, I die.'

When first those perjured lips of thine,
  Bepaled with blasting sighs, did seal
Their violated faith on mine, 10
  From the soft bosom that did heal
  Thee, thou my melting heart didst steal;
My soul, enflamed with thy false breath,
Poisoned with kisses, sucked in death.

Yet I nor hand nor lip will move, 15
  Revenge or mercy to procure
From the offended god of love;
  My curse is fatal, and my pure
  Love shall beyond thy scorn endure.
If I implore the gods, they 'll find 20
Thee too ungrateful, me too kind.

RED AND WHITE ROSES.

Read in these roses the sad story
Of my hard fate and your own glory:
In the white you may discover
The paleness of a fainting lover;
In the red, the flames still feeding 5
On my heart with fresh wounds bleeding.

The white will tell you how I languish,
And the red express my anguish:
The white my innocence displaying,
The red my martyrdom betraying. 10
The frowns that on your brow resided,
Have those roses thus divided;
O! let your smiles but clear the weather,
And then they both shall grow together.

EPITAPH ON LADY MARY WENTWORTH.

AND here the precious dust is laid,
Whose purely-tempered clay was made
So fine, that it the guest betrayed.

Else the soul grew so fast within,
It broke the outward shell of sin, 5
And so was hatched a cherubin.

In height, it soared to God above,
In depth, it did to knowledge move,
And spread in breadth to general love.

Before, a pious duty shined 10
To parents, courtesy behind,
On either side an equal mind.

Good to the poor, to kindred dear,
To servants kind, to friendship clear,
To nothing but herself severe. 15

So, though a virgin, yet a bride
To every grace, she justified
A chaste polygamy, and died.

Learn from hence, reader, what small trust
We owe this world, where virtue must, 20
Frail as our flesh, crumble to dust.

A SONG.

Ask me no more where Jove bestows,
When June is past, the fading rose;
For in your beauty's orient deep,
These flowers, as in their causes, sleep.

Ask me no more whither do stray 5
The golden atoms of the day;
For, in pure love, heaven did prepare
Those powders to enrich your hair.

Ask me no more whither doth haste
The nightingale, when May is past; 10
For in your sweet dividing throat
She winters, and keeps warm her note.

Ask me no more where those stars light,
That downwards fall in dead of night;
For in your eyes they sit, and there 15
Fixed become, as in their sphere.

Ask me no more if east or west,
The phœnix builds her spicy nest;
For unto you at last she flies,
And in your fragrant bosom dies. 20

MURDERING BEAUTY.

I 'LL gaze no more on that bewitchèd face,
Since ruin harbors there in every place,
For my enchanted soul alike she drowns,
With calms and tempests of her smiles and frowns.
I 'll love no more those cruel eyes of hers, 5
Which, pleased or angered, still are murderers;
For if she dart like lightning through the air
Her beams of wrath, she kills me with despair;
If she behold me with a pleasing eye,
I surfeit with excess of joy, and die. 10

ROBERT HERRICK, *Hesperides,* 1648; written between 1629 and 1640.

DELIGHT IN DISORDER.

A SWEET disorder in the dress
Kindles in clothes a wantonness.
A lawn about the shoulders thrown
Into a fine distractiòn;
An erring lace, which here and there 5
Enthralls the crimson stomacher;
A cuff neglectful, and thereby
Ribbands to flow confusedly;
A winning wave (deserving note)
In the tempestuous petticoat; 10
A careless shoe-string, in whose tie
I see a wild civility;
Do more bewitch me, than when art
Is too precise in every part.

TO LAURELS.

A FUNERAL stone
Or verse, I covet none;
But only crave
Of you that I may have
A sacred laurel springing from my grave; 5
Which being seen
Blest with perpetual green,
May grow to be
Not so much called a tree
As the eternal monument of me. 10

TO THE VIRGINS, TO MAKE MUCH OF TIME.

GATHER ye rosebuds while ye may,
Old time is still a-flying;
And this same flower that smiles to-day,
To-morrow will be dying.

The glorious lamp of heaven, the sun, 5
The higher he 's a-getting,
The sooner will his race be run,
And nearer he 's to setting.

That age is best which is the first,
When youth and blood are warmer; 10
But being spent, the worse, and worst
Times still succeed the former.

Then be not coy, but use your time,
And while ye may, go marry;
For having lost but once your prime, 15
You may forever tarry.

TO THE WESTERN WIND.

SWEET western wind, whose luck it is,
 Made rival with the air,
To give Perenna's lip a kiss,
 And fan her wanton hair,

Bring me but one, I 'll promise thee, 5
 Instead of common showers,
Thy wings shall be embalmed by me,
 And all beset with flowers.

TO PRIMROSES FILLED WITH MORNING DEW.

WHY do ye weep, sweet babes? Can tears
   Speak grief in you,
   Who were but born
  Just as the modest morn
  Teemed her refreshing dew? 5
 Alas, you have not known that shower
   That mars a flower,
   Nor felt the unkind
  Breath of a blasting wind,
  Nor are ye worn with years, 10
   Or warped, as we,
  Who think it strange to see
Such pretty flowers, like to orphans young,
To speak by tears before ye have a tongue.

Speak, whimpering younglings, and make known 15
   The reason why
   Ye droop and weep.
  Is it for want of sleep,
  Or childish lullaby?

Or that ye have not seen as yet 20
The violet?
Or brought a kiss
From that sweetheart to this?
No, no, this sorrow shown
By your tears shed 25
Would have this lecture read:
That things of greatest, so of meanest worth,
Conceived with grief are, and with tears brought forth.

TO ANTHEA,

WHO MAY COMMAND HIM ANYTHING.

Bid me to live, and I will live
Thy protestant to be;
Or bid me love, and I will give
A loving heart to thee.

A heart as soft, a heart as kind, 5
A heart as sound and free,
As in the whole world thou canst find,
That heart I 'll give to thee.

Bid that heart stay and it will stay,
To honor thy decree; 10
Or bid it languish quite away,
And 't shall do so for thee.

Bid me to weep, and I will weep,
While I have eyes to see;
And having none, yet I will keep 15
A heart to weep for thee.

Bid me despair, and I 'll despair,
Under that cypress tree;

Or bid me die, and I will dare
  E'en death, to die for thee. 20

Thou art my life, my love, my heart,
  The very eyes of me,
And hast command of every part
  To live and die for thee.

TO MEADOWS.

Ye have been fresh and green,
  Ye have been filled with flowers;
And ye the walks have been
  Where maids have spent their hours.

You have beheld how they 5
  With wicker arks did come,
To kiss and bear away
  The richer cowslips home.

Y 'ave heard them sweetly sing,
  And seen them in a round; 10
Each virgin, like a spring,
  With honeysuckles crowned.

But now, we see none here,
  Whose silv'ry feet did tread,
And with dishevelled hair 15
  Adorned this smoother mead.

Like unthrifts, having spent
  Your stock, and needy grown,
Y' are left here to lament
  Your poor estates, alone. 20

TO DAFFODILS.

FAIR daffodils, we weep to see
    You haste away so soon;
As yet the early rising sun
    Has not attained his noon.
        Stay, stay, 5
    Until the hasting day
            Has run
    But to the even-song;
And, having prayed together, we
        Will go with you along. 10

We have short time to stay, as you
    We have as short a spring;
As quick a growth to meet decay
    As you, or any thing.
        We die, 15
    As your hours do, and dry
            Away,
    Like to the summer's rain;
Or as the pearls of morning's dew,
        Ne'er to be found again. 20

TO BLOSSOMS.

FAIR pledges of a fruitful tree,
    Why do ye fall so fast?
    Your date is not so past
But you may stay yet here a while,
    To blush and gently smile, 5
            And go at last.

What, were ye born to be
An hour or half's delight,
And so to bid good-night?
'T was pity Nature brought ye forth, 10
Merely to show your worth,
And lose you quite.

But you are lovely leaves, where we
May read how soon things have
Their end, though ne'er so brave; 15
And after they have shown their pride
Like you awhile, they glide
Into the grave.

HIS GRANGE, OR PRIVATE WEALTH.

THOUGH clock,
To tell how night draws hence, I 've none,
A cock
I have to sing how day draws on.
I have 5
A maid, my Prue, by good luck sent,
To save
That little Fates me gave or lent.
A hen
I keep, which, creaking day by day, 10
Tells when
She goes her long white egg to lay.
A goose
I have, which, with a jealous ear,
Lets loose 15
Her tongue to tell what danger 's near.
A lamb
I keep, tame, with my morsels fed,

Whose dam
An orphan left him, lately dead. 20
A cat
I keep, that plays about my house,
Grown fat
With eating many a miching mouse;
To these 25
A Tracy I do keep, whereby
I please
The more my rural privacy:
Which are
But toys, to give my heart some ease. 30
Where care
None is, slight things do lightly please.

ROBERT HERRICK, *Noble Numbers*, 1647; written between 1629 and 1640.

TO DEATH.

THOU bidd'st me come away,
And I 'll no longer stay
Than for to shed some tears
For faults of former years,
And to repent some crimes 5
Done in the present times;
And next, to take a bit
Of bread, and wine with it;
To don my robes of love,
Fit for the place above; 10
To gird my loins about
With charity throughout,
And so to travel hence
With feet of innocence:

These done, I 'll only cry, 15
"God, mercy!" and so die.

A THANKSGIVING TO GOD FOR HIS HOUSE.

LORD, thou hast given me a cell
Wherein to dwell,
A little house, whose humble roof
Is weatherproof,
Under the spars of which I lie 5
Both soft and dry;
Where thou, my chamber for to ward,
Hast set a guard
Of harmless thoughts, to watch and keep
Me while I sleep. 10
Low is my porch, as is my fate,
Both void of state;
And yet the threshold of my door
Is worn by th' poor,
Who thither come and freely get 15
Good words or meat.
Like as my parlor so my hall
And kitchen 's small;
A little buttery, and therein
A little bin, 20
Which keeps my little loaf of bread
Unchipped, unfled;
Some brittle sticks of thorn or briar
Make me a fire,
Close by whose living coal I sit, 25
And glow like it.
Lord, I confess too, when I dine,
The pulse is thine,

And all those other bits that be
There placed by thee ; 30
The worts, the purslane, and the mess
Of water-cress,
Which of thy kindness thou hast sent ;
And my content
Makes those, and my belovèd beet, 35
To be more sweet.
'T is thou that crown'st my glittering hearth
With guiltless mirth,
And giv'st me wassail bowls to drink,
Spiced to the brink. 40
Lord, 't is thy plenty-dropping hand
That soils my land,
And giv'st me, for my bushel sown,
Twice ten for one ;
Thou mak'st my teeming hen to lay 45
Her egg each day ;
Besides my healthful ewes to bear
Me twins each year ;
The while the conduits of my kine
Run cream, for wine. 50
All these, and better thou dost send
Me, to this end,
That I should render, for my part,
A thankful heart,
Which, fired with incense, I resign, 55
As wholly thine ;
But the acceptance, — that must be,
My Christ, by thee.

William Habington, *Castara,*
Part III, 1639–40.

NOX NOCTI INDICAT SCIENTIAM.

When I survey the bright
Celestial sphere,
So rich with jewels hung, that night
Doth like an Ethiop bride appear,

My soul her wings doth spread, 5
And heavenward flies,
The Almighty's mysteries to read
In the large volume of the skies.

For the bright firmament
Shoots forth no flame 10
So silent, but is eloquent
In speaking the Creator's name.

No unregarded star
Contracts its light
Into so small a character, 15
Removed far from our human sight,

But, if we steadfast look,
We shall discern
In it, as in some holy book,
How man may heavenly knowledge learn. 20

It tells the conqueror,
That far-stretched power
Which his proud dangers traffic for,
Is but the triumph of an hour.

That from the farthest north 25
Some nation may,
Yet undiscovered, issue forth,
And o'er his new-got conquest sway.

Some nation yet shut in
With hills of ice 30
May be let out to scourge his sin,
Till they shall equal him in vice.

And then they likewise shall
Their ruin have;
For as yourselves your empires fall, 35
And every kingdom hath a grave.

Thus those celestial fires,
Though seeming mute
The fallacy of our desires
And all the pride of life confute. 40

For they have watched since first
The world had birth:
And found sin in itself accursed,
And nothing permanent on earth.

WILLIAM HABINGTON, *Cleodora, the Queen of Arragon*, 1640.

HIS MISTRESS FLOUTED.

FINE young folly, though you were
That fair beauty I did swear,
Yet you ne'er could reach my heart;
For we courtiers learn at school
Only with your sex to fool; 5
You 're not worth the serious part.

When I sigh and kiss your hand,
Cross my arms and wondering stand,
  Holding parley with your eye,
Then dilate on my desires, 10
Swear the sun ne'er shot such fires —
  All is but a handsome lie.

When I eye your curl or lace,
Gentle soul, you think your face
  Straight some murder doth commit; 15
And your virtue both begin
To grow scrupulous of my sin,
  When I talk to show my wit.

Therefore, madam, wear no cloud,
Nor to check my love grow proud; 20
  In sooth I much do doubt
'T is the powder in your hair,
Not your breath, perfumes the air,
  And your clothes that set you out.

Yet though truth has this confessed, 25
And I vow I love in jest,
  When I next begin to court,
And protest an amorous flame,
You will swear I in earnest am.
  Bedlam! this is pretty sport. 30

JAMES SHIRLEY, *The Imposture*,
1652; acted 1640.

PEACE RESTORED.

You virgins, that did late despair
  To keep your wealth from cruel men,

Tie up in silk your careless hair:
  Soft peace is come again.

Now lovers' eyes may gently shoot 5
  A flame that will not kill;
The drum was angry, but the lute
  Shall whisper what you will.

Sing Io, Io! for his sake,
  That hath restored your drooping heads; 10
With choice of sweetest flowers make
  A garden where he treads;

Whilst we whole groves of laurel bring,
  A petty triumph to his brow,
Who is the master of our spring 15
  And all the bloom we owe.

SONG OF THE NUNS.

O FLY, my soul! what hangs upon
    Thy drooping wings,
    And weighs them down
With love of gaudy mortal things?

The sun is now i' the east; each shade, 5
    As he doth rise,
    Is shorter made,
That earth may lessen to our eyes.

O, be not careless then and play
    Until the star of peace 10
Hide all his beams in dark recess.
Poor pilgrims needs must lose their way
When all the shadows do increase.

JAMES SHIRLEY, *The Contention of Ajax and Ulysses*, 1659; written about 1640.

NO ARMOR AGAINST FATE.

THE glories of our blood and state
Are shadows, not substantial things;
There is no armor against fate;
Death lays his icy hand on kings:
Sceptre and crown 5
Must tumble down,
And in the dust be equal made
With the poor crooked scythe and spade.

Some men with swords may reap the field,
And plant fresh laurels where they kill; 10
But their strong nerves at last must yield,
They tame but one another still:
Early or late
They stoop to fate
And must give up their murmuring breath 15
When they, pale captives, creep to death.

The garlands wither on your brow,
Then boast no more your mighty deeds;
Upon Death's purple altar now
See where the victor-victim bleeds: 20
Your heads must come
To the cold tomb;
Only the actions of the just
Smell sweet, and blossom in their dust.

ROBERT HERRICK, *Hesperides*, 1648; written before 1641.

HIS WINDING-SHEET.

COME thou, who art the wine and wit
Of all I 've writ;
The grace, the glory, and the best
Piece of the rest;
Thou art of what I did intend 5
The all and end;
And what was made, was made to meet
Thee, thee my sheet:
Come then, and be to my chaste side
Both bed and bride. 10
We two, as relics left, will have
One rest, one grave;
And, hugging close, we will not fear
Lust entering here,
Where all desires are dead or cold, 15
As is the mould;
And all affections are forgot,
Or trouble not.
Here, here the slaves and pris'ners be
From shackles free, 20
And weeping widows, long oppressed,
Do here find rest.
The wrongèd client ends his laws
Here, and his cause;
Here those long suits of Chancery lie 25
Quiet, or die,
And all Star Chamber bills do cease,
Or hold their peace.
Here needs no Court for our Request,
Where all are best, 30

All wise, all equal, and all just
Alike i' th' dust.
Nor need we here to fear the frown
Of court or crown:
Where Fortune bears no sway o'er things, 35
There all are kings.
In this securer place we 'll keep,
As lulled asleep;
Or for a little time we 'll lie,
As robes laid by, 40
To be another day re-worn,
Turned, but not torn;
Or like old testaments engrossed,
Locked up, not lost;
And for a while lie here concealed, 45
To be revealed
Next, at that great Platonic Year,
And then meet here.

GEORGE WITHER, *Haleluiah, or Britain's Second Remembrancer,* 1641.

A ROCKING HYMN.

SWEET baby sleep! what ails my dear,
What ails my darling thus to cry?
Be still, my child, and lend thine ear
To hear me sing thy lullaby:
My pretty lamb, forbear to weep, 5
Be still my dear, sweet baby sleep.

Thou blessed soul, what canst thou fear?
What thing to thee can mischief do?

Thy God is now thy father dear,
His holy spouse, thy mother too: 10
Sweet baby, then forbear to weep,
Be still my babe, sweet baby sleep.

Though thy conception was in sin,
A sacred bathing thou hast had;
And, though thy birth unclean hath been, 15
A blameless babe thou now art made:
Sweet baby, then forbear to weep,
Be still my dear, sweet baby sleep.

Whilst thus thy lullaby I sing,
For thee great blessings ripening be; 20
Thine eldest brother is a king,
And hath a kingdom bought for thee:
Sweet baby, then forbear to weep,
Be still my babe, sweet baby sleep.

Sweet baby sleep and nothing fear, 25
For whosoever thee offends,
By thy protector threat'ned are,
And God and angels are thy friends:
Sweet baby, then forbear to weep,
Be still my babe, sweet baby sleep. 30

When God with us was dwelling here,
In little babes he took delight;
Such innocents as thou, my dear,
Are ever precious in his sight:
Sweet baby, then forbear to weep, 35
Be still my babe, sweet baby sleep.

A little infant once was he,
And, strength in weakness, then was laid
Upon his virgin-mother's knee,

That power to thee might be conveyed: 40
Sweet baby, then forbear to weep,
Be still my babe, sweet baby sleep.

In this, thy frailty and thy need,
He friends and helpers doth prepare,
Which thee shall cherish, clothe and feed, 45
For of thy weal they tender are:
Sweet baby, then forbear to weep,
Be still my babe, sweet baby sleep.

The king of kings, when he was born,
Had not so much for outward ease; 50
By him such dressings were not worn,
Nor such like swaddling-clothes as these:
Sweet baby, then forbear to weep,
Be still my babe, sweet baby sleep.

Within a manger lodged thy lord 55
Where oxen lay and asses fed;
Warm rooms we do to thee afford,
An easy cradle or a bed:
Sweet baby, then forbear to weep,
Be still my babe, sweet baby sleep. 60

The wants that he did then sustain
Have purchased wealth, my babe, for thee;
And by his torments and his pain
Thy rest and ease securèd be:
My baby, then forbear to weep, 65
Be still my babe, sweet baby sleep.

Thou hast (yet more) to perfect this
A promise and an earnest got
Of gaining everlasting bliss,

Though thou, my babe, perceiv'st it not: 70
Sweet baby, then forbear to weep,
Be still my babe, sweet baby sleep.

WILLIAM CARTWRIGHT, *Comedies, Tragi-Comedies and Other Poems*, 1651; written before 1641.

TO CUPID.

THOU who didst never see the light,
Nor knowst the pleasure of the sight,
But always blinded, canst not say
Now it is night, or now 't is day,
So captivate her sense, so blind her eye, 5
That still she love me, yet she ne'er know why.

Thou who dost wound us with such art,
We see no blood drop from the heart,
And, subtly cruel, leav'st no sign
To tell the blow or hand was thine, 10
O gently, gently wound my fair, that she
May thence believe the wound did come from me.

VENUS.

VENUS, redress a wrong that 's done
By that young sprightful boy, thy son,
He wounds, and then laughs at the sore:
Hatred itself can do no more.
If I pursue, he 's small and light, 5
Both seen at once, and out of sight;
If I do fly, he 's wing'd, and then
At the third step I 'm caught again:

Lest one day thou thyself mayst suffer so,
Or clip the wanton's wings or break his bow. 10

TO CHLOE,

WHO WISHED HERSELF YOUNG ENOUGH FOR ME.

O CHLOE, why wish you that your years
Would backwards run till they meet mine,
That perfect likeness, which endears
Things unto things, might us combine?
Our ages so in date agree, 5
That twins do differ more than we.

There are two births, the one when light
First strikes the new awak'ned sense;
The other when two souls unite;
And we must count our life from thence: 10
When you loved me and I loved you,
Then both of us were born anew.

Love then to us new souls did give,
And in those souls did plant new powers;
Since when another life we live, 15
The breath we breathe is his, not ours;
Love makes those young whom age doth chill,
And whom he finds young, keeps young still.

Love, like that angel that shall call
Our bodies from the silent grave, 20
Unto one age doth raise us all,
None too much, none too little have;
Nay, that the difference may be none,
He makes two not alike, but one.

And now, since you and I are such, 25
Tell me what 's yours, and what is mine?
Our eyes, our ears, our taste, smell, touch,
Do — like our souls — in one combine;
So by this, I as well may be
Too old for you, as you for me. 30

A VALEDICTION.

Bid me not go where neither suns nor showers
Do make or cherish flowers;
Where discontented things in sadness lie
And Nature grieves as I;
When I am parted from those eyes, 5
From which my better day doth rise,
Though some propitious power
Should plant me in a bower,
Where amongst happy lovers I might see
How showers and sunbeams bring 10
One everlasting spring,
Nor would those fall nor these shine forth to me:
Nature to him is lost,
Who loseth her he honors most.

Then fairest to my parting view display 15
Your graces all in one full day,
Whose blessèd shapes I 'll snatch and keep, till when
I do return and view again:
So by this art fancy shall fortune cross,
And lovers live by thinking on their loss. 20

LOVE BUT ONE.

SEE these two little brooks that slowly creep
In snaky windings through the plains,
I knew them once one river, swift and deep,
Blessing and blest by poets' strains.

Then, touched with awe, we thought some god did pour 5
Those floods from out his sacred jar,
Transforming every weed into a flower,
And every flower into a star.

But since it broke itself, and double glides,
The naked banks no dress have worn, 10
And yon dry barren mountain now divides
These valleys which lost glories mourn.

O Chloris, think how this presents thy love,
Which, when it ran but in one stream,
We happy shepherds thence did thrive and prove, 15
And thou wast mine and all men's theme.

But since 't hath been imparted to one more,
And in two streams doth weakly creep,
Our common Muse is thence grown low and poor,
And mine as lean as these my sheep. 20

But think withal what honor thou hast lost,
Which we did to thy full stream pay,
Whiles now that swain that swears he loves thee most,
Slakes but his thirst, and goes away.

O in what narrow ways our minds must move ! 25
We may not hate, nor yet diffuse our love.

From *Wit's Recreations*, ed. 1641,
author unknown.

THE SAD LOVER.

WHY should I wrong my judgment so,
As for to love where I do know
There is no hold for to be taken?

For what her wish thirsts after most,
If once of it her heart can boast, 5
Straight by her folly 't is forsaken.

Thus, whilst I still pursue in vain,
Methinks I turn a child again,
And of my shadow am a-chasing.

For all her favors are to me 10
Like apparitions which I see,
But never can come near th' embracing.

Oft had I wished that there had been
Some almanac whereby to have seen,
When love with her had been in season. 15

But I perceive there is no art
Can find the epact of the heart,
That loves by chance, and not by reason.

Yet will I not for this despair,
For time her humor may prepare 20
To grace him who is now neglected.

And what unto my constancy
She now denies, one day may be
From her inconstancy expected.

RICHARD CRASHAW, *Delights of the Muses*, 1646; written before 1641.

WISHES TO HIS SUPPOSED MISTRESS.

WHOE'ER she be,
That not impossible she,
That shall command my heart and me;

Where'er she lie,
Locked up from mortal eye, 5
In shady leaves of destiny:

Till that ripe birth
Of studied fate stand forth
And teach her fair steps tread our earth;

Till that divine 10
Idea take a shrine
Of crystal flesh, through which to shine:

Meet you her, my wishes,
Bespeak her to my blisses,
And be ye called, my absent kisses. 15

I wish her beauty,
That owes not all its duty
To gaudy tire, or glist'ring shoe-tie.

Something more than
Taffeta or tissue can, 20
Or rampant feather, or rich fan.

More than the spoil
Of shop, or silkworm's toil,
Or a bought blush, or a set smile.

A face that 's best 25
By its own beauty drest,
And can alone commend the rest.

A face made up
Out of no other shop
Than what Nature's white hand sets ope. 30

A cheek where youth
And blood, with pen of truth,
Write what the reader sweetly ru'th.

A cheek where grows
More than a morning rose: 35
Which to no box his being owes.

Lips where all day
A lover's kiss may play,
Yet carry nothing thence away.

Looks that oppress 40
Their richest tires, but dress
Themselves in simple nakedness.

Eyes that displace
The neighbor diamond, and out-face
That sunshine by their own sweet grace. 45

Tresses that wear
Jewels, but to declare
How much themselves more precious are.

Whose native ray
Can tame the wanton day 50
Of gems, that in their bright shades play.

Each ruby there,
Or pearl that dares appear,
Be its own blush, be its own tear.

A well-tamed heart, 55
For whose more noble smart
Love may be long choosing a dart.

Eyes that bestow
Full quivers on Love's bow;
Yet pay less arrows than they owe. 60

Smiles that can warm
The blood, yet teach a charm,
That chastity shall take no harm.

Blushes that bin
The burnish of no sin, 65
Nor flames of aught too hot within.

Joys that confess
Virtue their mistress,
And have no other head to dress.

Fears, fond and flight 70
As the coy bride's, when night
First does the longing lover right.

Tears, quickly fled,
And vain, as those are shed
For a dying maidenhead. 75

Days that need borrow
No part of their good morrow,
From a fore-spent night of sorrow.

Days that in spite
Of darkness, by the light 80
Of a clear mind are day all night.

Nights, sweet as they,
Made short by lovers' play,
Yet long by th' absence of the day.

Life that dares send 85
A challenge to his end,
And when it comes, say, 'Welcome, friend.'

Sydneian showers
Of sweet discourse, whose powers
Can crown old Winter's head with flowers. 90

Soft silken hours,
Open suns, shady bowers,
'Bove all, nothing within that lowers.

Whate'er delight
Can make Day's forehead bright, 95
Or give down to the wings of Night.

In her whole frame
Have Nature all the name,
Art and ornament the shame.

Her flattery, 100
Picture and poesy:
Her counsel her own virtue be.

I wish her store
Of worth may leave her poor
Of wishes; and I wish — no more. 105

Now, if Time knows
That her, whose radiant brows
Weave them a garland of my vows;

Her whose just bays
My future hopes can raise, 110
A trophy to her present praise;

Her that dares be
What these lines wish to see:
I seek no further; it is she.

'T is she, and here 115
Lo! I unclothe and clear
My wishes' cloudy character.

May she enjoy it,
Whose merit dare apply it,
But modesty dares still deny it. 120

Such worth as this is,
Shall fix my flying wishes,
And determine them to kisses.

Let her full glory,
My fancies, fly before ye: 125
Be ye my fictions, but her story.

RICHARD BROME, *The Jovial Crew,* 1652; acted 1641.

THE MERRY BEGGARS.

COME, come; away! the spring,
By every bird that can but sing,
Or chirp a note, doth now invite
Us forth to taste of his delight,

In field, in grove, on hill, in dale; 5
But above all the nightingale,
Who in her sweetness strives t' outdo
The loudness of the hoarse cuckoo.
'Cuckoo,' cries he; 'jug, jug, jug,' sings she;
From bush to bush, from tree to tree: 10
Why in one place then tarry we?

Come away! why do we stay?
We have no debt or rent to pay;
No bargains or accounts to make,
Nor land or lease to let or take: 15
Or if we had, should that remore us
When all the world 's our own before us,
And where we pass and make resort,
It is our kingdom and our court.
'Cuckoo,' cries he; 'jug, jug, jug,' sings she 20
From bush to bush, from tree to tree:
Why in one place then tarry we?

Broad-sheet, 1641; author unknown.

LORD STRAFFORD'S MEDITATIONS IN THE TOWER.

Go empty joys,
With all your noise,
And leave me here alone,
In sad, sweet silence to bemoan
The fickle worldly height 5
Whose danger none can see aright,
Whilst your false splendors dim the sight.

Go, and ensnare
With your trim ware
Some other worldly wight, 10
And cheat him with your flattering light;
Rain on his head a shower
Of honor, greatness, wealth, and power;
Then snatch it from him in an hour.

Fill his big mind 15
With gallant wind
Of insolent applause;
Let him not fear the curbing laws,
Nor king, nor people's frown;
But dream of something like a crown, 20
Then, climbing upwards, tumble down.

Let him appear
In his bright sphere
Like Cynthia in her pride,
With starlike troops on every side; 25
For number and clear light
Such as may soon o'erwhelm quite,
And blind them both in one dead night.

Welcome, sad night,
Grief's sole delight, 30
Thy mourning best agrees
With honor's funeral obsequies.
In Thetis' lap he lies,
Mantled with soft securities,
Whose too much sunlight dims his eyes. 35

Was he too bold
Who needs would hold

With curbing reins the day,
And make Sol's fiery steeds obey?
Therefore as rash was I, 40
Who with Ambition's wings did fly
In Charles's wain too loftily.

I fall! I fall!
Whom shall I call?
Alas, shall I be heard 45
Who now am neither loved nor feared?
You, who have vowed the ground
To kiss where my blest steps were found,
Come, catch me at my last rebound.

How each admires 50
Heaven's twinkling fires
Whilst from their glorious seat
Their influence gives light and heat;
But O how few there are,
Though danger from the act be far, 55
Will run to catch a falling star!

O were 't our fate
To imitate
Those lights whose pallidness
Argues no guiltiness! 60
Their course is one way bent;
Which is the cause there 's no dissent
In Heaven's High Court of Parliament.

Sir John Suckling, *Fragmenta Aurea*, 1646; written between 1632 and 1641.

SONNET.

Dost see how unregarded now
That piece of beauty passes?
There was a time when I did vow
To that alone;
But mark the fate of faces; 5
The red and white works now no more on me,
Than if it could not charm, or I not see.

And yet the face continues good,
And I have still desires,
And still the self-same flesh and blood, 10
As apt to melt,
And suffer from those fires;
O, some kind power unriddle where it lies:
Whether my heart be faulty or her eyes?

She every day her man doth kill, 15
And I as often die;
Neither her power then or my will
Can questioned be.
What is the mystery?
Sure beauty's empire, like to greater states, 20
Have certain periods set, and hidden fates.

SONG.

I prithee spare me, gentle boy,
Press me no more for that slight toy,
That foolish trifle of an heart;
I swear it will not do its part,
Though thou dost thine, employ'st thy power and art. 5

For through long custom it has known
The little secrets, and is grown
Sullen and wise, will have its will,
And, like old hawks, pursues that still
That makes least sport, flies only where 't can kill. 10

Some youth that has not made his story,
Will think, perchance, the pain 's the glory;
And mannerly sit out love's feast;
I shall be carving of the best,
Rudely call for the last course 'fore the rest. 15

And, O, when once that course is past,
How short a time the feast doth last!
Men rise away, and scarce say grace,
Or civilly once thank the face
That did invite; but seek another place. 20

THE SIEGE.

'T IS now since I sat down before
That foolish fort, a heart,
(Time strangely spent) a year or more,
And still I did my part:

Made my approaches, from her hand 5
Unto her lip did rise,
And did already understand
The language of her eyes.

Proceeded on with no less art
(My tongue was engineer) 10
I thought to undermine the heart
By whispering in the ear.

When this did nothing, I brought down
  Great cannon-oaths, and shot
A thousand thousand to the town, 15
  And still it yielded not.

I then resolved to starve the place
  By cutting off all kisses,
Praying, and gazing on her face,
  And all such little blisses. 20

To draw her out, and from her strength,
  I drew all batteries in:
And brought myself to lie, at length,
  As if no siege had been.

When I had done what man could do, 25
  And thought the place mine own,
The enemy lay quiet too,
  And smiled at all was done.

I sent to know from whence and where
  These hopes and this relief. 30
A spy informed, Honor was there,
  And did command in chief.

'March, march,' quoth I, 'the word straight give,
  Let 's lose no time, but leave her;
That giant upon air will live, 35
  And hold it out for ever.

To such a place our camp remove
  As will no siege abide;
I hate a fool that starves her love,
  Only to feed her pride.' 40

SONG.

HONEST lover whatsoever,
If in all thy love there ever
Was one wav'ring thought, if thy flame
Were not still even, still the same:
Know this, 5
Thou lov'st amiss,
And, to love true,
Thou must begin again, and love anew.

If when she appears i' th' room,
Thou dost not quake, and art struck dumb, 10
And in striving this to cover,
Dost not speak thy words twice over:
Know this,
Thou lov'st amiss,
And to love true, 15
Thou must begin again, and love anew.

If fondly thou dost not mistake,
And all defects for graces take,
Persuad'st thyself that jests are broken
When she hath little or nothing spoken: 20
Know this,
Thou lov'st amiss,
And to love true,
Thou must begin again, and love anew.

If when thou appear'st to be within, 25
And lett'st not men ask and ask again;
And when thou answerest, if it be
To what was asked thee, properly:
Know this,
Thou lov'st amiss, 30

And to love true,
Thou must begin again, and love anew.

If when thy stomach calls to eat,
Thou cutt'st not fingers 'stead of meat,
And with much gazing on her face 35
Dost not rise hungry from the place:
Know this,
Thou lov'st amiss,
And to love true,
Thou must begin again, and love anew. 40

If by this thou dost discover
That thou art no perfect lover,
And desiring to love true,
Thou dost begin to love anew:
Know this, 45
Thou lov'st amiss,
And to love true,
Thou must begin again, and love anew.

Sir John Suckling, *Last Remains*, 1659; written before 1642.

CONSTANCY.

Out upon it, I have loved
Three whole days together;
And am like to love three more,
If it prove fair weather.

Time shall moult away his wings, 5
Ere he shall discover
In the whole wide world again
Such a constant lover.

But the spite on 't is, no praise
  Is due at all to me: 10
Love with me had made no stays,
  Had it any been but she.

Had it any been but she,
  And that very face,
There had been at least ere this 15
  A dozen dozen in her place.

SONG.

I PRITHEE send me back my heart,
  Since I cannot have thine;
For if from yours you will not part,
  Why then shouldst thou have mine?

Yet, now I think on 't, let it lie; 5
  To find it were in vain,
For th' hast a thief in either eye
  Would steal it back again.

Why should two hearts in one breast lie,
  And yet not lodge together? 10
O love, where is thy sympathy,
  If thus our breasts thou sever?

But love is such a mystery,
  I cannot find it out:
For when I think I 'm best resolv'd, 15
  I then am most in doubt.

Then farewell care, and farewell woe!
  I will no longer pine;
For I 'll believe I have her heart
  As much as she hath mine. 20

JOHN MILTON, *Poems, English and Latin*, 1645; written 1642.

SONNET.

WHEN THE ASSAULT WAS INTENDED TO THE CITY.

CAPTAIN or colonel, or knight in arms,
Whose chance on these defenceless doors may seize,
If deed of honor did thee ever please,
Guard them, and him within protect from harms.
He can requite thee, for he knows the charms 5
That call fame on such gentle acts as these,
And he can spread thy name o'er lands and seas,
Whatever clime the sun's bright circle warms.
Lift not thy spear against the Muses' bower:
The great Emathian conqueror bid spare 10
The house of Pindarus, when temple and tower
Went to the ground; and the repeated air
Of sad Electra's poet had the power
To save the Athenian walls from ruin bare.

RICHARD CRASHAW, *Steps to the Temple*, 1646; written before 1643.

A HYMN OF THE NATIVITY,

SUNG BY THE SHEPHERDS.

Chorus.

COME, we shepherds whose blest sight
Hath met Love's noon in Nature's night,
Come, lift we up our loftier song
And wake the sun that lies too long.

To all our world of well-stol'n joy 5
He slept, and dreamt of no such thing,
While we found out heaven's fairer eye,
And kissed the cradle of our King;
Tell him he rises now too late
To show us aught worth looking at. 10

Tell him we now can show him more
Than he e'er showed to mortal sight,
Than he himself e'er saw before,
Which to be seen needs not his light:
Tell him, Tityrus, where th' hast been, 15
Tell him, Thyrsis, what th' hast seen.

Tityrus.

Gloomy night embraced the place
Where the noble infant lay:
The babe looked up, and showed his face;
In spite of darkness it was day. 20
It was thy day, sweet, and did rise,
Not from the east but from thine eyes.

Chorus. It was thy day, sweet, etc.

Thyrsis.

Winter chid aloud, and sent
The angry North to wage his wars: 25
The North forgot his fierce intent,
And left perfumes instead of scars.
By those sweet eyes' persuasive powers,
Where he meant frosts he scattered flowers.

Chorus. By those sweet eyes, etc. 30

Both.

We saw thee in thy balmy nest,
  Young dawn of our eternal day;
We saw thine eyes break from the east,
  And chase the trembling shades away:
We saw thee, and we blest the sight, 35
We saw thee by thine own sweet light.

Tityrus.

Poor world, said I, what wilt thou do
  To entertain this starry stranger?
Is this the best thou canst bestow —
  A cold and not too cleanly manger? 40
Contend, the powers of heaven and earth,
To fit a bed for this huge birth.

  Chorus. Contend, the powers, etc.

Thyrsis.

Proud world, said I, cease your contest,
  And let the mighty babe alone, 45
The phœnix builds the phœnix' nest,
  Love's architecture is his own.
The babe, whose birth embraves this morn,
Made his own bed ere he was born.

  Chorus. The babe, whose birth, etc. 50

Tityrus.

I saw the curled drops, soft and slow,
  Come hovering o'er the place's head,
Offering their whitest sheets of snow,
  To furnish the fair infant's bed.
Forbear, said I, be not too bold; 55
Your fleece is white, but 't is too cold.

  Chorus. Forbear, said I, etc.

Thyrsis.

I saw the obsequious seraphim
  Their rosy fleece of fire bestow,
For well they now can spare their wing, 60
  Since heaven itself lies here below.
Well done, said I; but are you sure
Your down, so warm, will pass for pure?
  Chorus. Well done, said I, etc.

Both.

No, no, your King's not yet to seek 65
  Where to repose his royal head;
See, see how soon his new-bloomed cheek
  'Twixt mother's breasts is gone to bed.
Sweet choice, said we, no way but so
Not to lie cold, yet sleep in snow! 70
  Chorus. Sweet choice, said we, etc.

Full Chorus.

Welcome all wonders in our sight!
  Eternity shut in a span!
Summer in winter! day in night!
  Heaven in earth! and God in man! 75
Great little one, whose all-embracing birth
Lifts earth to heaven, stoops heaven to earth!

Welcome, though nor to gold nor silk,
  To more than Cæsar's birthright is:
Two sister seas of virgin's milk, 80
  With many a rarely-temper'd kiss,
That breathes at once both maid and mother,
Warms in the one, cools in the other.

She sings thy tears asleep, and dips
  Her kisses in thy weeping eye; 85
She spreads the red leaves of thy lips,
  That in their buds yet blushing lie.
She 'gainst those mother diamonds tries
The points of her young eagle's eyes.

Welcome — though not to those gay flies, 90
  Gilded i' th' beams of earthly kings,
Slippery souls in smiling eyes —
  But to poor shepherds' homespun things,
Whose wealth 's their flocks, whose wit to be
Well read in their simplicity. 95

Yet when young April's husband showers
  Shall bless the fruitful Maia's bed,
We 'll bring the first-born of her flowers,
  To kiss thy feet, and crown thy head.
To thee, dread Lamb! whose love must keep 100
The shepherds while they feed their sheep.

To thee, meek Majesty, soft King
  Of simple graces and sweet loves,
Each of us his lamb will bring,
  Each his pair of silver doves; 105
Till burnt at last, in fire of thy fair eyes,
Ourselves become our own best sacrifice.

ON THE ASSUMPTION OF THE VIRGIN MARY.

Hark! she is called, the parting hour is come;
Take thy farewell, poor world. Heaven must go home.
A piece of heavenly earth; purer and brighter
Than the chaste stars, whose choice lamps come to light
    her,

Whilst through the crystal orbs, clearer than they, 5
She climbs, and makes a far more milky way.
She 's called again; hark how the dear immortal dove
Sighs to his silver mate, 'Rise up, my love,
Rise up, my fair, my spotless one,
The winter 's past, the rain is gone; 10
The spring is come, the flowers appear,
No sweets, save thou, are wanting here.
Come away, my love,
Come away, my dove,
Cast off delay; 15
The court of heaven is come
To wait upon thee home;
Come away, come away!
The flowers appear,
Or quickly would, wert thou once here. 20
The spring is come, or if it stay
'T is to keep time with thy delay.
The rain is gone, except so much as we
Detain in needful tears to weep the want of thee.
The winter 's past, 25
Or if he make less haste,
His answer is, 'Why, she does so;
If summer come not, how can winter go?
Come away, come away!
The shrill winds chide, the waters weep thy stay, 30
The fountains murmur, and each loftiest tree
Bows lowest his leafy top to look for thee.
Come away, my love,
Come away, my dove,
Cast off delay; 35
The court of heaven is come
To wait upon thee home;
Come, come away.'

She 's called again. And will she go?
When heaven bids come, who can say no? 40
Heaven calls her, and she must away,
Heaven will not, and she cannot stay.
Go then; go, glorious on the golden wings
Of the bright youth of heaven, that sings
Under so sweet a burden. Go, 45
Since thy dread son will have it so.
And while thou goest, our song and we
Will, as we may, reach after thee.
Hail, holy queen of humble hearts!
We in thy praise will have our parts. 50
And though thy dearest looks must now give light
To none but the blest heavens, whose bright
Beholders, lost in sweet delight,
Feed for ever their fair sight
With those divinest eyes, which we 55
And our dark world no more shall see;
Though our poor joys are parted so,
Yet shall our lips never let go
Thy gracious name, but to the last
Our loving song shall hold it fast. 60

Thy precious name shall be
Thyself to us, and we
With holy care will keep it by us.
We to the last
Will hold it fast, 65
And no assumption shall deny us.
All the sweetest showers
Of our fairest flowers
Will we strow upon it.
Though our sweets cannot make 70
It sweeter, they can take
Themselves new sweetness from it.

Maria, men and angels sing,
Maria, mother of our king.
Live, rosy princess, live, and may the bright 75
Crown of a most incomparable light
Embrace thy radiant brows! O may the best
Of everlasting joys bathe thy white breast.
Live, our chaste love, the holy mirth
Of heaven; the humble pride of earth. 80
Live, crown of women; queen of men;
Live, mistress of our song; and when
Our weak desires have done their best,
Sweet angels come, and sing the rest.

RICHARD CRASHAW, *The Delights of the Muses*, 1646; written before 1644.

LOVE'S HOROSCOPE.

LOVE, brave Virtue's younger brother,
Erst hath made my heart a mother.
She consults the conscious spheres,
To calculate her young son's years;
She asks if sad or saving powers 5
Gave omen to his infant hours;
She asks each star that then stood by
If poor Love shall live or die.

Ah, my heart, is that the way?
Are these the beams that rule the day? 10
Thou knowst a face in whose each look
Beauty lays ope Love's fortune-book,
On whose fair revolutions wait
The obsequious motions of man's fate.

Ah, my heart! her eyes and she 15
Have taught thee new astrology.
Howe'er Love's native hours were set,
Whatever starry synod met,
'T is in the mercy of her eye,
If poor Love shall live or die. 20

If those sharp rays, putting on
Points of death, bid Love be gone;
Though the heavens in council sate
To crown an uncontrollèd fate,
Though their best aspects twined upon 25
The kindest constellatiòn,
Cast amorous glances on his birth,
And whispered the confederate earth
To pave his paths with all the good
That warms the bed of youth and blood — 30
Love has no plea against her eye;
Beauty frowns, and Love must die.

But if her milder influence move,
And gild the hopes of humble Love; —
Though heaven's inauspicious eye 35
Lay black on Love's nativity;
Though every diamond in Jove's crown
Fixed his forehead to a frown; —
Her eye a strong appeal can give,
Beauty smiles, and Love shall live. 40

O, if Love shall live, O where
But in her eye, or in her ear,
In her breast, or in her breath,
Shall I hide poor Love from death?
For in the life aught else can give, 45
Love shall die, although he live.

Or, if Love shall die, O, where
But in her eye, or in her ear,
In her breath, or in her breast,
Shall I build his funeral nest? 50
While Love shall thus entombèd lie
Love shall live, although he die.

JOHN MILTON, *Poems, English and Latin*, 1645; written 1644.

SONNET.

TO A VIRTUOUS YOUNG LADY.

LADY, that in the prime of earliest youth
Wisely hast shunned the broad way and the green,
And with those few art eminently seen
That labor up the hill of heavenly truth,
The better part, with Mary and with Ruth, 5
Chosen thou hast; and they that overween,
And at thy growing virtues fret their spleen,
No anger find in thee, but pity and ruth.
Thy care is fixed, and zealously attends
To fill thy odorous lamp with deeds of light, 10
And hope that reaps not shame. Therefore be sure
Thou, when the Bridegroom with his feastful friends
Passes to bliss at the mid-hour of night,
Hast gained thy entrance, virgin wise and pure.

EDMUND WALLER, *Poems upon Several Occasions*, 1645; date of writing uncertain.

TO PHYLLIS.

PHYLLIS, why should we delay,
Pleasures shorter than the day?
Could we (which we never can)
Stretch our lives beyond their span,
Beauty like a shadow flies, 5
And our youth before us dies;
Or, would youth and beauty stay,
Love hath wings, and will away.
Love hath swifter wings than Time:
Change in love to heaven does climb; 10
Gods, that never change their state,
Vary oft their love and hate.
  Phyllis, to this truth we owe
All the love betwixt us two.
Let not you and I enquire 15
What has been our past desire;
On what shepherds you have smiled,
Or what nymphs I have beguiled;
Leave it to the planets too,
What we shall hereafter do: 20
For the joys we now may prove,
Take advice of present love.

ON A GIRDLE.

THAT which her slender waist confined
Shall now my joyful temples bind;
No monarch but would give his crown,
His arms might do what this has done.

It was my heaven's extremest sphere, 5
The pale which held that lovely deer;
My joy, my grief, my hope, my love,
Did all within this circle move.

A narrow compass, and yet there
Dwelt all that 's good and all that 's fair; 10
Give me but what this ribband bound,
Take all the rest the sun goes round!

TO FLAVIA.

A SONG.

'Tis not your beauty can engage
My wary heart:
The sun, in all his pride and rage,
Has not that art;
And yet he shines as bright as you, 5
If brightness could our souls subdue.

'T is not the pretty things you say,
Nor those you write,
Which can make Thyrsis' heart your prey;
For that delight, 10
The graces of a well-taught mind,
In some of our own sex we find.

No, Flavia, 't is your love I fear;
Love's surest darts,
Those which so seldom fail him, are 15
Headed with hearts;
Their very shadows make us yield;
Dissemble well, and win the field.

ON THE ROSE.

Go, lovely rose,
Tell her that wastes her time and me,
That now she knows,
When I resemble her to thee,
How sweet and fair she seems to be. 5

Tell her that 's young,
And shuns to have her graces spied,
That had'st thou sprung
In deserts where no men abide,
Thou must have uncommended died. 10

Small is the worth
Of beauty from the light retired;
Bid her come forth,
Suffer herself to be desired,
And not blush so to be admired. 15

Then die, that she
The common fate of all things rare
May read in thee:
How small a part of time they share,
That are so wondrous sweet and fair. 20

JAMES SHIRLEY, *Poems*, 1646.

GOOD MORROW.

GOOD morrow unto her who in the night
Shoots from her silver brow more light
Than Cynthia, upon whose state
All other servile stars of beauty wait.

Good morrow unto her who gives the day, 5
Whose eyes preserve a clearer ray
Than Phœbus, when in Thetis' streams
He hath new bathed himself and washed his beams.

The day and night are only thine, and we
Were lost in darkness but for thee; 10
For thee we live, all hearts are thine,
But none so full of faith and flame as mine.

FIE ON LOVE.

Now fie on love! it ill befits
Or man or woman know it:
Love was not meant for people in their wits,
And they that fondly show it
Betray their too much feathered brains, 5
And shall have only Bedlam for their pains.

To love is to distract my sleep,
And waking to wear fetters;
To love is but to go to school to weep;
I 'll leave it to my betters. 10
If single, love be such a curse,
To marry is to make it ten times worse.

HENRY VAUGHAN, *Poems*, 1646.

TO AMORET, GONE FROM HOME.

FANCY and I last evening walked,
And, Amoret, of thee we talked.
The west just then had stol'n the sun,
And his last blushes were begun.

We sate, and marked how every thing 5
Did mourn his absence; how the spring
That smiled and curled about his beams,
Whilst he was here, now checked her streams;
The wanton eddies of her face
Were taught less noise and smoother grace; 10
And in a slow, sad channel went,
Whisp'ring the banks their discontent.
The careless banks of flowers that spread
Their perfumed bosoms to his head,
And with an open, free embrace, 15
Did entertain his beamy face,
Like absent friends point to the west,
And on that weak reflection feast.

If creatures then that have no sense,
But the loose tie of influence — 20
Though fate and time each day remove
Those things that element their love —
At such vast distance can agree,
Why, Amoret, why should not we?

ABRAHAM COWLEY, *The Mistress*, 1647.

THE INCONSTANT.

I NEVER yet could see that face
Which had no dart for me;
From fifteen years, to fifty's space,
They all victorious be.
Love, thou 'rt a devil, if I may call thee *one;* 5
For sure in me thy name is Legion.

Color or shape, good limbs or face,
Goodness or wit, in all I find;
In motion or in speech a grace;
If all fail, yet 't is womankind; 10
And I 'm so weak, the pistol need not be
Double or treble charged to murder me.

If tall, the name of 'proper' slays;
If fair, she 's pleasant in the light;
If low, her prettiness does please; 15
If black, what lover loves not night?
If yellow-haired, I love lest it should be
Th' excuse to others for not loving me.

The fat, like plenty, fills my heart;
The lean, with love makes me too so; 20
If straight, her body 's Cupid's dart
To me; if crooked, 't is his bow:
Nay, age itself does me to rage incline,
And strength to women gives, as well as wine.

Just half as large as Charity 25
My richly landed Love 's become;
And, judged aright, is Constancy,
Though it take up a larger room:
Him, who loves always one, why should they call
More constant than the man loves always all? 30

Thus with unwearied wings I flee
Through all Love's gardens and his fields;
And, like the wise, industrious bee,
No weed but honey to me yields!
Honey still spent this dil'gence still supplies, 35
Though I return not home with laden thighs.

My soul at first indeed did prove
Of pretty strength against a dart,
Till I this habit got of love;
But my consumed and wasted heart, 40
Once burnt to tinder with a strong desire,
Since that, by every spark is set on fire.

THOMAS STANLEY, *Poems and Translations*, 1647.

THE TOMB.

WHEN, cruel fair one, I am slain
By thy disdain,
And, as a trophy of thy scorn,
To some old tomb am borne,
Thy fetters must their power bequeath 5
To those of death;
Nor can thy flame immortal burn,
Like monumental fires within an urn;
Thus freed from thy proud empire, I shall prove
There is more liberty in death than love. 10

And when forsaken lovers come
To see my tomb,
Take heed thou mix not with the crowd
And, as a victor, proud
To view the spoils thy beauty made 15
Press near my shade,
Lest thy too cruel breath or name
Should fan my ashes back into a flame,
And thou, devoured by this revengeful fire,
His sacrifice, who died as thine, expire. 20

But if cold earth or marble must
Conceal my dust,
Whilst hid in some dark ruins, I
Dumb and forgotten lie,
The pride of all thy victory 25
Will sleep with me;
And they who should attest thy glory,
Will, or forget, or not believe this story,
Then to increase thy triumph, let me rest,
Since by thine eye slain, buried in thy breast. 30

THE RELAPSE.

O TURN away those cruel eyes,
The stars of my undoing;
Or death in such a bright disguise
May tempt a second wooing.

Punish their blind and impious pride 5
Who dare contemn thy glory;
It was my fall that deified
Thy name and sealed thy story.

Yet no new suffering can prepare
A higher praise to crown thee; 10
Though my first death proclaim thee fair,
My second will unthrone thee.

Lovers will doubt thou can'st entice
No other for thy fuel,
And if thou burn one victim twice, 15
Both think thee poor and cruel.

CELIA SINGING.

Roses in breathing forth their scent,
Or stars their borrowed ornament,
Nymphs in watery sphere that move,
Or angels in their orbs above,
The wingèd chariot of the light, 5
Or the slow, silent wheels of night,
The shade which from the swifter sun
Doth in a circular motion run,
Or souls that their eternal rest do keep,
Make far more noise than Celia's breath in sleep. 10

But if the angel, which inspires
This subtle flame with active fires,
Should mould his breath to words, and those
Into a harmony dispose,
The music of this heavenly sphere 15
Would steal each soul out at the ear,
And into plants and stones infuse
A life that cherubim would choose,
And with new powers invert the laws of fate,
Kill those that live, and dead things animate. 20

Richard Lovelace, *Lucasta, Epodes, Odes, Sonnets, and Songs,* 1649; written before 1648.

TO LUCASTA, GOING BEYOND THE SEAS.

If to be absent were to be
Away from thee;
Or that when I am gone,
You or I were alone;

Then my Lucasta might I crave 5
Pity from blust'ring wind or swallowing wave.

But I 'll not sigh one blast or gale
To swell my sail,
Or pay a tear to 'suage
The foaming blow-god's rage; 10
For whether he will let me pass
Or no, I 'm still as happy as I was.

Though seas and land betwixt us both,
Our faith and troth,
Like separated souls, 15
All time and space controls:
Above the highest sphere we meet,
Unseen, unknown, and greet as angels greet.

So then we do anticipate
Our after-fate, 20
And are alive i' th' skies,
If thus our lips and eyes
Can speak like spirits unconfined
In heaven, their earthly bodies left behind.

SONG.

TO LUCASTA, ON GOING TO THE WARS.

Tell me not, sweet, I am unkind,
That from the nunnery
Of thy chaste breast and quiet mind
To war and arms I fly.

True, a new mistress now I chase, 5
The first foe in the field;
And with a stronger faith embrace
A sword, a horse, a shield.

Yet this inconstancy is such
As you too shall adore: 10
I could not love thee, dear, so much
Loved I not honor more.

SONG.

AMARANTHA, sweet and fair,
Ah braid no more that shining hair;
As my curious hand or eye,
Hovering round thee, let it fly:
Let it fly as unconfined 5
As its ravisher the wind,
Who has left his darling east
To wanton o'er this spicy nest.

Every tress must be confessed
But neatly tangled at the best, 10
Like a clew of golden thread,
Most excellently ravellèd,
Do not then wind up that light
In ribands, and o'ercloud the night;
Like the sun in 's early ray, 15
But shake your head and scatter day.

THE SCRUTINY.

WHY should'st thou swear I am forsworn,
Since thine I vowed to be?
Lady, it is already morn,
And 't was last night I swore to thee
That fond impossibility. 5

Have I not loved thee much and long,
A tedious twelve hours' space?

I should all other beauties wrong,
And rob thee of a new embrace,
Should I still dote upon thy face. 10

Not but all joy in thy brown hair
By others may be found;
But I must search the black and fair,
Like skilful min'ralists that sound
For treasure in un-plowed-up ground. 15

Then if, when I have loved my round,
Thou prov'st the pleasant she,
With spoils of meaner beauties crowned,
I laden will return to thee,
E'en sated with variety. 20

TO ALTHEA FROM PRISON.

When Love with unconfinèd wings,
Hovers within my gates,
And my divine Althea brings
To whisper at the grates;
When I lie tangled in her hair 5
And fettered to her eye,
The gods that wanton in the air
Know no such liberty.

When flowing cups run swiftly round
With no allaying Thames, 10
Our careless heads with roses crowned,
Our hearts with loyal flames;
When thirsty grief in wine we steep,
When healths and draughts go free,
Fishes that tipple in the deep 15
Know no such liberty.

When, like committed linnets, I
  With shriller throat shall sing
The sweetness, mercy, majesty,
  And glories of my king; 20
When I shall voice aloud how good
  He is, how great should be,
Enlargèd winds, that curl the flood,
  Know no such liberty.

Stone walls do not a prison make, 25
  Nor iron bars a cage;
Minds innocent and quiet take
  That for an hermitage:
If I have freedom in my love,
  And in my soul am free, 30
Angels alone, that soar above,
  Enjoy such liberty.

THOMAS FORDE, *Love's Labyrinth,*
1660; written before 1648.

THE BUSY MAN IS FREE.

FOND Love, no more
Will I adore
    Thy feignèd deity;
Go throw thy darts
At simple hearts, 5
    And prove thy victory.

Whilst I do keep
My harmless sheep,
    Love hath no power on me:

'T is idle souls 10
Which he controls;
The busy man is free.

ROBERT HERRICK, *Hesperides*, 1648; written between 1640 and 1648.

TO PERILLA.

AH, my Perilla! dost thou grieve to see
Me, day by day, to steal away from thee?
Age calls me hence, and my grey hairs bid come
And haste away to mine eternal home;
'T will not be long, Perilla, after this, 5
That I must give thee the supremest kiss.
Dead when I am, first cast in salt, and bring
Part of the cream from that religious spring,
With which, Perilla, wash my hands and feet;
That done, then wind me in that very sheet 10
Which wrapped thy smooth limbs when thou didst implore
The gods' protection but the night before;
Follow me weeping to my turf, and there
Let fall a primrose, and with it a tear:
Then lastly, let some weekly strewings be 15
Devoted to the memory of me;
Then shall my ghost not walk about, but keep
Still in the cool and silent shades of sleep.

UPON THE LOSS OF HIS MISTRESSES.

I HAVE lost, and lately, these
Many dainty mistresses;
Stately Julia, prime of all:
Sappho next, a principal;
Smooth Anthea, for a skin 5
White and heaven-like crystalline;
Sweet Electra, and the choice
Myrrha, for the lute and voice.
Next, Corinna, for her wit,
And the graceful use of it; 10
With Perilla: all are gone,
Only Herrick 's left alone,
For to number sorrow by
Their departures hence, and die.

HIS POETRY HIS PILLAR.

ONLY a little more
I have to write,
Then I 'll give o'er,
And bid the world good-night.

'T is but a flying minute 5
That I must stay,
Or linger in it;
And then I must away.

O Time, that cut'st down all,
And scarce leav'st here 10
Memorial
Of any men that were!

How many lie forgot
In vaults beneath,
And piecemeal rot 15
Without a fame in death!

Behold this living stone
I rear for me,
Ne'er to be thrown
Down, envious Time, by thee. 20

Pillars let some set up,
If so they please,
Here is my hope,
And my pyramides.

JASPER MAYNE, *The Amorous War*, 1648.

TIME IS THE FEATHERED THING.

TIME is the feathered thing,
And, whilst I praise
The sparklings of thy looks and call them rays,
Takes wing,
Leaving behind him as he flies 5
An unperceivèd dimness in thine eyes.
His minutes whilst th' are told
Do make us old;
And every sand of his fleet glass,
Increasing age as it doth pass, 10
Insensibly sows wrinkles there
Where flowers and roses do appear.
Whilst we do speak, our fire
Doth into ice expire;

Flames turn to frost, 15
And ere we can
Know how our crow turns swan,
Or how a silver snow
Springs there where jet did grow,
Our fading spring is in dull winter lost. 20

Since then the night hath hurled
Darkness, love's shade,
Over its enemy the day, and made
The world
Just such a blind and shapeless thing 25
As 't was before light did from darkness spring,
Let us employ its treasure
And make shade pleasure;
Let 's number out the hours by blisses,
And count the minutes by our kisses; 30
Let the heavens new motions feel
And by our embraces wheel;
And whilst we try the way
By which love doth convey
Soul into soul, 35
And mingling so
Makes them such raptures know
As makes them entrancèd lie
In mutual ecstasy,
Let the harmonious spheres in music roll. 40

RICHARD CRASHAW, *Carmen Deo Nostro*, 1652; written before 1649.

A SONG.

LORD, when the sense of thy sweet grace
Sends up my soul to seek thy face,
Thy blessed eyes breed such desire
I die in love's delicious fire.
O love, I am thy sacrifice, 5
Be still triumphant, blessed eyes;
Still shine on me, fair suns, that I
Still may behold though still I die.

Though still I die, I live again,
Still longing so to be still slain; 10
So painful is such loss of breath,
I die even in desire of death.
Still live in me this loving strife
Of living death and dying life:
For while thou sweetly slayest me, 15
Dead to myself, I live in thee.

JAMES GRAHAM, Marquess of Montrose; first printed in 1711, written before 1650.

MY DEAR AND ONLY LOVE.

MY dear and only love, I pray
That little world of thee
Be governed by no other sway
Than purest monarchy;

For if confusion have a part, 5
Which virtuous souls abhor,
And hold a synod in thy heart,
I 'll never love thee more.

As Alexander I will reign,
And I will reign alone; 10
My thoughts did evermore disdain
A rival on my throne.
He either fears his fate too much,
Or his deserts are small,
That dares not put it to the touch, 15
To gain or lose it all.

But I will reign and govern still,
And always give the law,
And have each subject at my will,
And all to stand in awe; 20
But 'gainst my batteries if I find
Thou kick, or vex me sore,
As that thou set me up a blind,
I 'll never love thee more.

And in the empire of thine heart, 25
Where I should solely be,
If others do pretend a part,
Or dare to vie with me,
Or if committees thou erect,
And go on such a score, 30
I 'll laugh and sing at thy neglect,
And never love thee more.

But if thou wilt prove faithful, then,
And constant of thy word,

I 'll make thee glorious by my pen, 35
And famous by my sword;
I 'll serve thee in such noble ways
Was never heard before;
I 'll crown and deck thee all with bays,
And love thee more and more. 40

PHINEAS FLETCHER, *A Father's Testament*, 1670; written before 1650 (?).

TO THE SOUL.

FOND soul is this
Thy way to bliss?
Grasp both the Indies, let thy mighty hand
The iron North and golden South command;
Transcend the moon, 5
Fasten thy throne
Above the fixèd stars; above expressions,
Above thy thought enlarge thy vast possessions:
Fond soul, all this
Can not make up thy bliss. 10

All these are vain,
Full, but with pain;
All creatures have their ends to serve, not bless thee;
As servants they may help, as lords oppress thee;
They vex in getting 15
Used, lost with fretting;
Can slaves advance? shades fill? can grief give rest?
That which was cursed for thee can't make thee blest:
They all are vain
And bring not bliss but pain. 20

Fond soul, thy birth
Is not of earth
Or heaven; thou earth and heaven itself survivest;
Though born in time, thou, dying, Time out-livest.
They fail, deceive thee, 25
They age, die, leave thee;
Soar up immortal spirit, and mounting fly
Into the arms of great Eternity:
Not heaven or earth,
He, he thy end and birth. 30

HENRY VAUGHAN, *Silex Scintillans*, Part I, 1650.

THE RETREAT.

HAPPY those early days, when I
Shined in my angel-infancy,
Before I understood this place
Appointed for my second race,
Or taught my soul to fancy ought 5
But a white, celestial thought;
When yet I had not walked above
A mile or two from my first love,
And looking back, at that short space,
Could see a glimpse of his bright face; 10
When on some gilded cloud, or flower
My gazing soul would dwell an hour,
And in those weaker glories spy
Some shadows of eternity;
Before I taught my tongue to wound 15
My conscience with a sinful sound,
Or had the black art to dispense
A sev'ral sin to ev'ry sense,

But felt through all this fleshly dress
Bright shoots of everlastingness. 20
O how I long to travel back,
And tread again that ancient track!
That I might once more reach that plain
Where first I left my glorious train;
From whence th' enlightened spirit sees 25
That shady City of palm-trees.
But ah, my soul with too much stay
Is drunk, and staggers in the way!
Some men a forward motion love,
But I by backward steps would move; 30
And, when this dust falls to the urn,
In that state I came, return.

PEACE.

My soul, there is a country
Afar beyond the stars,
Where stands a wingèd sentry
All skilful in the wars.
There, above noise and danger, 5
Sweet Peace sits crowned with smiles,
And one born in a manger
Commands the beauteous files.
He is thy gracious friend
And — O my soul, awake! — 10
Did in pure love descend
To die here for thy sake.
If thou canst get but thither,
There grows the flower of peace,
The rose that can not wither, 15
Thy fortress and thy ease.
Leave then thy foolish ranges;

For none can thee secure,
But one, who never changes,
Thy God, thy life, thy cure. 20

LOVE, AND DISCIPLINE.

SINCE in a land not barren still —
Because thou dost thy grace distil —
My lot is fall'n, blest be thy will.

And since these biting frosts but kill
Some tares in me which choke or spill 5
That seed thou sow'st, blest be thy skill.

Blest be thy dew, and blest thy frost,
And happy I to be so crost,
And cured by crosses at thy cost.

The dew doth cheer what is distrest, 10
The frosts ill weeds nip and molest,
In both thou work'st unto the best.

Thus while thy several mercies plot,
And work on me, now cold now hot,
The work goes on and slacketh not; 15

For as thy hand the weather steers,
So thrive I best 'twixt joys and tears,
And all the year have some green ears.

THE WORLD.

I SAW Eternity the other night
Like a great ring of pure and endless light,
All calm, as it was bright;
And round beneath it, Time in hours, days, years,

Driv'n by the spheres, 5
Like a vast shadow moved, in which the world
And all her train were hurled.
The doating lover in his quaintest strain
Did there complain;
Near him, his lute, his fancy, and his flights, 10
Wit's four delights,
With gloves and knots, the silly snares of pleasure;
Yet his dear treasure
All scattered lay, while he his eyes did pour
Upon a flower. 15

The darksome statesman, hung with weights and woe,
Like a thick midnight-fog, moved there so slow
He did nor stay nor go;
Condemning thoughts, like sad eclipses, scowl
Upon his soul, 20
And clouds of crying witnesses without
Pursued him with one shout;
Yet digged the mole, and, lest his ways be found,
Worked under ground,
Where he did clutch his prey. But one did see 25
That policy:
Churches and altars fed him; perjuries
Were gnats and flies;
It rained about him blood and tears; but he
Drank them as free. 30

The fearful miser on a heap of rust
Sate pining all his life there, did scarce trust
His own hands with the dust;
Yet would not place one piece above, but lives
In fear of thieves. 35
Thousands there were as frantic as himself
And hugged each one his pelf;

The downright epicure placed heaven in sense,
And scorned pretence;
While others, slipped into a wide excess, 40
Said little less;
The weaker sort slight, trivial wares enslave,
Who think them brave;
And poor, despisèd Truth sate counting by
Their victory. 45

Yet some, who all this time did weep and sing,
And sing and weep, soared up into the ring;
But most would use no wing.
O fools, said I, thus to prefer dark night
Before true light! 50
To live in grots and caves, and hate the day
Because it shows the way,
The way, which from this dead and dark abode
Leads up to God;
A way where you might tread the sun, and be 55
As bright as he!
But, as I did their madness so discuss,
One whispered thus:
"This ring the bridegroom did for none provide
But for his bride." 60

THE HIDDEN FLOWER.

I WALKED the other day to spend my hour
Into a field
Where I sometimes had seen the soil to yield
A gallant flower;
But winter now had ruffled all the bower 5
And curious store
I knew there heretofore.

Yet I, whose search loved not to peep and peer
I' th' face of things,
Thought with myself, there might be other springs 10
Besides this here,
Which, like cold friends, sees us but once a year;
And so the flower
Might have some other bower.

Then, taking up what I could nearest spy, 15
I digged about
That place where I had seen him to grow out;
And by and by
I saw the warm recluse alone to lie
Where fresh and green 20
He lived of us unseen.

Many a question intricate and rare
Did I there strow;
But all I could extort was, that he now
Did there repair 25
Such losses as befel him in this air,
And would ere long
Come forth most fair and young.

This past, I threw the clothes quite o'er his head;
And, stung with fear 30
Of my own frailty, dropped down many a tear
Upon his bed;
Then sighing whispered, 'Happy are the dead!
What peace doth now
Rock him asleep below!' 35

And yet, how few believe such doctrine springs
From a poor root,
Which all the winter sleeps here under foot,

And hath no wings
To raise it to the truth and light of things, 40
But is still trod
By every wand'ring clod.

O Thou! whose spirit did at first inflame
And warm the dead,
And by a sacred incubation fed 45
With life this frame,
Which once had neither being, form, nor name, —
Grant I may so
Thy steps track here below,

That in these masques and shadows I may see 50
Thy sacred way;
And by those hid ascents climb to that day,
Which breaks from thee
Who art in all things, though invisibly!
Show me thy peace, 55
Thy mercy, love, and ease!

And from this care, where dreams and sorrows reign,
Lead me above,
Where light, joy, leisure, and true comforts move
Without all pain; 60
There, hid in thee, show me his life again,
At whose dumb urn
Thus all the year I mourn.

ANDREW MARVELL, *Miscellaneous Poems*, 1681; written before 1651.

THE CORONET.

WHEN for the thorns with which I long, too long,
With many a piercing wound,
My Saviour's head have crowned,
I seek with garlands to redress that wrong, —
Through every garden, every mead, 5
I gather flowers (my fruits are only flowers),
Dismantling all the fragrant towers
That once adorned my shepherdess's head;
And now, when I have summed up all my store,
Thinking (so I myself deceive), 10
So rich a chaplet thence to weave
As never yet the King of Glory wore,
Alas! I find the Serpent old,
That, twining in his speckled breast,
About the flowers disguised does fold 15
With wreaths of fame and interest.
Ah foolish man, that wouldst debase with them
And mortal glory, heaven's diadem!
But thou who only couldst the Serpent tame,
Either his slipp'ry knots at once untie, 20
And disentangle all his winding snare;
Or shatter too with him my curious frame,
And let these wither — so that he may die —
Though set with skill, and chosen out with care:
That they while thou on both their spoils dost tread, 25
May crown thy feet, that could not crown thy head.

BERMUDAS.

WHERE the remote Bermudas ride
In the ocean's bosom unespied,
From a small boat, that rowed along,
The listening winds received this song:

What should we do but sing his praise, 5
That led us through the watery maze,
Unto an isle so long unknown,
And yet far kinder than our own?
Where he the huge sea-monsters wracks,
That lift the deep upon their backs, 10
He lands us on a grassy stage,
Safe from the storms' and prelates' rage.
He gave us this eternal spring,
Which here enamels everything,
And sends the fowls to us in care 15
On daily visits through the air;
He hangs in shades the orange bright,
Like golden lamps in a green night,
And does in the pomegranates close
Jewels more rich than Ormus shows; 20
He makes the figs our mouths to meet,
And throws the melons at our feet;
But apples plants of such a price
No tree could ever bear them twice;
With cedars chosen by his hand 25
From Lebanon, he stores the land,
And makes the hollow seas, that roar,
Proclaim the ambergris on shore;
He cast (of which we rather boast)
The gospel's pearl upon our coast, 30
And in these rocks for us did frame

A temple, where to sound his name.
O let our voice his praise exalt,
Till it arrive at heaven's vault,
Which, thence (perhaps) rebounding may 35
Echo beyond the Mexique bay.

Thus sung they in the English boat,
A holy and a cheerful note;
And all the way to guide their chime
With falling oars they kept the time. 40

CLORINDA AND DAMON.

Clorinda.

DAMON, come drive thy flocks this way.

Damon.

No, 't is too late they went astray.

Clorinda.

I have a grassy scutcheon spied,
Where Flora blazons all her pride;
The grass I aim to feast thy sheep, 5
The flowers I for thy temples keep.

Damon.

Grass withers, and the flowers too fade.

Clorinda.

Seize the short joys then, ere they vade.
Seest thou that unfrequented cave?

Damon.

That den? 10

Clorinda.

Love's shrine.

Damon.

But virtue's grave.

Clorinda.

In whose cool bosom we may lie,
Safe from the sun.

Damon.

Not heaven's eye.

Clorinda.

Near this, a fountain's liquid bell
Tinkles within the concave shell.

Damon.

Might a soul bathe there and be clean, 15
Or slake its drought?

Clorinda.

What is 't you mean?

Damon.

These once had been enticing things,
Clorinda — pastures, caves, and springs.

Clorinda.

And what late change?

Damon.

The other day
Pan met me. 20

Clorinda.

What did great Pan say?

Damon.

Words that transcend poor shepherd's skill;
But he e'er since my songs does fill,
And his name swells my slender oat.

Clorinda.

Sweet must Pan sound in Damon's note.

Damon.

Clorinda's voice might make it sweet. 25

Clorinda.

Who would not in Pan's praises meet?

Chorus.

Of Pan the flowery pastures sing,
Caves echo, and the fountains ring.
Sing then while he doth us inspire;
For all the world is our Pan's choir. 30

A DIALOGUE BETWEEN THYRSIS AND DORINDA.

Dorinda.

WHEN death shall snatch us from these kids,
And shut up our divided lids,
Tell me, Thyrsis, prithee do,
Whither thou and I must go.

Thyrsis.

To the Elysium. 5

Dorinda.

O where is 't?

Thyrsis.

A chaste soul can never miss 't.

Dorinda.

I know no way but one: our home
Is our Elysium.

Thyrsis.

Cast thine eye to yonder sky;
There the milky way doth lie: 10
'T is a sure but rugged way
That leads to everlasting day.

Dorinda.

There birds may nest, but how can I
That have no wings and cannot fly?

Thyrsis.

Do not sigh, fair nymph, for fire 15
Hath no wings, yet doth aspire
Till it hit against the pole:
Heaven 's the centre of the soul.

Dorinda.

But in Elysium how do they
Pass eternity away? 20

Thyrsis.

O there 's neither hope nor fear;
There 's no wolf, no fox, no bear;
No need of dog to fetch our stray,
Our Lightfoot we may give away;
And there most sweetly may thine ear 25
Feast with the music of the sphere.

Dorinda.

How I my future state
By silent thinking antedate!
I prithee let us spend our time [to] come
In talking of Elysium. 30

Thyrsis.

Then I 'll go on: there, sheep are full
Of softest grass and softest wool;
There birds sing consorts, garlands grow,
Cool winds do whisper, springs do flow;
There always is a rising sun, 35
And day is ever but begun;
Shepherds there bear equal sway,
And every nymph 's a queen of May.

Dorinda.

Ah me! ah me!

Thyrsis.

Dorinda, why dost cry?

Dorinda.

I 'm sick, I 'm sick, and fain would die. 40

Thyrsis.

Convince me now that this is true,
By bidding with me all adieu.

Dorinda.

I cannot live without thee, I
Will for thee, much more with thee, die.

Thyrsis.

Then let us give Corellia charge o' th' sheep, 45
And thou and I'll pick poppies, and them steep
In wine, and drink on 't even till we weep:
So shall we smoothly pass away in sleep.

THE FAIR SINGER.

To make a final conquest of all me,
Love did compose so sweet an enemy,
In whom both beauties to my death agree,
Joining themselves in fatal harmony;
That, while she with her eyes my heart does bind, 5
She with her voice might captivate my mind.

I could have fled from one but singly fair;
My disentangled soul itself might save,
Breaking the curlèd trammels of her hair;
But how should I avoid to be her slave 10
Whose subtle art invisibly can wreathe
My fetters of the very air I breathe?

It had been easy fighting in some plain,
Where victory might hang in equal choice;
But all resistance against her is vain 15
Who has th' advantage both of eyes and voice;

And all my forces needs must be undone,
She having gainèd both the wind and sun.

TO HIS COY MISTRESS.

HAD we but world enough and time,
This coyness, lady, were no crime.
We would sit down and think which way
To walk and pass our long love's day.
Thou by the Indian Ganges' side 5
Shouldst rubies find; I by the tide
Of Humber would complain. I would
Love you ten years before the Flood;
And you should, if you please, refuse
Till the conversion of the Jews. 10
My vegetable love should grow
Vaster than empires, and more slow;
An hundred years should go to praise
Thine eyes and on thy forehead gaze;
Two hundred to adore each breast, 15
But thirty thousand to the rest;
An age at least to every part,
And the last age should show your heart.
For, lady, you deserve this state,
Nor would I love at lower rate. 20

But at my back I always hear
Time's wingèd chariot hurrying near;
And yonder all before us lie
Deserts of vast eternity.
Thy beauty shall no more be found, 25
Nor, in thy marble vault, shall sound
My echoing song; then worms shall try
That long preserved virginity;

And your quaint honor turn to dust,
And into ashes all my lust: 30
The grave 's a fine and private place,
But none, I think, do there embrace.

Now therefore while the youthful hue
Sits on thy skin like morning dew,
And while thy willing soul transpires 35
At every pore with instant fires,
Now let us sport us while we may,
And now, like amorous birds of prey,
Rather at once our time devour
Than languish in his slow-chapt power. 40
Let us roll all our strength, and all
Our sweetness up into one ball;
And tear our pleasures with rough strife
Thorough the iron gates of life:
Thus, though we cannot make our sun 45
Stand still, yet we will make him run.

THE PICTURE OF LITTLE T. C. IN A PROSPECT OF FLOWERS.

See with what simplicity
This nymph begins her golden days!
In the green grass she loves to lie,
And there with her fair aspect tames
The wilder flowers and gives them names, 5
But only with the roses plays,
And them does tell
What colors best become them and what smell.

Who can foretell for what high cause,
This darling of the gods was born? 10

Yet this is she whose chaster laws
The wanton Love shall one day fear,
And, under her command severe,
See his bow broke, and ensigns torn.
        Happy who can 15
Appease this virtuous enemy of man!

O then let me in time compound
And parley with those conquering eyes,
Ere they have tried their force to wound;
Ere with their glancing wheels they drive 20
In triumph over hearts that strive,
And them that yield but more despise:
        Let me be laid,
Where I may see the glories from some shade.

Meantime, whilst every verdant thing 25
Itself does at thy beauty charm,
Reform the errors of the spring;
Make that the tulips may have share
Of sweetness, seeing they are fair;
And roses of their thorns disarm; 30
        But most procure
That violets may a longer age endure.

But O, young beauty of the woods,
Whom nature courts with fruit and flowers,
Gather the flowers, but spare the buds, 35
Lest Flora, angry at thy crime
To kill her infants in their prime,
Do quickly make th' example yours;
        And ere we see,
Nip, in the blossom, all our hopes and thee. 40

THE MOWER TO THE GLOW-WORMS.

Ye living lamps, by whose dear light
The nightingale does sit so late,
And studying all the summer night,
Her matchless songs does meditate;

Ye country comets, that portend 5
No war nor prince's funeral,
Shining unto no higher end
Than to presage the grass's fall;

Ye glow-worms, whose officious flame
To wandering mowers shows the way, 10
That in the night have lost their aim,
And after foolish fires do stray;

Your courteous lights in vain you waste,
Since Juliana here is come;
For she my mind hath so displaced, 15
That I shall never find my home.

THE MOWER'S SONG.

My mind was once the true survey
Of all these meadows fresh and gay,
And in the greenness of the grass
Did see its hopes as in a glass;
When Juliana came, and she, 5
What I do to the grass, does to my thoughts and me.

But these, while I with sorrow pine,
Grew more luxuriant still and fine,
That not one blade of grass you spied
But had a flower on either side; 10
When Juliana came, and she,
What I do to the grass, does to my thoughts and me.

Unthankful meadows, could you so
A fellowship so true forego,
And in your gaudy May-games meet, 15
While I lay trodden under feet —
When Juliana came, and she,
What I do to the grass, does to my thoughts and me?

But what you in compassion ought,
Shall now by my revenge be wrought; 20
And flowers, and grass, and I, and all,
Will in one common ruin fall;
For Juliana comes, and she,
What I do to the grass, does to my thoughts and me.

And thus, ye meadows, which have been 25
Companions of my thoughts more green,
Shall now the heraldry become
With which I shall adorn my tomb;
For Juliana came, and she,
What I do to the grass, does to my thoughts and me. 30

MAKING HAY-ROPES.

Ametas.

THINK'ST thou that this love can stand,
Whilst thou still dost say me nay?
Love unpaid does soon disband:
Love binds love as hay binds hay.

Thestylis.

Think'st thou that this rope would twine 5
If we both should turn one way?
Where both parties so combine,
Neither love will twist nor hay.

Ametas.

Thus you vain excuses find,
  Which yourself and us delay; 10
And love ties a woman's mind
  Looser than with ropes of hay.

Thestylis.

What you cannot constant hope
  Must be taken as you may.

Ametas.

Then let 's both lay by our rope 15
  And go kiss within the hay.

SIR EDWARD SHERBURNE, *Salmasis, Lyrian and Sylvia*, 1651.

THE VOW.

By my life I vow,
That my life art thou,
By my heart and by my eyes;
But thy faith denies
To my juster oath t' incline, 5
For thou say'st I swear by thine.

By this sigh I swear,
By this falling tear,
By the undeservèd pains
My griev'd soul sustains: 10
Now thou may'st believe my moan,
These are too too much my own.

WEEPING AND KISSING.

A KISS I begged, but smiling she
Denied it me;
When straight, her cheeks with tears o'erflown —
Now kinder grown —
What smiling she 'd not let one have 5
She weeping gave.
Then you whom scornful beauties awe,
Hope yet relief
From Love, who tears from smiles can draw,
Pleasure from grief. 10

NOVO INAMORAMENTO.

AND yet anew entangled, see
Him who escaped the snare so late!
A truce, no league, thou mad'st with me,
False love, which now is out of date:
Fool, to believe the fire quite out, alas, 5
Which only laid asleep in embers was.

The sickness not at first past cure,
By this relapse despiseth art.
Now, treacherous boy, thou hast me sure,
Playing the wanton with my heart, 10
As foolish children that a bird have got
Slacken the thread, but not untie the knot.

THE SWEETMEAT.

THOU gav'st me late to eat
A sweet without, but within, bitter meat:
As if thou would'st have said 'Here, taste in this
What Celia is.'

But if there ought to be 5
A likeness, dearest, 'twixt thy gift and thee,
Why first what 's sweet in thee should I not taste,
The bitter last?

CHANGE DEFENDED.

Leave, Chloris, leave; I pray no more
With want of love or lightness charge me.
'Cause thy looks captived me before,
May not another's now enlarge me?

He whose misguided zeal hath long 5
Paid homage to some pale star's light,
Better informed, may without wrong
Leave that t' adore the queen of night.

Then if my heart, which long served thee,
Will to Carintha now incline; 10
Why termed inconstant should it be
For bowing 'fore a richer shrine?

Censure those lovers so, whose will
Inferior objects can entice;
Who changes for the better still, 15
Makes that a virtue, you call vice.

THE FOUNTAIN.

Stranger, whoe'er thou art, that stoop'st to taste
These sweeter streams, let me arrest thy haste;
Nor of their fall
The murmurs (though the lyre
Less sweet be) stand to admire. 5

But as you shall
See from this marble tun
The liquid crystal run,
And mark withal
How fixed the one abides, 10
How fast the other glides;
Instructed thus, the difference learn to see
'Twixt mortal life and immortality.

JOHN MILTON, *Letters of State,*
1694, written 1652.

SONNET.

XVI.

TO THE LORD GENERAL CROMWELL.

CROMWELL, our chief of men, who through a cloud
Not of war only, but detractions rude,
Guided by faith and matchless fortitude,
To peace and truth thy glorious way hast ploughed,
And on the neck of crownèd Fortune proud 5
Hast reared God's trophies, and his work pursued,
While Darwen stream, with blood of Scots imbrued,
And Dunbar field, resounds thy praises loud,
And Worcester's laureate wreath: yet much remains
To conquer still; peace hath her victories 10
No less renowned than war: new foes arise,
Threatening to bind our souls with secular chains.
Help us to save free conscience from the paw
Of hireling wolves, whose Gospel is their maw.

JAMES SHIRLEY, *Cupid and Death*, 1653.

DEATH'S SUBTLE WAYS.

VICTORIOUS men of earth, no more
Proclaim how wide your empires are;
Though you bind in every shore
And your triumphs reach as far
As night or day, 5
Yet you, proud monarchs, must obey
And mingle with forgotten ashes when
Death calls ye to the crowd of common men.

Devouring famine, plague, and war,
Each able to undo mankind, 10
Death's servile emissaries are;
Nor to these alone confined,
He hath at will
More quaint and subtle ways to kill:
A smile or kiss, as he will use the art, 15
Shall have the cunning skill to break a heart.

JOHN MILTON, *Poems upon Several Occasions*, 1673; written 1655.

SONNETS.

XVIII.

ON THE LATE MASSACRE IN PIEDMONT.

AVENGE, O Lord, thy slaughtered saints, whose bones
Lie scattered on the Alpine mountains cold;
Even them who kept thy truth so pure of old,
When all our fathers worshipped stocks and stones,

Forget not: in thy book record their groans 5
Who were thy sheep, and in their ancient fold
Slain by the bloody Piedmontese, that rolled
Mother and infant down the rocks. Their moans
The vales redoubled to the hills, and they
To heaven. Their martyred blood and ashes sow 10
O'er all th' Italian fields, where still doth sway
The triple Tyrant; that from these may grow
A hundredfold, who, having learnt thy way,
Early may fly the Babylonian woe.

XIX.

ON HIS BLINDNESS.

When I consider how my light is spent,
Ere half my days, in this dark world and wide,
And that one talent which is death to hide
Lodged with me useless, though my soul more bent
To serve therewith my Maker, and present 5
My true account, lest he returning chide,
'Doth God exact day-labor, light denied?'
I fondly ask. But patience, to prevent
That murmur, soon replies, 'God doth not need
Either man's work or his own gifts. Who best 10
Bear his mild yoke, they serve him best. His state
Is kingly: thousands at his bidding speed,
And post o'er land and ocean without rest;
They also serve who only stand and wait.'

HENRY VAUGHAN, *Silex Scintillans, Part II*, 1655.

DEPARTED FRIENDS.

THEY are all gone into the world of light,
  And I alone sit ling'ring here.
Their very memory is fair and bright,
  And my sad thoughts doth clear.

It glows and glitters in my cloudy breast 5
  Like stars upon some gloomy grove,
Or those faint beams in which this hill is drest
  After the sun's remove.

I see them walking in an air of glory,
  Whose light doth trample on my days; 10
My days, which are at best but dull and hoary,
  Mere glimmerings and decays.

O holy hope! and high humility!
  High as the heavens above;
These are your walks, and you have show'd them me, 15
  To kindle my cold love.

Dear, beauteous death, the jewel of the just,
  Shining nowhere but in the dark;
What mysteries do lie beyond thy dust,
  Could man outlook that mark! 20

He that hath found some fledged bird's nest may know
  At first sight if the bird be flown;
But what fair well or grove he sings in now,
  That is to him unknown.

And yet, as angels in some brighter dreams 25
  Call to the soul when man doth sleep,

So some strange thoughts transcend our wonted themes,
And into glory peep.

If a star were confined into a tomb,
Her captive flames must needs burn there; 30
But when the hand that locked her up gives room,
She 'll shine through all the sphere.

O Father of eternal life, and all
Created glories under thee!
Resume thy spirit from this world of thrall 35
Into true liberty!

Either disperse these mists, which blot and fill
My perspective still as they pass;
Or else remove me hence unto that hill,
Where I shall need no glass. 40

THE THRONE.

WHEN with these eyes, closed now by thee,
But then restored,
The great and white throne I shall see
Of my dread Lord;
And lowly kneeling — for the most 5
Stiff then must kneel —
Shall look on him at whose high cost,
Unseen, such joys I feel;

Whatever arguments or skill
Wise heads shall use, 10
Tears and my blushes still
Will I produce.
And should these speechless beggars fail,
Which oft have won,
Then, taught by thee, I will prevail 15
And say: "Thy will be done."

CHARLES COTTON, *Poems on Several Occasions*, 1689; written about 1655.

ODE.

THE day is set did earth adorn,
  To drink the brewing of the main;
And, hot with travel, will ere morn
  Carouse it to an ebb again.
Then let us drink, time to improve, 5
  Secure of Cromwell and his spies;
Night will conceal our healths and love,
  For all her thousand thousand eyes.

Chorus.

Then let us drink, secure of spies,
To Phœbus and his second rise. 10

Without the evening dew and showers
  The earth would be a barren place,
Of trees and plants, of herbs and flowers,
  To crown her now enamelled face;
Nor can wit spring, nor fancies grow, 15
  Unless we dew our heads in wine,
Plump autumn's wealthy overflow
  And sprightly issue of the vine.

Chorus.

Then let us drink, secure of spies,
To Phœbus and his second rise. 20

Wine is the cure of cares and sloth,
  That rust the metal of the mind;
The juice that man to man does both
  In freedom and in friendship bind.
This clears the monarch's cloudy brows, 25

And cheers the hearts of sullen swains,
To wearied souls repose allows,
And makes slaves caper in their chains.

Chorus.

Then let us drink, secure of spies,
To Phœbus and his second rise. 30

Wine, that distributes to each part
Its heat and motion, is the spring,
The poet's head, the subject's heart,
'T was wine made old Anacreon sing.
Then let us quaff it while the night 35
Serves but to hide such guilty souls,
As fly the beauty of the light
Or dare not pledge our loyal bowls.

Chorus.

Then let us revel, quaff and sing,
Health and his sceptre to the king. 40

ODE.

FAIR Isabel, if aught but thee
I could, or would, or like, or love;
If other beauties but approve
To sweeten my captivity:
I might those passions be above, 5
Those powerful passions, that combine
To make and keep me only thine.

Or if for tempting treasure, I
Of the world's god, prevailing gold,
Could see thy love and my truth sold, 10
A greater, nobler treasury:
My flame to thee might then grow cold,
And I, like one whose love is sense,
Exchange thee for convenience.

But when I vow to thee I do 15
Love thee above or health or peace,
Gold, joy, and all such toys as these,
'Bove happiness and honor too:
Thou then must know, this love can cease
Nor change, for all the glorious show 20
Wealth and discretion bribes us to.

What such a love deserves, thou, sweet,
As knowing best, mayst best reward;
I, for thy bounty well prepared,
With open arms my blessing meet. 25
Then do not, dear, our joys detard;
But unto him propitious be
That knows no love, nor life, but thee.

ABRAHAM COWLEY, *Miscellanies*, 1656.

THE CHRONICLE.

A BALLAD.

MARGARITA first possessed,
If I remember well, my breast,
Margarita first of all;
But when awhile the wanton maid
With my restless heart had played, 5
Martha took the flying ball.

Martha soon did it resign
To the beauteous Catherine.
Beauteous Catherine gave place
(Though loth and angry she to part 10
With the possession of my heart)
To Elisa's conquering face.

Elisa till this hour might reign
Had she not evil counsels ta'en.
    Fundamental laws she broke, 15
And still new favorites she chose,
Till up in arms my passions rose,
    And cast away her yoke.

Mary then and gentle Ann
Both to reign at once began, 20
    Alternately they swayed;
And sometimes Mary was the fair,
And sometimes Ann the crown did wear;
    And sometimes both I obeyed.

Another Mary then arose 25
And did rigorous laws impose.
    A mighty tyrant she!
Long, alas, should I have been
Under that iron-sceptred Queen,
    Had not Rebecca set me free. 30

When fair Rebecca set me free,
'T was then a golden time with me,
    But soon those pleasures fled;
For the gracious princess died
In her youth and beauty's pride, 35
    And Judith reigned in her stead.

One month, three days and half an hour
Judith held the sovereign power,
    Wondrous beautiful her face;
But so small and weak her wit, 40
That she to govern was unfit,
    And so Susanna took her place.

But when Isabella came
Armed with a resistless flame
And th' artillery of her eye; 45
Whilst she proudly marched about
Greater conquests to find out,
She beat out Susan by the by.

But in her place I then obeyed
Black-eyed Bess, her viceroy-maid, 50
To whom ensued a vacancy.
Thousand worse passions then possessed
The interregnum of my breast.
Bless me from such an anarchy!

Gentle Henrietta than 55
And a third Mary next began,
Then Joan, and Jane, and Audria.
And then a pretty Thomasine,
And then another Catherine,
And then a long *et cætera.* 60

But should I now to you relate,
The strength and riches of their state,
The powder, patches, and the pins,
The ribbands, jewels, and the rings,
The lace, the paint, and warlike things 65
That make up all their magazines;

If I should tell the politic arts
To take and keep men's hearts,
The letters, embassies and spies,
The frowns, and smiles, and flatteries, 70
The quarrels, tears and perjuries,
Numberless, nameless mysteries!

And all the little lime-twigs laid
By Matchavil, the waiting-maid;
  I more voluminous should grow 75
(Chiefly if I like them should tell
All change of weathers that befell)
  Than Holinshed or Stow.

But I will briefer with them be,
Since few of them were long with me. 80
  An higher and a nobler strain
My present Emperess does claim,
Heleonora, first o' th' name;
  Whom God grant long to reign!

ANACRÉONTIQUE II.

DRINKING.

The thirsty earth soaks up the rain,
And drinks, and gapes for drink again.
The plants suck in the earth, and are
With constant drinking fresh and fair.
The sea itself, which one would think 5
Should have but little need of drink,
Drinks ten thousand rivers up,
So filled that they o'erflow the cup.
The busy sun — and one would guess
By 's drunken fiery face no less — 10
Drinks up the sea, and when he has done,
The moon and stars drink up the sun;
They drink and dance by their own light,
They drink and revel all the night.
Nothing in nature 's sober found, 15
But an eternal health goes round.

Fill up the bowl then, fill it high;
Fill all the glasses there, for why
Should every creature drink but I —
Why, men of morals, tell me why? 20

HENRY KING, *Poems, Elegies,*
Paradoxes, and Sonnets, 1657.

SONNET.

TELL me no more how fair she is,
I have no mind to hear
The story of that distant bliss
I never shall come near:
By sad experience I have found 5
That her perfection is my wound.

And tell me not how fond I am
To tempt my daring fate,
From whence no triumph ever came,
But to repent too late: 10
There is some hope ere long I may
In silence dote myself away.

I ask no pity, Love, from thee,
Nor will thy justice blame,
So that thou wilt not envy me 15
The glory of my flame,
Which crowns my heart whene'er it dies,
In that it falls her sacrifice.

HENRY HARRINGTON, in *Henry Lawe's Airs and Dialogues, Third Book*, 1658.

SONG.

TRUST the form of airy things,
Or a siren when she sings,
Trust the sly hyena's voice,
Or of all distrust make choice,—
And believe these sooner than 5
Truth in women, faith in men.

JOHN MILTON, *Poems on Several Occasions*, 1673; written 1658.

SONNET.

XXIII.

ON HIS DECEASED WIFE.

METHOUGHT I saw my late espousèd saint
Brought to me like Alcestis from the grave,
Whom Jove's great son to her glad husband gave,
Rescued from Death by force, though pale and faint.
Mine, as whom washed from spot of child-bed taint 5
Purification in the Old Law did save,
And such as yet once more I trust to have
Full sight of her in heaven without restraint,
Came vested all in white, pure as her mind.
Her face was veiled; yet to my fancied sight 10
Love, sweetness, goodness, in her person shined
So clear as in no face with more delight.
But, O! as to embrace me she inclined,
I waked, she fled, and day brought back my night.

THOMAS FLATMAN, *Poems and Songs*, 1674; written 1659.

FOR THOUGHTS.

THOUGHTS! what are they?
They are my constant friends,
Who, when harsh Fate its dull brow bends,
Uncloud me with a smiling ray,
And in the depth of midnight force a day. 5

When I retire and flee
The busy throngs of company
To hug myself in privacy,
O the discourse! the pleasant talk
'Twixt us, my thoughts, along a lonely walk! 10

You (like the stupefying wine
The dying malefactors sip
With trembling lip,
T' abate the rigor of their doom
By a less troublous cut to their long home) 15
Make me slight crosses, though they piled up lie,
All by the magic of an ecstasy.

Do I desire to see
The throne and awful majesty
Of that proud one, 20
Brother and uncle to the stars and sun?
These can conduct me where such toys reside
And waft me 'cross the main, sans wind and tide.

Would I descry
Those radiant mansions 'bove the sky, 25
Invisible to mortal eye,
My thoughts can eas'ly lay

A shining track thereto,
And nimbly flitting go;
Through all th' eleven orbs can shove a way. 30
My thoughts like Jacob's ladder are
A most angelic thoroughfare.

The wealth that shines
In th' oriental mines;
Those sparkling gems which Nature keeps 35
Within her cabinets, the deeps;
The verdant fields,
Those rarities the rich world yields,
Huge structures, whose each gilded spire
Glisters like lightning, which while men admire 40
They deem the neighboring sky on fire —
These can I dwell upon and 'live mine eyes
With millions of varieties.
As on the front of Pisgah I
Can th' Holy Land through these my optics spy. 45

Contemn we then
The peevish rage of men,
Whose violence can ne'er divorce
Our mutual amity,
Or lay so damned a curse 50
As non-addresses 'twixt my thoughts and me;
For though I sigh in irons, they
Use their old freedom, readily obey,
And, when my bosom friends desert me, stay.

Come then, my darlings, I 'll embrace 55
My privilege; make known
The high prerogative I own,
By making all allurements give you place,

Whose sweet society to me
A sanctuary and a shield shall be 60
'Gainst the full quivers of my Destiny.

A WISH.

Not to the hills where cedars move
Their cloudy heads; not to the grove
Of myrtles in th' Elysian shade,
Nor Tempe which the poets made,
Not on the spicy mountains play, 5
Or travel to Arabia,
I aim not at the careful throne
Which Fortune's darlings sit upon:
No, no, the best this fickle world can give
Has but a little, little time to live. 10

But let me soar, O let me fly
Beyond poor earth's benighted eye,
Beyond the pitch swift eagles tower,
Beyond the reach of human power,
Above the clouds, above the way 15
Whence the sun darts his piercing ray,
O let me tread those courts that are
So bright, so pure, so blest, so fair,
As neither thou nor I must ever know
On earth: 't is thither, thither would I go. 20

ALEXANDER BROME, *Songs and Other Poems*, 1661; written before 1660.

THE RESOLVE.

TELL me not of a face that 's fair,
Nor lip and cheek that 's red,
Nor of the tresses of her hair,
Nor curls in order laid;
Nor of a rare seraphic voice, 5
That like an angel sings;
Though, if I were to take my choice,
I would have all these things.
But if that thou wilt have me love,
And it must be a she, 10
The only argument can move
Is, that she will love me.

The glories of your ladies be
But metaphors of things,
And but resemble what we see 15
Each common object brings.
Roses out-red their lips and cheeks,
Lilies their whiteness stain:
What fool is he that shadows seeks,
And may the substance gain! 20
Then if thou 'lt have me love a lass,
Let it be one that 's kind,
Else I 'm a servant to the glass
That 's with Canary lined.

A MOCK SONG.

'TIS true I never was in love;
But now I mean to be,

For there 's no art
Can shield a heart
From love's supremacy. 5

Though in my nonage I have seen
A world of taking faces,
I had not age or wit to ken
Their several hidden graces.

Those virtues which, though thinly set, 10
In others are admirèd,
In thee are altogether met,
Which make thee so desirèd;

That though I never was in love,
Nor never meant to be, 15
Thyself and parts
Above my arts
Have drawn my heart to thee.

SIR WILLIAM DAVENANT, *Poems on Several Occasions*, 1672; written before 1660.

SONG,

AGAINST WOMAN'S PRIDE.

WHY dost thou seem to boast, vainglorious sun?
Why should thy bright complexion make thee proud?
Think but how often since thy race begun
Thou wert eclipsed, then blush behind a cloud.

Or why look you, fair Empress of the night, 5
So big upon 't, when you at full appear?
Remember yours is but a borrowed light,
Then shrink with paleness in your giddy sphere.

If neither sun nor moon can justify
  Their pride, how ill it women then befits   10
That are on earth but *ignes fatui*
  That lead poor men to wander from their wits.

SONG.

The lark now leaves his wat'ry nest,
  And, climbing, shakes his dewy wings,
He takes this window for the east,
  And to implore your light, he sings:
Awake, awake, the morn will never rise   5
Till she can dress her beauty at your eyes.

The merchant bows unto the seaman's star,
  The ploughman from the sun his season takes;
But still the lover wonders what they are
  Who look for day before his mistress wakes.   10
Awake, awake, break through your veils of lawn,
Then draw your curtains, and begin the dawn.

Katherine Philips, *Poems by ... the Matchless Orinda*, 1667; written before 1664.

AN ANSWER TO ANOTHER PERSUADING A LADY TO MARRIAGE.

Forbear, bold youth; all 's heaven here,
  And what do you aver,
To others courtship may appear;
  'T is sacrilege to her.

She is a public deity,   5
  And were 't not very odd

She should depose herself to be
  A petty household god?

First make the sun in private shine
  And bid the world adieu, 10
That so he may his beams confine
  In compliment to you.

But if of that you do despair,
  Think how you did amiss
To strive to fix her beams, which are 15
  More bright and large than his.

SIR WILLIAM KILLEGREW, *Selindra,* 1665; acted 1664.

SONG.

COME, come, thou glorious object of my sight,
O my joy, my life, my own delight!
    May this glad minute be
    Blessed to eternity!
See how the glimmering tapers of the sky 5
Do gaze, and wonder at our constancy,
    How they crowd to behold
    What our arms do unfold!
How do all envy our felicities,
And grudge the triumphs of Selindra's eyes! 10
    How Cynthia seeks to shroud
    Her crescent in yon cloud!
Where sad night puts her sable mantle on,
Thy light mistaking, hasteth to be gone;
    Her gloomy shades give way, 15
    As at the approach of day;

And all the planets shrink, in doubt to be
Eclipsèd by a brighter deity.

Look, O look!
How the small 20
Lights do fall,
And adore
What before
The heavens have not shown,
Nor their godheads known! 25

Such a faith,
Such a love
As may move
From above
To descend, and remain 30
Amongst mortals again.

SIR GEORGE ETHERIDGE, *Love in a Tub*, 1664.

SONG.

LADIES, though to your conquering eyes
Love owes his chiefest victories,
And borrows those bright arms from you
With which he does the world subdue;
Yet you yourselves are not above 5
The empire nor the griefs of love.

Then rack not lovers with disdain,
Lest love on you revenge their pain;
You are not free because you 're fair,
The Boy did not his Mother spare. 10
Beauty's but an offensive dart;
It is no armor for the heart.

JOHN DRYDEN, *The Indian Queen*, acted 1664.

INCANTATION.

You twice ten hundred deities,
To whom we daily sacrifice;
You powers that dwell with fate below,
And see what men are doomed to do,
Where elements in discord dwell; 5
Thou god of sleep, arise and tell
Great Zempoalla what strange fate
Must on her dismal vision wait!
By the croaking of the toad,
In their caves that make abode; 10
Earthy, dun, that pants for breath,
With her swelled sides full of death;
By the crested adders' pride,
That along the clifts do glide;
By thy visage fierce and black; 15
By the death's head on thy back;
By the twisted serpents placed
For a girdle round thy waist;
By the hearts of gold that deck
Thy breast, thy shoulders, and thy neck: 20
From thy sleepy mansion rise,
And open thy unwilling eyes,
While bubbling springs their music keep,
That use to lull thee in thy sleep.

JOHN DRYDEN, *The Indian Emperor*, 1665.

SONG.

AH, fading joy! how quickly art thou past!
Yet we thy ruin haste.
As if the cares of human life were few,
We seek out new:
And follow fate that does too fast pursue. 5

See how on every bough the birds express
In their sweet notes their happiness.
They all enjoy and nothing spare,
But on their mother nature lay their care:
Why then should man, the lord of all below, 10
Such troubles choose to know
As none of all his subjects undergo?

Hark, hark, the waters fall, fall, fall,
And with a murmuring sound
Dash, dash, upon the ground, 15
To gentle slumbers call.

SIR CHARLES SEDLEY, *The Mulberry Garden*, 1668.

TO A VERY YOUNG LADY.

AH, Chloris! that I now could sit
As unconcerned, as when
Your infant beauty could beget
No pleasure nor no pain.

When I the dawn used to admire, 5
And praised the coming day,
I little thought the growing fire
Must take my rest away.

Your charms in harmless childhood lay,
  Like metals in the mine; 10
Age from no face took more away,
  Than youth concealed in thine.

But as your charms insensibly
  To their perfections pressed,
Fond love as unperceived did fly, 15
  And in my bosom rest.

My passion with your beauty grew,
  And Cupid at my heart,
Still, as his mother favored you,
  Threw a new flaming dart. 20

Each gloried in their wanton part:
  To make a lover, he
Employed the utmost of his art;
  To make a beauty, she.

Though now I slowly bend to love, 25
  Uncertain of my fate,
If your fair self my chains approve,
  I shall my freedom hate.

Lovers, like dying men, may well
  At first disordered be; 30
Since none alive can truly tell
  What fortune they might see.

Sir Charles Sedley, *Plays, Poems, Songs, etc.*, 1702; written between 1668–1687.

SONG.

Not, Celia, that I juster am
  Or better than the rest;
For I would change each hour like them,
  Were not my heart at rest.

But I am tied to very thee 5
By every thought I have;
Thy face I only care to see,
Thy heart I only crave.

All that in woman is adored
In thy dear self I find; 10
For the whole sex can but afford
The handsome and the kind.

Why then should I seek further store,
And still make love anew?
When change itself can give no more 15
'T is easy to be true.

LOVE STILL HAS SOMETHING OF THE SEA.

Love still has something of the sea,
From whence his mother rose;
No time his slaves from love can free,
Nor give their thoughts repose.

They are becalmed in clearest days, 5
And in rough weather tossed;
They wither under cold delays,
Or are in tempests lost.

One while they seem to touch the port,
Then straight into the main 10
Some angry wind in cruel sport
The vessel drives again.

At first Disdain and Pride they fear,
Which, if they chance to 'scape,
Rivals and Falsehood soon appear 15
In a more dreadful shape.

By such degrees to joy they come,
  And are so long withstood,
So slowly they receive the sum,
  It hardly does them good. 20

'T is cruel to prolong a pain,
  And to defer a joy,
Believe me, gentle Celemene,
  Offends the wingèd boy.

An hundred thousand oaths your fears 25
  Perhaps would not remove,
And if I gazed a thousand years
  I could no deeper love.

PHYLLIS KNOTTING.

"Hears not my Phyllis how the birds
  Their feathered mates salute?
They tell their passion in their words:
  Must I alone be mute?"
    Phyllis, without frown or smile, 5
    Sat and knotted all the while.

"The god of love in thy bright eyes
  Does like a tyrant reign;
But in thy heart a child he lies
  Without his dart or flame." 10
    Phyllis, without frown or smile,
    Sat and knotted all the while.

"So many months in silence past,
  And yet in raging love,
Might well deserve one word at last 15
  My passion should approve."
    Phyllis, without frown or smile,
    Sat and knotted all the while.

"Must then your faithful swain expire
And not one look obtain, 20
Which he to soothe his fond desire
Might pleasingly explain?"
Phyllis, without frown or smile,
Sat and knotted all the while!

PHYLLIS IS MY ONLY JOY.

PHYLLIS is my only joy,
Faithless as the winds or seas,
Sometimes coming, sometimes coy,
Yet she never fails to please;
If with a frown 5
I am cast down,
Phyllis smiling
And beguiling
Makes me happier than before.

Though alas! too late I find 10
Nothing can her fancy fix,
Yet the moment she is kind
I forgive her all her tricks;
Which though I see,
I can't get free. 15
She deceiving,
I believing,
What need lovers wish for more?

A SONG.

PHYLLIS, men say that all my vows
Are to thy fortune paid:
Alas! my heart he little knows
Who thinks my love a trade.

Were I of all these woods the lord, 5
One berry from thy hand
More real pleasure would afford
Than all my large command.

My humble love has learned to live
On what the nicest maid, 10
Without a conscious blush, may give
Beneath the myrtle shade.

JOHN DRYDEN, *Tyrannic Love*,
1670; acted 1668–69.

YOU PLEASING DREAMS OF LOVE.

YOU pleasing dreams of love and sweet delight,
Appear before this slumbering virgin's sight;
Soft visions set her free
From mournful piety.
Let her sad thoughts from heaven retire, 5
And let the melancholy love
Of those remoter joys above
Give place to your more sprightly fire.
Let purling streams be in her fancy seen,
And flowery meads, and vales of cheerful green, 10
And in the midst of deathless groves
Soft sighing wishes lie,
And smiling hopes fast by,
And just beyond them ever-laughing loves.

JOHN DRYDEN, *An Evening's Love*, 1671.

YOU CHARMED ME NOT WITH THAT FAIR FACE.

You charmed me not with that fair face,
  Though it was all divine:
To be another's is the grace
  That makes me wish you mine.
The gods and fortune take their part 5
  Who, like young monarchs, fight,
And boldly dare invade that heart
  Which is another's right.
First, mad with hope, we undertake
  To pull up every bar; 10
But, once possessed, we faintly make
  A dull defensive war.
Now, every friend is turned a foe,
  In hope to get our store:
And passion makes us cowards grow, 15
  Which made us brave before.

JOHN WILMOT, Earl of Rochester,
Poems on Several Occasions, 1680;
date of writing uncertain.

A SONG.

Absent from thee I languish still,
  Then ask me not, 'when I return?'
The straying fool 't will plainly kill
  To wish all day, all night to mourn.

Dear, from thine arms then let me fly, 5
That my fantastic mind may prove
The torments it deserves to try,
That tears my fixed heart from my love.

When, wearied with a world of woe,
To thy safe bosom I retire, 10
Where love, and peace, and truth does flow,
May I, contented, there expire.

Lest once more wandering from that heaven,
I fall on some base heart unblest,
Faithless to thee, false, unforgiven, 15
And lose my everlasting rest.

LOVE AND LIFE.

All my past life is mine no more,
The flying hours are gone,
Like transitory dreams given o'er,
Whose images are kept in store
By memory alone. 5

The time that is to come is not:
How can it then be mine?
The present moment 's all my lot,
And that, as fast as it is got,
Phyllis, is only thine. 10

Then talk not of inconstancy,
False hearts, and broken vows,
If I, by miracle, can be
This live-long minute true to thee,
'T is all that heaven allows. 15

UPON DRINKING IN A BOWL.

VULCAN, contrive me such a cup
  As Nestor used of old;
Show all thy skill to trim it up,
  Damask it round with gold.

Make it so large that, filled with sack   5
  Up to the swelling brim,
Vast toasts on the delicious lake,
  Like ships at sea may swim.

Engrave not battle on his cheek,
  With war I 've naught to do: 10
I 'm none of those that took Maestrick,
  Nor Yarmouth leaguer knew.

Let it no name of planets tell,
  Fixed stars or constellations;
For I am no Sir Sidrophel,   15
  Nor none of his relations.

But carve thereon a spreading vine,
  Then add two lovely boys;
Their limbs in amorous folds entwine,
  The type of future joys.   20

Cupid and Bacchus my saints are,
  May Drink and Love still reign!
With wine I wash away my care,
  And then to love again.

CONSTANCY.

I cannot change, as others do,
Though you unjustly scorn,
Since that poor swain that sighs for you,
For you alone was born;
No, Phyllis, no, your heart to move 5
A surer way I 'll try,
And to revenge my slighted love,
Will still love on, and die.

When, killed with grief, Amyntas lies,
And you to mind shall call 10
The sighs that now unpitied rise,
The tears that vainly fall:
That welcome hour that ends his smart,
Will then begin your pain,
For such a faithful tender heart 15
Can never break in vain.

A SONG.

My dear mistress has a heart
Soft as those kind looks she gave me;
When with love's resistless art,
And her eyes, she did enslave me.
But her constancy 's so weak 5
She 's so wild and apt to wander;
That my jealous heart would break,
Should we live one day asunder.

Melting joys about her move,
Killing pleasures, wounding blisses; 10
She can dress her eyes in love,
And her lips can arm with kisses.

Angels listen when she speaks,
She 's my delight, all mankind's wonder;
But my jealous heart would break, 15
Should we live one day asunder.

THOMAS FLATMAN, *Poems and Songs*, 1674; date of writing uncertain.

THE DEFIANCE.

Be not too proud, imperious dame,
Your charms are transitory things,
May melt, while you at heaven aim,
Like Icarus's waxen wings;
And you a part in his misfortune bear, 5
Drowned in a briny ocean of despair.

You think your beauties are above
The poet's brain and painter's hand,
As if upon the throne of love
You only should the world command: 15
Yet know, though you presume your title true,
There are pretenders that will rival you.

There 's an experienced rebel, Time,
And in his squadron 's Poverty;
There 's Age that brings along with him 15
A terrible artillery:
And if against all these thou keep'st thy crown,
Th' usurper Death will make thee lay it down.

Sir George Etheridge, *A Collection of Poems*, 1701; written before 1675.

TO A LADY,

ASKING HOW LONG HE WOULD LOVE HER.

It is not, Celia, in our power
  To say how long our love will last;
It may be we within this hour
  May lose those joys we now do taste:
The blessed that immortal be, 5
From change in love are only free.

Then since we mortal lovers are,
  Ask not how long our love may last;
But while it does, let us take care
  Each minute be with pleasure passed: 10
Were it not madness to deny
To live because we 're sure to die?

A SONG.

Ye happy swains whose hearts are free
  From Love's imperial chain,
Take warning and be taught by me
  T' avoid th' enchanting pain;
Fatal the wolves to trembling flocks, 5
  Fierce winds to blossoms prove,
To careless seamen, hidden rocks,
  To human quiet, love.

Fly the fair sex, if bliss you prize;
  The snake's beneath the flower: 10

Whoever gazed on beauteous eyes,
That tasted quiet more?
How faithless is the lovers' joy!
How constant is their care
The kind with falsehood to destroy, 15
The cruel, with despair!

APHARA BEHN, *Abdelazer, or the Moor's Revenge*, 1677; acted 1676.

SONG.

LOVE in fantastic triumph sat,
Whilst bleeding hearts around him flowed,
For whom fresh pains he did create,
And strange tyrannic power he showed;
From thy bright eyes he took his fires, 5
Which round about in sport he hurled;
But 't was from mine he took desires
Enough t' undo the amorous world.

From me he took his sighs and tears,
From thee his pride and cruelty; 10
From me his languishments and fears,
And every killing dart from thee:
Thus thou and I the god have armed,
And set him up a deity,
But my poor heart alone is harmed, 15
Whilst thine the victor is, and free.

JOHN DRYDEN, *Troilus and Cressida*, 1679.

CAN LIFE BE A BLESSING?

CAN life be a blessing,
Or worth the possessing,
Can life be a blessing, if love were away?
Ah, no! though our love all night keep us waking,
And though he torment us with cares all the day, 5
Yet he sweetens, he sweetens our pains in the taking;
There 's an hour at the last, there 's an hour to repay.

In every possessing,
The ravishing blessing,
In every possessing, the fruit of our pain, 10
Poor lovers forget long ages of anguish,
Whate'er they have suffered and done to obtain;
'T is a pleasure, a pleasure to sigh and to languish,
When we hope, when we hope to be happy again.

CHARLES SACKVILLE, *Earl of Dorset, A New Miscellany of Poems on Several Occasions*, 1701; written before 1680.

ON A LADY WHO FANCIED HERSELF A BEAUTY.

DORINDA'S sparkling wit and eyes,
United cast too fierce a light,
Which blazes high, but quickly dies,
Pains not the heart, but hurts the sight.

Love is a calmer, gentler joy, 5
Smooth are his looks, and soft his pace:
Her Cupid is a blackguard boy,
That runs his link full in your face.

The same in *Works of Celebrated Authors*, 1750; written before 1680.

SONG.

PHYLLIS, for shame! let us improve
A thousand different ways
Those few short moments snatched by love
From many tedious days.

If you want courage to despise 5
The censure of the grave,
Though Love's a tyrant in your eyes
Your heart is but a slave.

My love is full of noble pride,
Nor can it e'er submit 10
To let that fop, Discretion, ride
In triumph over it.

False friends I have, as well as you,
Who daily counsel me
Fame and ambition to pursue, 15
And leave off loving thee.

But when the least regard I show
To fools who thus advise,
May I be dull enough to grow
Most miserably wise! 20

JOHN DRYDEN, *The Spanish Friar*, 1681.

FAREWELL, UNGRATEFUL TRAITOR.

FAREWELL, ungrateful traitor!
  Farewell, my perjured swain!
Let never injured creature
  Believe a man again.
The pleasure of possessing 5
Surpasses all expressing,
But 'tis too short a blessing,
  And love too long a pain.

'Tis easy to deceive us,
  In pity of your pain; 10
But when we love, you leave us
  To rail at you in vain.
Before we have descried it,
There is no bliss beside it,
But she, that once has tried it, 15
  Will never love again.

The passion you pretended,
  Was only to obtain;
But when the charm is ended,
  The charmer you disdain. 20
Your love by ours we measure,
Till we have lost our treasure;
But dying is a pleasure,
  When living is a pain.

JOHN DRYDEN, *The Duke of Guise*, 1683; acted 1682.

SONG.

BETWIXT A SHEPHERD AND A SHEPHERDESS.

Shepherdess.

TELL me, Thyrsis, tell your anguish,
Why you sigh, and why you languish;
When the nymph whom you adore
Grants the blessing
Of possessing, 5
What can love and I do more?

Shepherd.

Think it 's love beyond all measure
Makes me faint away with pleasure;
Strength of cordial may destroy,
And the blessing 10
Of possessing
Kills me with excess of joy.

Shepherdess.

Thyrsis, how can I believe you?
But confess, and I 'll forgive you:
Men are false, and so are you. 15
Never Nature
Framed a creature
To enjoy, and yet be true.

Shepherd.

Mine 's a flame beyond expiring,
Still possessing, still desiring, 20

Fit for Love's imperial crown;
Ever shining
And refining
Still the more 't is melted down.

Chorus.

Mine's a flame beyond expiring, 25
Still possessing, still desiring,
Fit for Love's imperial crown;
Ever shining
And refining
Still the more 't is melted down. 30

JOHN NORRIS, *Poems and Discourses*, 1684.

HYMN TO DARKNESS.

HAIL, thou most sacred venerable thing!
What Muse is worthy thee to sing?
Thee, from whose pregnant universal womb
All things, even Light, thy rival, first did come.
What dares he not attempt that sings of thee, 5
Thou first and greatest mystery?
Who can the secrets of thy essence tell?
Thou, like the light of God, art inaccessible.

Before great Love this monument did raise,
This ample theatre of praise; 10
Before the folding circles of the sky
Were tuned by him who is all harmony;
Before the morning stars their hymn began
Before the council held for man;

Before the birth of either Time or Place 15
Thou reign'st unquestioned monarch in the empty space.

Thy native lot thou didst to Light resign,
But still half of the globe is thine.
Here with a quiet, and yet awful hand,
Like the best emperors, thou dost command. 20
To thee the stars above their brightness owe,
And mortals their repose below.
To thy protection Fear and Sorrow flee
And those that weary are of light find rest in thee.

Though light and glory be th' Almighty's throne, 25
Darkness is his pavilion.
From that his radiant beauty, but from thee
He has his terror and his majesty.
Thus when he first proclaimed his sacred law,
And would his rebel subjects awe, 30
Like princes on some great solemnity,
H' appeared in 's robes of state and clad himself with thee.

The blest above do thy sweet umbrage prize,
When, cloyed with light, they veil their eyes;
The vision of the Deity is made 35
More sweet and beatific by thy shade.
But we, poor tenants of this orb below
Don't here thy excellencies know,
Till death our understandings does improve,
And then our wiser ghosts thy silent night-walks love. 40

But thee I now admire, thee would I choose
For my religion, or my Muse.
'T is hard to tell whether thy reverend shade
Has more good votaries or poets made,

From thy dark caves were inspirations given, 45
And from thick groves went vows to Heaven.
Hail then, thou Muse's and devotion's spring!
'T is just we should adore, 't is just we should thee sing.

CHARLES COTTON, *Poems on Several Occasions*, 1689; written before 1687.

THE MORNING QUATRAINS.

THE cock has crowed an hour ago,
'T is time we now dull sleep forgo;
Tired nature is by sleep redressed
And labor 's overcome by rest.

We have out-done the work of night; 5
'T is time we rise t' attend the light,
And ere he shall his beams display,
To plot new business for the day.

None but the slothful or unsound
Are by the sun in feathers found, 10
Nor, without rising with the sun,
Can the world's business e'er be done.

Hark, hark! the watchful chanticler
Tells us the day's bright harbinger
Peeps o'er the eastern hills, to awe 15
And warn night's sov'reign to withdraw.

The morning curtains now are drawn,
And now appears the blushing dawn;
Aurora has her roses shed,
To strew the way Sol's steeds must tread. 20

Xanthus and Æthon harnessed are
To roll away the burning car,
And, snorting flame, impatient bear
The dressing of the charioteer.

The sable cheeks of sullen Night 25
Are streaked with rosy streams of light,
Whilst she retires away in fear
To shade the other hemisphere.

The merry lark now takes her wings,
And longed-for day's loud welcome sings, 30
Mounting her body out of sight,
As if she meant to meet the light.

Now doors and windows are unbarred,
Each-where are cheerful voices heard,
And round about "good-morrows" fly, 35
As if day taught humanity.

The chimneys now to smoke begin,
And the old wife sits down to spin,
Whilst Kate, taking her pail, does trip
Mull's swoll'n and straddling paps to strip. 40

Vulcan now makes his anvil ring,
Dick whistles loud and Maud doth sing,
And Silvio with his bugle horn
Winds an imprime unto the morn.

Now through the morning doors behold 45
Phœbus arrayed in burning gold,
Lashing his fiery steeds, displays
His warm and all-enlight'ning rays.

Now each one to his work repairs,
All that have hands are laborers, 50
And manufactures of each trade
By op'ning shops are open laid.

Hob yokes his oxen to the team,
The angler goes unto the stream,
The woodman to the purlieus hies, 55
The lab'ring bees to load their thighs.

Fair Amaryllis drives her flocks,
All night safe folded from the fox,
To flow'ry downs, where Colin stays
To court her with his roundelays. 60

The traveller now leaves his inn
A new day's journey to begin,
As he would post it with the day,
And early rising makes good way.

The slick-faced schoolboy satchel takes, 65
And with slow pace small riddance makes;
For why, the haste we make, you know,
To knowledge and to virtue 's slow.

The fore-horse jingles on the road,
The waggoner lugs on his load, 70
The field with busy people snies,
And city rings with various cries.

The world is now a busy swarm,
All doing good, or doing harm;
But let 's take heed our acts be true, 75
For heaven's eye sees all we do.

None can that piercing sight evade,
It penetrates the darkest shade,
And sin, though it should 'scape the eye,
Would be discovered by the cry. 80

RONDEAU.

Forbear, fair Phyllis, O forbear
Those deadly killing frowns, and spare
A heart so loving, and so true,
By none to be subdued, but you,
Who my poor life's sole princess are. 5
You only can create my care;
But offend you, I all things dare.
Then, lest your cruelty you rue,
Forbear;
And lest you kill that heart, beware, 10
To which there is some pity due,
If but because I humbly sue.
Your anger, therefore, sweetest fair,
Though mercy in your sex is rare,
Forbear. 15

SONG.

Why, dearest, shouldst thou weep when I relate
The story of my woe?
Let not the swarthy mists of my black fate
O'ercast thy beauty so:
For each rich pearl lost on that score, 5
Adds to mischance, and wounds your servant more.

Quench not those stars that to my bliss should guide:
O spare that precious tear!

Nor let those drops unto a deluge tide,
To drown your beauty there; 10
That cloud of sorrow makes it night,
You lose your lustre, but the world its light.

LES AMOURS.

SHE that I pursue, still flies me;
Her that follows me, I fly;
She that I still court, denies me;
Her that courts me, I deny:
Thus in one web we 're subtly wove, 5
And yet we mutiny in love.

She that can save me, must not do it;
She that cannot, fain would do;
Her love is bound, yet I still woo it;
Hers by love is bound in woe: 10
Yet how can I of love complain,
Since I have love for love again?

This is thy work, imperious Child,
Thine 's this labyrinth of love,
That thus hast our desires beguiled, 15
Nor seest how thine arrows rove.
Then prithee, to compose this stir,
Make her love me, or me love her.

But, if irrevocable are
Those keen shafts that wound us so, 20
Let me prevail with thee thus far,
That thou once more take thy bow;
Wound her hard heart, and by my troth,
I 'll be content to take them both.

SONG.

Join once again, my Celia, join
Thy rosy lips to these of mine,
  Which, though they be not such,
Are full as sensible of bliss,
That is, as soon can taste a kiss, 5
  As thine of softer touch.

Each kiss of thine creates desire,
Thy odorous breath inflames love's fire,
  And wakes the sleeping coal:
Such a kiss to be I find 10
The conversation of the mind,
  And whisper of the soul.

Thanks, sweetest, now thou 'rt perfect grown,
For by this last kiss I 'm undone;
  Thou breathest silent darts, 15
Henceforth each little touch will prove
A dangerous stratagem in love,
  And thou wilt blow up hearts.

TO CELIA.

ODE.

When, Celia, must my old days set,
  And my young morning rise
In beams of joy, so bright, as yet
  Ne'er blessed a lover's eyes?
My state is more advanced than when 5
  I first attempted thee;
I sued to be a servant then,
  But now to be made free.

I 've served my time, faithful and true,
  Expecting to be placed 10
In happy freedom, as my due,
  To all the joys thou hast :
Ill husbandry in love is such
  A scandal to love's power,
We ought not to mispend so much 15
  As one poor short-lived hour.

Yet think not, sweet, I 'm weary grown,
  That I pretend such haste,
Since none to surfeit e'er was known
  Before he had a taste ; 20
My infant love could humbly wait,
  When young it scarce knew how
To plead ; but grown to man's estate
  He is impatient now.

LAURA SLEEPING.

WINDS, whisper gently whilst she sleeps,
  And fan her with your cooling wings,
Whilst she her drops of beauty weeps
  From pure and yet unrivalled springs.

Glide over beauty's field, her face, 5
  To kiss her lip and cheek be bold,
But with a calm and stealing pace,
  Neither too rude nor yet too cold.

Play in her beams and crisp her hair
  With such a gale as wings soft love, 10
And with so sweet, so rich an air
  As breathes from the Arabian grove.

A breath as hushed as lover's sigh,
  Or that unfolds the morning door;
Sweet as the winds that gently fly 15
  To sweep the spring's enamelled floor.

Murmur soft music to her dreams,
  That pure and unpolluted run,
Like to the new-born crystal streams
  Under the bright enamoured sun. 20

But when she waking shall display
  Her light, retire within your bar.
Her breath is life, her eyes are day,
  And all mankind her creatures are.

APHARA BEHN, *The Lover's Watch*, 1686.

THE CHARM FOR CONSTANCY.

IRIS, to keep my soul entire and true,
It thinks each moment of the day on you;
  And when a charming face I see
    That does all other eyes incline,
  It has no influence on me: 5
    I think it e'en deformed to thine.
My eyes, my soul, and sense regardless move
To all but the dear object of my love.

APHARA BEHN, *The Lucky Chance*, 1687.

O LOVE THAT STRONGER ART THAN WINE.

O LOVE! that stronger art than wine,
Pleasing delusion, witchery divine,
Wont to be prized above all wealth,
Disease that has more joys than health:
Though we blaspheme thee in our pain, 5
And of thy tyranny complain,
We all are bettered by thy reign.

What reason never can bestow
We to this useful passion owe:
Love wakes the dull from sluggish ease, 10
And learns a clown the art to please,
Humbles the vain, kindles the cold,
Makes misers free, and cowards bold;
'T is he reforms the sot from drink,
And teaches airy fops to think. 15

When full brute appetite is fed,
And choked the glutton lies and dead,
Thou new spirits dost dispense
And finest the gross delights of sense:
Virtue's unconquerable aid 20
That against Nature can persuade,
And makes a roving mind retire
Within the bounds of just desire;
Cheerer of age, youth's kind unrest,
And half the heaven of the blest! 25

EDMUND WALLER, *The Second Part of Mr. Waller's Poems*, 1690; written after 1686.

OF THE LAST VERSES IN THE BOOK.

WHEN we for age could neither read nor write,
The subject made us able to indite;
The soul, with nobler resolutions decked,
The body stooping, does herself erect.
No mortal parts are requisite to raise 5
Her that, unbodied, can her Maker praise.

The seas are quiet when the winds give o'er;
So, calm are we when passions are no more!
For then we know how vain it was to boast
Of fleeting things, so certain to be lost. 10
Clouds of affection from our younger eyes
Conceal that emptiness which age descries.

The soul's dark cottage, battered and decayed,
Lets in new light through chinks that time has made;
Stronger by weakness, wiser men become, 15
As they draw near to their eternal home.
Leaving the old, both worlds at once they view,
That stand upon the threshold of the new.

JOHN DRYDEN, *Poems on Various Occasions*, 1701.

A SONG.

FOR SAINT CECILIA'S DAY, 1687.

FROM harmony, from heavenly harmony,
This universal frame began:
When nature underneath a heap

Of jarring atoms lay,
And could not heave her head, 5
The tuneful voice was heard from high,
'Arise, ye more than dead.'
Then cold, and hot and moist, and dry,
In order to their stations leap,
And Music's power obey. 10
From harmony, from heavenly harmony,
This universal frame began:
From harmony to harmony
Through all the compass of the notes it ran,
The diapason closing full in man. 15

What passion cannot music raise and quell?
When Jubal struck the chorded shell,
His listening brethren stood around,
And, wondering, on their faces fell
To worship that celestial sound. 20
Less than a god they thought there could not dwell
Within the hollow of that shell
That spoke so sweetly and so well.
What passion cannot music raise and quell?

The trumpet's loud clangor 25
Excites us to arms,
With shrill notes of anger
And mortal alarms.
The double, double, double beat
Of the thundering drum, 30
Cries, hark! the foes come:
Charge, charge! 't is too late to retreat.

The soft complaining flute
In dying notes discovers

The woes of hopeless lovers, 35
Whose dirge is whispered by the warbling lute.

Sharp violins proclaim
Their jealous pangs and desperation,
Fury, frantic indignation,
Depths of pains and height of passion 40
For the fair, disdainful dame.

But, O! what art can teach,
What human voice can reach
The sacred organ's praise?
Notes inspiring holy love, 45
Notes that wing their heavenly ways
To mend the choirs above.

Orpheus could lead the savage race,
And trees unrooted left their place
Sequacious to the lyre: 50
But bright Cecilia raised the wonder higher;
When to her organ vocal breath was given,
An angel heard, and straight appeared
Mistaking earth for heaven.

Grand Chorus.

As from the power of sacred lays 55
The spheres began to move,
And sung the great Creator's praise
To all the bless'd above;
So when the last and dreadful hour
This crumbling pageant shall devour, 60
The trumpet shall be heard on high,
The dead shall live, the living die,
And Music shall untune the sky.

JOHN DRYDEN, *King Arthur*, 1691.

FAIREST ISLE, ALL ISLES EXCELLING.

FAIREST isle, all isles excelling,
  Seat of pleasures and of loves;
Venus here will choose her dwelling,
  And forsake her Cyprian groves.

Cupid from his favorite nation 5
  Care and envy will remove;
Jealousy, that poisons passion,
  And despair, that dies for love.

Gentle murmurs, sweet complaining,
  Sighs that blow the fire of love; 10
Soft repulses, kind disdaining,
  Shall be all the pains you prove.

Every swain shall pay his duty,
  Grateful every nymph shall prove;
And as these excel in beauty, 15
  Those shall be renowned for love.

JOHN DRYDEN, *Cleomenes*, 1692.

NO, NO, POOR SUFFERING HEART.

No, no, poor suffering heart, no change endeavor;
Choose to sustain the smart, rather than leave her.
My ravished eyes behold such charms about her,
I can die with her, but not live without her;
One tender sigh of hers to see me languish, 5
Will more than pay the price of my past anguish.

Beware, O cruel fair, how you smile on me,
'T was a kind look of yours that has undone me.

Love has in store for me one happy minute,
And she will end my pain who did begin it; 10
Then no day void of bliss or pleasure leaving,
Ages shall slide away without perceiving:
Cupid shall guard the door, the more to please us,
And keep out Time and Death, when they would seize us:
Time and Death shall depart, and say, in flying, 15
Love has found out a way to live by dying.

JOHN DRYDEN, *Third Miscellany*, 1693.

A SONG.

TO A FAIR YOUNG LADY GOING OUT OF TOWN IN SPRING.

ASK not the cause why sullen spring
So long delays her flowers to bear;
Why warbling birds forget to sing,
And winter storms invert the year:
Chloris is gone, and Fate provides 5
To make it spring where she resides.

Chloris is gone, the cruel fair;
She cast not back a pitying eye,
But left her lover in despair,
To sigh, to languish, and to die. 10
Ah, how can those fair eyes endure,
To give the wounds they will not cure?

Great god of love, why hast thou made
A face that can all hearts command,

That all religions can invade, 15
  And change the laws of every land?
Where thou hadst placed such power before,
Thou shouldst have made her mercy more.

When Chloris to the temple comes,
  Adoring crowds before her fall; 20
She can restore the dead from tombs,
  And every life but mine recall.
I only am by love designed
To be the victim for mankind.

MATTHEW PRIOR, *Poems on Several Occasions*, 1709; written about 1693.

A SONG.

In vain you tell your parting lover
You wish fair winds may waft him over.
Alas! what winds can happy prove
That bear me far from what I love?
Alas! what dangers on the main 5
Can equal those that I sustain
From slighted vows and cold disdain?

Be gentle, and in pity choose
To wish the wildest tempests loose;
That, thrown again upon the coast 10
Where first my shipwrecked heart was lost,
I may once more repeat my pain,
Once more in dying notes complain
Of slighted vows and cold disdain.

JOHN DRYDEN, *Love Triumphant*, 1693–94.

SONG OF JEALOUSY.

WHAT state of life can be so blest
As love, that warms a lover's breast?
Two souls in one, the same desire
To grant the bliss, and to require.
But if in heaven a hell we find, 5
'T is all from thee,
O Jealousy!
'T is all from thee,
O Jealousy!
Thou tyrant, tyrant Jealousy, 10
Thou tyrant of the mind.

All other ills, though sharp they prove,
Serve to refine and perfect love:
In absence, or unkind disdain,
Sweet hope relieves the lover's pain. 15
But, ah! no cure but death we find,
To set us free
From Jealousy:
O Jealousy!
Thou tyrant, tyrant Jealousy, 20
Thou tyrant of the mind.

False in thy glass all objects are,
Some set too near, and some too far;
Thou art the fire of endless night,
The fire that burns, and gives no light. 25
All torments of the damned we find
In only thee,

O Jealousy!
Thou tyrant, tyrant Jealousy,
Thou tyrant of the mind. 30

MATTHEW PRIOR, *Poems on Several Occasions*, 1709; written about 1695–96.

AN ODE.

THE merchant, to secure his treasure,
Conveys it in a borrowed name:
Euphelia serves to grace my measure,
But Chloe is my real flame.

My softest verse, my darling lyre 5
Upon Euphelia's toilet lay,
When Chloe noted her desire
That I should sing, that I should play.

My lyre I tune, my voice I raise;
But with my numbers mix my sighs; 10
And whilst I sing Euphelia's praise,
I fix my soul on Chloe's eyes.

Fair Chloe blushed, Euphelia frowned,
I sung and gazed, I played and trembled:
And Venus to the Loves around 15
Remarked how ill we all dissembled.

TO CHLOE WEEPING.

SEE, whilst thou weep'st, fair Chloe, see
The world in sympathy with thee!

The cheerful birds no longer sing,
Each droops his head, and hangs his wing;
The clouds have bent their bosom lower, 5
And shed their sorrows in a shower;
The brooks beyond their limits flow,
And louder murmurs speak their woe.
The nymphs and swains adopt thy cares,
They heave thy sighs and weep thy tears. 10
Fantastic nymph, that grief should move
Thy heart obdurate against love!
Strange tears, whose power can soften all
But that dear breast on which they fall!

A SONG.

If wine and music have the power
To ease the sickness of the soul,
Let Phœbus every string explore,
And Bacchus fill the sprightly bowl.
Let them their friendly aid employ 5
To make my Chloe's absence light,
And seek for pleasure to destroy
The sorrows of this live-long night.

But she to-morrow will return.
Venus be thou to-morrow great, 10
Thy myrtles strew, thy odors burn,
And meet thy favorite nymph in state.
Kind goddess, to no other powers
Let us to-morrow's blessings own;
Thy darling loves shall guide the hours, 15
And all the day be thine alone.

George Granville, Lord Lansdowne, *A Collection of Poems*, 1701; written before 1689.

SONG.

The happiest mortals once were we,
I loved Myra, Myra me;
Each desirous of the blessing,
Nothing wanting but possessing;
I loved Myra, Myra me: 5
The happiest mortals once were we.

But since cruel fates dissever,
Torn from love, and torn forever,
Tortures end me,
Death befriend me! 10
Of all pain, the greatest pain
Is to love, and love in vain.

William Congreve, *Works*, 1710; written before 1700.

SONG.

See, see, she wakes, Sabina wakes!
And now the sun begins to rise;
Less glorious is the morn that breaks
From his bright beams, than her fair eyes.

With light united, day they give, 5
But different fates ere night fulfil;
How many by his warmth will live!
How many will her coldness kill!

AMORET.

FAIR Amoret is gone astray:
  Pursue and seek her, every lover!
I 'll tell the signs by which you may
  The wandering shepherdess discover.

Coquet and coy at once her air, 5
  Both studied, though both seem neglected;
Careless she is, with artful care,
  Affecting to seem unaffected.

With skill her eyes dart every glance,
  Yet change so soon you 'd ne'er suspect them; 10
For she 'd persuade they wound by chance,
  Though certain aim and art direct them.

She likes herself, yet others hates
  For that which in herself she prizes;
And while she laughs at them, forgets 15
  She is the thing that she despises.

JOHN DRYDEN, *The Secular Masque*, 1700.

HUNTING SONG.

Diana.

WITH horns and hounds, I waken the day,
And hie to the woodland walks away;
I tuck up my robe, and am buskined soon,
And tie to my forehead a wexing moon;

I course the fleet stag, and unkennel the fox, 5
And chase the wild goats o'er the summits of rocks ;
With shouting and hooting we pierce through the sky,
And Echo turns hunter and doubles the cry.

Chorus.

With shouting and hooting we pierce through the sky,
And Echo turns hunter and doubles the cry. 10

NOTES.

1. **Pan's Anniversary.** The title of this masque, as printed in the folio of 1631–1641, bears: "As it was presented at Court before King James, 1625." James died in March of that year, and as this masque is more appropriate to summer, Nichols has assigned it to the summer of 1624, Mr. Fleay to June 19, 1623. This was one of the masques in which Inigo Jones, the famous architect, assisted Jonson. As to Jonson, see the editor's *Elizabethan Lyrics*, Athenæum Press Series, pp. xxxi, lxvi, and 259.

1. **The Shepherds' Holiday.** In the original the three stanzas are assigned to successive "nymphs," young women of marriageable age.

1 1. **Rites Are due.** Note the omission of the relative. See Abbott's *Shakespeare Grammar*, § 244, and cf. below, pp. 4 3, 9 2, 18 5, 94 9, 107 4.

1 9. **Primrose-drop.** Appropriately so called from the appearance of the blossoms as placed on separate peduncles.

1 10. **Day's-eyes and the lips of cows.** Daisies and cowslips.

1 11. **Garden-star.** Probably the flower popularly known as the star-of-Bethlehem.

2. **Hymn, To Pan.** Here, too, the stanzas in the original are assigned to successive nymphs, the refrain being in chorus.

2 3. **Can.** Knows, is able to perform. Cf. 99 20.

2 7. **Hermes** would appropriately lead the dance, from the lightness of his winged feet.

2 18. **Rebound.** Echo back, resound, a not uncommon meaning. Cf. Child, *Ballads*, ed. 1871, III, 340, and, especially, *The Spanish Tragedy*, i. 1. 30:

> Both raising dreadful clamors to the sky,
> That valleys, hills and rivers made rebound.

2. **Thomas Dekker.** See *Elizabethan Lyrics*, p. 232.

2. **The Sun's Darling** is described as "a moral masque," and is the work of Dekker and Ford. These two vigorous songs are assuredly Dekker's.

2. **Country Glee.** The title is Mr. Bullen's.

2 7. **Bravely.** Finely, beautifully.

3 16. **Princes' courts.** Mr. Bullen, on I know not what authority, reads *a prince's courts*. The ed. of Ford, 1840, and the reprint of Dekker read as in the text.

3 20. **Echo's holloa.** Ed. 1870 reads *echo's hollow.*

3 27. **Spring up . . . the partridges.** Start, raise.

3 35. **Sousing.** Swooping down, a term in falconry.

4. **Cast away Care.** This lively drinking song is put into the mouth of the character Folly.

4 6. **Play it off.** A term in the old jargon of boon-companionship. Cf. *1 Henry IV*, ii. 4. 18.

4 9. Cf. Falstaff's praise of sack, *2 Henry IV*, iv. 3. 92.

4. **Christ Church MS.** This poem was first printed by Mr. Bullen in his *More Lyrics from Elizabethan Song Books*, 1888, p. 125.

4 6. **Years Are yet untold.** Note the omission of the relative and cf. 1 2.

5. **Thomas May,** the historian of the Long Parliament, wrote several plays in his youth. Mr. Fleay places the composition of *The Old Couple* before *The Heir*, which was acted in 1620. The poem in the text appears also in Porter's *Madrigals and Airs*, 1632.

5. **Love's Prime.** Mr. Bullen (*More Lyrics*, p. 153) doubts whether May wrote this song. The title is that given in *Wit's Recreations*, ed. 1641 (not 1640, if I read the Preface to Park's reprint of that interesting work, p. ix, aright). This poem was also printed in John Cotgrave's *Wit's Interpreter*, 1655, and in Stafford Smith's *Musica Antiqua*, of about the same date. Both of these versions exhibit several variant readings of minor importance.

5 5. **Flaming beams.** This is the reading of *Wit's Recreations;* Bullen reads *inflaming beams*, etc.

5 9. **Still young.** Ever young. Cf. 33 12.

5 9 10. These lines are omitted in the version of *Wit's Recreations.*

5. **Edmund Waller,** in the *Biographica Britannica*, ed. 1766, startlingly described as "the most celebrated lyric poet that England ever produced," has of late been almost as perversely dignified by Mr. Gosse (in his *From Shakespeare to Pope*) as the absolute founder of the classic school of poetry. I would commend a consideration of this little lyric of Waller's (which his first editor, Fenton, assigns to the year 1627, and which is wholly in the old, free manner) to those who believe that Waller's "earliest verses . . . possess the formal character, the precise prosody without irregularity or overflow, which we find in

the ordinary verse of Dryden, Pope or Darwin" (*Eighteenth Century Literature*, p. 3).

5 1. **Stay, Phoebus, stay!** Cotton begins a poem with the same words (*Poems*, ed. 1689, p. 339).

5 6. **De Mornay.** Probably one of Queen Henrietta's attendants, who upon the misbehavior of Monseigneur Saint George and the Bishop of Mende quitted England (Fenton).

6 7. **Well does this prove.** The same excellent commentator remarks: "The latter stanza of these verses . . . alludes to the Copernican system, in which the earth is supposed to be a planet, and to move on its own axis around the sun, the center of the universe. Dr. Donne and Mr. Cowley industriously affected to entertain the fair sex with such philosophical allusions, which in his riper age Mr. Waller as industriously avoided." Cf. with this stanza Wordsworth's *Poems*, ed. Dowden, p. 54:

> No motion has she now, no force;
> She neither hears nor sees;
> Rolled round in earth's diurnal course
> With rocks, and stones, and trees.

Or more poetically Tennyson's beautiful lines beginning (*Poems*, ed. 1830, p. 377):

> Move eastward, happy earth, and leave
> Yon orange sunset.

6. **Love's Hue and Cry.** This poem appears in several places,— first in Shirley's *Witty Fair One*, published in 1633, in the *Poems of Carew*, 1640, and in Shirley's octavo volume of 1646. The versions differ considerably. I have preferred the first — that of the play — which seems to me, barring the conclusion, the simplest and the best. The title is that of Shirley's octavo, in which the poem is thus concluded:

> That, that is she; O straight surprise
> And bring her unto Love's assize;
> But lose no time, for fear that she
> Ruin all mankind, like me,
> Fate and philosophy control,
> And leave the world without a soul.

The question of authorship is not easily decided and is rendered the more difficult as this is not the only poem in which there is a confusion of authorship between Shirley and Carew. Shirley edited his poems in 1646 with greater care than was usual in his age. In a *Postscript to the Reader* he says in excuse for setting forth his volume: "When I observed most of these copies [of his verses] corrupted in their transcripts, and the rest fleeting from me, which were by some indiscreet collector, not acquainted with distributive justice, mingled with other men's (some eminent) conceptions in print, I thought myself concerned to use some vindication" (*Works of Shirley*, ed. Gifford and Dyce, VI, 461). On the other hand, there is every reason to believe that the poetry of Carew was not only printed but prepared for the press after the poet's death. Dyce in his notes on Shirley's poems does not venture an opinion; Hazlitt claims the poem for the poet he happens to be editing; includes a well-known poem of Drayton's, from its similar title, in his collection, claiming it also for Carew; says that Dyce did not know of the insertion of the *Hue and Cry* in the works of Carew; and, happening upon Dyce's notes before his own ed. of Carew appeared, concludes by retracting his own words in his *Index of Names*. (See Hazlitt's *Carew*, pp. 128, and 244 under *Shirley*.) Such external evidence as we have at hand, then, would assign the authorship of this poem, together with the two others mentioned below, to Shirley rather than to Carew. When we consider the style of the poems, this view is substantiated. *Love's Hue and Cry* is an imitation, though not a slavish one, of Drayton's *Crier* (see *Elizabethan Lyrics*, p. 195), whilst *To his Mistress Confined* is decidedly Donnian, and the *Song*, "Would you know what is soft?" a variation on the third stanza of Jonson's *Triumph of Charis*. Now such imitations, adaptations, or reminiscences of the literature of the past are characteristics of the dramatic work of Shirley, characteristics, by the way, which take less from his praise than might be supposed. (See Ward's estimate, *History of the English Drama*, first edition, II, 334.) Reminiscence is emphatically not a trait of the undoubted poetry of Carew, whose delicately wrought and finely polished lyrics elude the paternity of both Jonson and Donne, and sparkle with an originality their own.

6 12. **As.** That. Cf. 7 8.

6 16. **Weed.** Garment. This is the reading of the original ed. Gifford reads *red*.

6 17. **As.** As if. But see *Shakespeare Grammar*, § 107.

7. **John Ford,** the famous dramatist, tried his hand at other forms of literature, even moral treatises. Of his life little is known save that he was matriculated at Oxford and was later admitted a member of the Middle Temple. He does not seem to have depended upon the stage for a livelihood, and most of his work is characterized by elaborated

care in conception and in diction. Ford retained not a little of the great lyrical touch of the previous age.

7. **The Lover's Melancholy** was the first play that Ford printed, although many preceded it on the stage.

7 8. **As.** That. Cf. 6 12.

7. **The Broken Heart.** There is no account of the first appearance of this famous play.

7 2. **Hours.** Dissyllabic, as generally.

7 4. **Envying.** Accent on the penult. Cf. Campion's *Song*, "Silly boy 't is full moon yet," *Elizabethan Lyrics*, p. 187:

> He that holds his sweetheart true unto his day of dying,
> Lives, of all that ever breathed, most worthy the *envy̆ing*.

8 7. **So graced, not,** etc. So graced as not, etc. See *Shakespeare Grammar*, § 281, and cf. *Merchant of Venice*, iii. 3. 9.

9. **Thomas Goffe** was a clergyman, who, in his youth, wrote several plays, some of them performed by the students of his own college, Christ Church, Oxford. *The Careless Shepherdess* was acted before the king and queen, apparently after Goffe's death. This may possibly not be Goffe's own.

9 1. **Impale.** Encircle, surround. Cf. *3 Henry VI*, iii. 2. 171.

9 2. **Flowers the time allows.** Cf. 1 2, 4 3.

9. **Hesperides.** The title of Herrick's collected poetry. The chronology of Herrick is attended with peculiar difficulties, as there is little attempt at order or arrangement in either of the divisions of his work that he has left us. He began to write in the twenties, perhaps earlier; and we have nothing certainly his after 1649. Some of his poems, many of his epigrams — more it is likely than appear in his accredited work — strayed into publications like *Wit's Recreations* (a hodge-podge of everything the bookseller could lay his hands on), whether before publication elsewhere or not, it is often not easy to determine. In the arrangement of Herrick's poems in this volume I have followed Professor Hale. See his *Dissertation*, *Die Chronologische Anordnung der Dichtungen Robert Herricks*, Halle, 1892.

10. **Corinna 's Going A-Maying.** Mr. Palgrave says of this poem: "A lyric more faultless and sweet than this cannot be found in any literature. Keeping with profound instinctive art within the limits of the key chosen, Herrick has reached a perfection very rare at any period of literature in the tones of playfulness, natural description, passion, and seriousness which introduce and follow each other, like the motives in

a sonata by Weber or Beethoven, throughout this little masterpiece of music without notes" (Ed. *Herrick*, *Golden Treasury*, p. 190).

10 2. **God unshorn.** Apollo.

10 4. **Fresh-quilted colors.** Here referable to the bright and variegated colors of sunrise. Cf. Milton's *tissued clouds*, *Ode on the Morning of Christ's Nativity*, v. 146.

10 5. **Slug-a-bed.** Cf. *Romeo and Juliet*, iv. 5. 2.

11 25. **Titan.** The sun.

11 28. **Beads.** Prayers.

11 33. **Each porch,** etc. It is an ancient custom, still observed in Devonshire and Cornwall, to deck the porches of houses with boughs of sycamore and hawthorn on May-day (Grosart).

11 40. **Proclamation made for May.** Probably some local ceremonial preceding the May revels, for an account of which latter see Brand's *Popular Antiquities*, ed. 1813, I, 179.

11 45. **Deal of youth.** A goodly number of youth.

12 57. **Come, let us go.** Nott refers to Catullus, *Carmen* v, for a parallel to this passage.

12. **To Julia.** A larger number of Herrick's verses are addressed to Julia than to any other of his "many dainty mistresses."

12 3. **And the elves also.** Cf. Herrick's fairy poetry, ed. Hale, Athenæum Press Series, pp. 38–48.

12 7. **Slow-worm.** A harmless species of lizard, but popularly supposed to be very venomous; also called a blind worm.

12 11. **Cumber.** Trouble, perplex.

13. **A Hymn to Love.** This poem occurs in *Wit's Recreations*, from its position probably in an early ed., that of 1641 or 1645.

13 3. **Likes me.** This impersonal use of like was very common.

13 8. **Blubb'ring.** Weeping. Not formerly a vulgar or ludicrous word. Cf. Prior's *The Better Answer:*

> Dear Chloe, how blubbered is that pretty face.

14. **London's Tempe, or The Field of Happiness** was composed for the Mayor's festival of 1629, while Dekker was city poet.

14 1. **Hammer, from your sound,** etc. In allusion to the Jewish legend of later times which associates Tubal-cain, "a furbisher of every cutting instrument of copper and iron," with his father Lamech's song.

15 10. **Dragons of the moon.** Cf. "Night's swift dragons," *Midsummer Night's Dream*, iii. 2. 379, and *Il Penseroso*, v. 59.

15 15. **Lemnian hammers.** The island of Lemnos was sacred to Hephaestus as the place on which he fell when hurled from Heaven.

15 27. **Sparrowbills.** Sparable, a headless nail used in soling shoes. The form sparable occurs in Herrick's *Upon Cob.*, ed. Hazlitt, I, 242.

15 30. **Venus' . . . brawls and bans.** *Bans*, curses. As to Venus' brawls with her husband, Vulcan, see Valerius Flaccus, *Argonautica*, II, 98, 175, 312, *et passim*.

16. **The New Inn** was so complete a failure that it was not even heard to a conclusion. Two years later Jonson, who did not include it in the folio then printing, put it forth with this title: *The New Inn: or the Light Heart, a Comedy. As it was never acted, but most negligently played by some, the King's servants; and more squeamishly beheld and censured by others, the King's subjects. . . . Now at last set at liberty to the readers, his Majesty's servants and subjects, to be judged of.* The most interesting outcome of the failure of this play and the consequent attacks on its author was Jonson's vigorous *Ode, To Himself*, beginning: "Come leave the loathed stage," and the answers which it inspired among such "sons of Ben" as Randolph, Carew, and others. See Cunningham's *Jonson*, V, p. 415 f.

16. **Dr. John Wilson's Cheerful Airs** was not published until 1660, but the spirit of the poetry is almost wholly Elizabethan and Jacobean, a spirit which continued into the earlier part of the reign of Charles.

17 28. **That goes into the clear.** Probably *clear* equals the light, blaze of the furnace or refiner's fire.

18 5. **Witty.** Wise. Cf. 35 17.

18 5. **Words her sweet tongue.** Cf. 1 2, 4 3, 9 2.

18 5. **So wove, four eyes in one.** Cf. Donne's *The Ecstacy*, ed. 1650, p. 42:

> Our eye-beams twisted, and did thread
> Our eyes upon one double string.

19. **Egerton MS., 2013.** This MS. contains songs, the music of which was written by Dr. John Wilson (1594–1673); and by John Hilton, who died in 1657. Save for some small matters of punctuation, I follow the text of Arber's *English Garner*, III, 395–397.

20. **Upon a Maid.** This epitaph is found in *Wit's Recreations*, ed. Park, p. 245. From its position before several of the epitaphs on Hobson, the Cambridge carrier, by Milton and several lesser poets in 1630, I have no hesitation in placing it early.

20 1. **In bed of spice.** Cf. *The Dirge of Jephtha's Daughter, Herrick*, ed. Hale, 147 61.

20. **On Time.** The words "To be set on a clock-case" are found following this title in Milton's MS. in his own hand (Warton).

20 2. **Leaden-stepping.** Cf. Carew's *A Pastoral Dialogue*, where the hours are said to "move with leaden feet." Reprint 1824, p. 56 (Dyce).

20 12. **Individual.** Inseparable. Cf. *Paradise Lost*, iv. 486: "An individual solace dear"; and also *ibid.* v. 610 (Warton).

21 18. **Happy-making sight.** The plain English of *beatific vision* (Newton).

21. **Song on May Morning.** This little lyric is usually assigned to May 1, 1630.

21 3. **Flowery May,** etc. Cf. the *Faery Queen*, *Of Mutability*, vii. 34:

> Then came fair May, the fairest maid on ground,
> Decked all with dainties of her season's pride,
> And throwing flowers out of her lap around.

21. **An Epitaph.** These commendatory verses were prefixed to the second folio of Shakespeare. "Milton's couplets, however," as the late Mr. Mark Pattison remarks, "differ from these pieces [others, prefixed] in not having been written to order, but being the spontaneous outcome of his own admiration for Shakespeare" (*Milton's Sonnets*, p. 78).

21 1. **Need.** The Shakespeare folio reads *neede*. See *Shakespeare Grammar*, § 297, and cf. *Much Ado*, i. 1. 318:

> *What need* the bridge much broader than the flood?

21 4. **Star-ypointing.** The prefix *y* answers to the Old English *ge* and "is etymologically equivalent to Latin *con*, *cum*. It is usually prefixed to past participles, but also to past tenses, present tenses, adjectives and adverbs" (Skeat, *Etymological Dictionary*, *s.v.*).

22 10. **Heart.** The folio reads *part*.

22 11. **Unvalued,** invaluable. Cf. *unexpressive*, inexpressible, *Ode on the Nativity*, 116, *Lycidas*, 176, and Shelley's *Arethusa:* over heaps of *unvalued* (i.e., valueless) stones. I am indebted for this and many other notes and parallels to Pattison's excellent edition of *Milton's Sonnets*.

22 15. **And, so sepulchred,** etc. Pattison refers this 'conceit' to the funeral oration of Pericles, *Thucydides*, ii. 43; and calls attention to Pope's imitation of it in his *Epitaph on Gay*. *Sepùlchred* is the usual accent in Shakespeare; cf. *Richard II*, i. 3. 195.

22 16. **That kings,** etc. Cf. Donne's *Letters*, ed. 1651, p. 244: "No prince would be loth to die that were assured of so fair a tomb to preserve his memory."

22. **To the Nightingale.** This title is not found in either the edition of 1645 or that of 1673. "In this sonnet and the Shakespeare epitaph," says Pattison, "Milton had not yet shaken himself free from the trick of contriving *concetti*, as was the fashion of the previous age, and especially of his models, the Italians. After these two juvenile pieces his sense of reality asserted itself, and he never again, in the sonnets, lapses into frigid and far-fetched ingenuities" (*Milton's Sonnets*, p. 84).

22 4. **Jolly.** Festive or almost in the sense of the French *joli*, pleasing, pretty. Cf. *The Faery Queen*, *Of Mutability*, vii. 29: "Then came the jolly summer," and *ibid.* 35, where the same adjective is applied to June. Cf. Milton's poem *In Adventum Veris*, 25, 26, and Gray's *Ode to Spring*.

22 5. **Close the eye of day.** Cf. *Comus*, 978, and Crashaw, *To the Morning*, ed. Trumbull, p. 113 (Todd).

22 6. **First heard,** etc. Cf. *The Cuckoo and the Nightingale*, 51–56:

> But as I lay this other night waking,
> I thought how lovers had a tokening,
> And among hem it was a commune tale
> That it would good to hear the nightingale
> Rather than the leud cuckoo sing.

Pattison calls this whole sonnet "only an amplification of this stanza."

22 9. **Rude bird of hate.** The cuckoo, from its habit of leaving its eggs in the nests of other birds and deserting its offspring, became in all literatures the type of the enemy of love. Cf. Brand's *Popular Antiquities*, ed. 1813, II, 114.

22 13. **His mate.** *His* agreeing with *Love* in gender.

23 1. **How soon hath Time.** This sonnet has every appearance of having been written on Milton's twenty-third birthday, Dec. 9, 1631, although the heading of the text is not found in either of the editions printed during the poet's lifetime. The sonnet appears to have been prompted by a friend's expostulation that Milton do something better than study. See Masson's *Milton*, I, 289, where this letter is quoted entire.

23 1. **The subtle thief of youth.** Cf. Pope's *Sat.* VI, 76.

23 2. **Stolen on his wing.** Cf. Pope's *Transl. of Martial's Epigram on Antonius Primus*, X, 23:

> While Time with still career
> Wafts on his gentle wing his eightieth year.

23 5. **My semblance.** In allusion to his youthful face and figure. It is said that when forty Milton was taken for thirty.

23 8. **Endu'th.** Endoweth.

23 9. **It.** I.e., inward ripeness, v. 7.

23 10. **It shall be still in strictest measure even.** "Nothing in Milton's life is more noteworthy than his deliberate intention to be a great poet, and the preparation he made with that intention from the earliest period. Here we have a solemn record of self-dedication, without specification of the nature of the performance" (Pattison, *Milton's Sonnets*, p. 98).

23 10 11. **Even to.** Conformable with.

23 14. **Taskmaster's eye.** An allusion to the parable of the laborers in the vineyard, *Matthew* XX.

23. **Philip Massinger** was sometime page in the household of the Earl of Pembroke. The limits and extent of his dramatic labors are difficult to define, owing to his habit of collaboration. A close friendship existed between him and Fletcher. He is said to have become a convert to Roman Catholicism in middle life. This play is one of the fifteen in which Massinger is supposed to have been unaided by others.

23. **Death Invoked.** This is Mr. Bullen's title. The song is sung, in the play, by the empress Eudocia.

24. **Richard Brome** was in early life a servant and later a protégé of Ben Jonson. *The Northern Lass* was his most successful play.

24 4. **Mickle.** This form, later confined chiefly to the north, was not uncommon in Elizabethan English.

25. **Richard Brathwaite** was a voluminous author in his day, his works ranging through the usual popular and trivial subjects of the pamphleteer in verse and prose. He appears to have written for pleasure, as he was a man of substantial wealth and position. His best-known work is his *Barnabae Itinerarium or Barnabee's Journal*, an account of a journey in English and Latin doggerel verses of considerable spirit. *The English Gentleman* and *The English Gentlewoman* are made up of "sundry excellent rules and exquisite observations, tending to direction of every gentleman of selecter rank and quality, how to demean, or accommodate himself in the management of public and private affairs."

25. **Celestina, or the tragi-comedy of Calisto and Melibea,** a dramatic romance in dialogue, is regarded by historians of Spanish literature as the source of their national drama. The work was completed about the year 1492, by Fernando de Rojas, by the addition of twenty acts to the first, which was ascribed to Rodrigo Cota. James Mabbe, who translated his own name into Don Diego Puer-de-ser on the title, was the first to translate the story into English, although the plot had been more than once previously employed in the drama. Though no more than translations, the first from the thirteenth act, the second from the nineteenth, these two little lyrics have a grace of manner and a poetical spirit which I think justifies their reappearance here. The former reads thus in the original (*La Celestina*, Barcelona, 1883, p. 228):

> Duerme y descansa, penado.
> Desde azora ;
> Pues te ama tu señora
> De su grado ;
> Venza placer al cuidado,
> Y no le vea,
> Pues te ha hecho su privado
> Melibea.

Mr. Bullen, who is apparently not aware that these lyrics are translations, finds a more remote resemblance in one of the fragments of *Sappho*.

26. **Albion's Triumph.** This masque was "presented by the King and his lords, Sunday after Twelfth Night." Inigo Jones contrived it and procured Townsend to write it. The flattery of royalty by obvious classical allusion needs no explanation here.

27. **Love in thy Youth.** There is a MS. copy of this poem, *Ashmole MS.* 38, No. 188.

28. **Peter Hausted,** a Cambridge clergyman, "was killed on the ramparts of Banbury, while the Roundheads were vigorously besieging it" (Gosse). *The Rival Friends* is described on the title as "cried down by boys, faction, envy and confident ignorance; approved by the judicious, and now exposed to public censure by the author"; and dedicated "To the Right Honourable, Right Reverend, Right Worshipful, or whatever he be, or shall be, whom I hereafter may call patron."

29. **William Habington,** says Anthony à Wood, "was educated at S. Omers and Paris; in the first of which he was earnestly invited to take upon him the habit of the Jesuits, but by excuses, got free and left them. After his return from Paris, being at man's estate,

he was instructed at home in matters of history by his father, and became an accomplished gentleman" (*Athenae Oxon.*, ed. 1817, III, 223). Wood relates further that Habington, during the Commonwealth, "did run with the times, and was not unknown to Oliver the Usurper." Besides *Castara*, Habington wrote a play and some *Observations upon History*.

29. **Castara.** The text is from Professor Arber's reprint of the ed. 1634–1640. *Castara* was Lady Lucy Herbert, daughter of Lord Powis, whom the poet married between 1630 and 1633. The poems are largely autobiographical, and smack strongly of the characteristics of the Elizabethan sonnet sequences, though few of them are in anything even approaching the sonnet form. Professor Masson assigns the earlier poems of *Castara* to the year 1632; the later ones were written after Habington's marriage (*Life of Milton*, I, 454).

29 2. **In the chaste nunn'ry of her breasts.** Cf. Lovelace's use of the same figure below, — *To Lucasta, on Going to the Wars*, 132 2.

29 5. **Transplanted thus, how bright ye grow.** Cf. Carew, *On a Damask Rose, sticking upon a Lady's Breast.*

29 7. **Close.** Walled in, protected.

29 14. **Your glorious sepulchre shall be.** Cf. with this verse and the whole poem, Herrick's lines *Upon the Roses in Julia's Bosom:*

> Thrice happy roses, so much graced, to have
> Within the bosom of my love your grave!
> Die when ye will, your sepulchre is known,
> Your grave her bosom is, the lawn the stone.

30 16. **The withered marigold.** In allusion to the popular belief that the marigold closes its petals with the setting of the sun. Cf. Carew, *The Marigold*, below, p. 43.

30 5. **Some cherubim.** Often used as a singular in Shakespeare's day and later. Cf. *Tempest*, i. 2. 152, and 73 6, below.

31. **Against them that lay Unchastity to the Sex of Woman.** This poem is written in direct answer to Donne's *Song*, "Go and catch a falling star." See *Elizabethan Lyrics*, p. 97.

31 3. **They hear but when the mermaid sings.** Donne: "Teach me to hear mermaid's singing."

31 5. **Who ever dare affirm.** Donne:

> And swear
> Nowhere
> Lives a woman true and fair.

31 11. **Right ones.** True ones, real ones.

32. **George Herbert** enjoyed a distinguished career at Cambridge, procuring in 1619 the public oratorship of the University. This, with the high position of his family, brought him into contact with the court, where he was held in high favor by James, and enjoyed the personal friendship of Bacon and Dr. Donne. Having entered the church, in 1630 he became rector of Fuggelstone, after which he survived only three years. His life was pure and saint-like and has been beautifully told by Isaak Walton.

32. **The Temple, Sacred Poems and Private Ejaculations** is the title of Herbert's volume of devotional poetry. This title appears to have been given the work after Herbert's death by his friend and literary executor, Nicholas Ferrar. One of the two extant MSS. of *The Temple*, that in the Williams Library, London, bears the title, *The Church*, the later title having been given the work from *Psalm* XXIX, "In his Temple doth every man speak of his honor," which appears in the printed title. The book enjoyed from the first a great popularity, a second edition following in the same year, with no less than eleven successors up to 1709.

32. **The Altar, Easter Wings.** Both of these poems were printed in the original editions to shape their titles. A chapter, interesting to the curious, might be written on these shaped verses. Puttenham in his *The Art of English Poesie* devotes considerable space to a grave discussion of "the lozange, fuzie, tricquet, pillaster, piramis"; and derives their invention from "the Courts of the great princes of China and Tartary." Such devices, with acrostics, anagrams, and other exercises of ingenuity, were very popular in the days of Elizabeth and James (see Sylvester, ed. Grosart, I, 4, 15; II, 321, etc., Wither, Arber's *English Garner*, IV, 476–478, and *Musarum Deliciae*, II, 295, *et passim*), but were ridiculed by such men as Jonson and Nashe. See the editor's *Poetic and Verse Criticism of the Reign of Elizabeth*, pp. 54, 55, for a fuller account of this fashion.

32 2. **Cemented.** Accent on the first syllable.

32 10. **The fall further the flight,** i.e., "So shall the fall of man give me an opportunity for a longer and higher flight than would otherwise have been possible."

33 12. **Still.** Ever. Cf. 5 9.

33 19. **Imp.** In falconry, to mend or extend a deficient wing by the insertion of a feather. Cf. Carew's *Ingrateful Beauty Threatened*, v. 6.

33 5. **The sweetness** (of the flower) **and the praise** (for the act of grace).

33 14. **To thy praise.** With respect to; we should say "in thy praise." Cf. *Shakespeare Grammar*, § 186.

34 19. **That.** The honey. **These.** The flowers.

34 22. **All my company.** "All the company or companionship that I furnish is that of a weed among flowers." I am indebted for this note and that on 32 10 to Professor Kittredge.

34 23. **Consort.** Cf. a consort of music, an orchestra, with a play on the meaning, — those that live in agreement and harmony with thee.

34 2. **Bridal.** Bridal day. This word was originally bride ale, bride's feast, and had not yet lost its etymological meaning in Herbert's day.

34 5. **Angry.** Red, the color of anger.

34 5. **Brave.** Beautiful, here perhaps gaudy. Cf. 81 15.

34 11. **Closes.** In music the end of a strain or cadence. Cf. Dryden's *Flower and the Leaf*, 197.

34 2. **Train-bands.** Citizen soldiers of London.

35 11. **I heard in music you had skill.** Herbert is reported to have been an excellent musician, "not only singing, but playing on the lute and viol."

35 17. **Wit.** In the usual contemporary meaning, mind, understanding. Cf. witty, 18 5.

36 9. **Regiments.** Rules, governments. Cf. the title of John Knox's book, *First Blast of the Trumpet against the Monstrous Regiment of Women*.

36 13. **Weeds.** Garments.

36 2. **Your sense.** Your senses in modern English. Cf. 37 30, 94 5, and 127 19.

37 20. **Propagation.** The termination dissyllabic, as usual. Cf. 75 4.

37 23. **Commérce.** So accentuated by Shakespeare; see *Troilus and Cressida*, i. 3. 105: "Peaceful commerce from dividable shores."

38. **Arcades.** "Part of an entertainment presented to the Countess Dowager of Derby at Harefield by some noble persons of her family, who appear on the scene in pastoral habit." This was Milton's first masque. He seems to have been invited to write it by his friend, Henry Lawes, the famous musician. The piece, as we have it, is not complete, the prose parts being probably not Milton's.

38 1. **Enamelled.** A favorite word of the age. Bright, variegated is a secondary and probably later sense.

38 2. **Print of step.** Cf. *Comus*, 897: "printless feet."

38 4. **Warbled.** Tuneful. Cf. *Comus*, 854.

38 6. **Star-proof elm.** Cf. *Faery Queen*, i. 1. 7. This is one of several of Milton's trivial inaccuracies in the observation of nature, as the foliage of the elm is notably light.

38 2. **Sandy Ladon.** Ladon, a river in Arcadia. Cf. Browne's *Britannia's Pastorals*, ii. 4.

38 2. **Lilied.** Cf. Sylvester, *Bethulia's Rescue*, ed. Grosart, II, 194.

38 3. **Lycæus.** A mountain of Arcadia sacred to Zeus and to Pan. *Cyllene* was the highest mountain of the Peloponnesus.

38 5. **Erymanth.** Probably here neither particularly the stream nor mountain of that name, but the region in which both are situated.

38 7. **Mænalus.** Also a mountain in Arcadia, especially sacred to Pan.

38 9. **Have greater grace.** Meet with greater favor.

38 11. **Syrinx.** The story of this Arcadian nymph, pursued by Pan and turned into a reed, is a familiar classical fable.

39. **A Masque.** This is the title of Lawes' edition of 1637, of Milton's first edition of his poems, and his second edition of 1673. Thomas Warton in his excellent ed. of Milton, 1785, says: "I have ventured to insert this title [*Comus*], which has the full sanction of use." The original music of the songs of *Comus*, written by Lawes, who was himself one of the performers at its presentation, is preserved in the British Museum, *Add. MS.* 115–118. The music of the *Song*, "Sweet Echo," is printed in Hawkins' *History of Music*, IV, 53.

39 2. **Airy shell.** Vault or convex of the heavens. Cf. *Ode on the Nativity*, stanza x, where a similar expression is applied to the moon's sphere:

> Nature that heard such sound,
> Beneath the *hollow round*
> Of Cynthia's seat the airy region thrilling.

39 3. **Margent.** A doublet of *margin*.

39 4. **Violet-embroidered.** Compounds such as these were less common among the poets of Milton's day than a generation earlier.

39 5. **Love-lorn.** Deprived of her mate. Cf. *Tempest*, iv. 1. 68: "lass-lorn."

39 7. **A gentle pair.** Warton directs our attention to these very words in *The Faithful Shepherdess*, i. 1, as one instance of many "which prove Milton's intimate familiarity with Fletcher's play."

39 14. **Give resounding grace,** i.e., the grace of an echo. Warton

notes Lawes' 'professional alteration' of this verse to "And hold a counterpoint to all heaven's harmonies."

39 1. **Sabrina fair.** Cf. line 824, above:

> There is a gentle Nymph not far from hence,
> That with moist curb sways the smooth Severn stream:
> Sabrina is her name: a virgin pure;
> Whilom she was the daughter of Locrine,
> That had the sceptre from his father Brute.
> She, guiltless damsel, flying the mad pursuit
> Of her enragèd stepdame, Guendolen,
> Commended her fair innocence to the flood
> That stayed her flight with his cross-flowing course.

See Mr. Swinburne's fine tragedy on this old theme.

39 3. **Glassy . . . wave.** Cf. *Hamlet*, iv. 7. 168.

39 5. **Amber-dropping.** The water dripping from her hair, partaking its color by reflection. Todd gives the following parallel from Nashe's *Terrors of the Night*, 1594: "Their hair they wear loose unrowled about their shoulders, whose dangling amber trammells reaching down beneath their knees, seem to drop baulm on their delicious bodies." Milton is very fond of the word *amber*. Cf. *L'Allegro*, 61, *Paradise Lost*, iii. 359, *Paradise Regained*, iii. 288, and *Comus*, 333.

39 10–21. **Great Oceanus.** Hesiod, *Theog.* 20; repeated again and again by such English poets as Drayton in the *Polyolbion*, and Jonson in the *Queen's Masque*. See Warton's note. In the lines following we have a long list of the ancient deities of the sea: Tethys, the aged wife of Oceanus; Nereus, the old man of the sea, who sits at the bottom in ooze and slime; the prophetic (wizard) Proteus, called the Carpathian, from the island Carpathos, in which, according to one of the legends, he was supposed to have been born, with the shepherd's crook (hook) with which he tended his flocks of seals; the merman Triton, with his conch; Glaucus, the immortal fisherman, god of mariners; Leucothea, otherwise Ino, who, like Sappho, jumped into the sea, and, like Arion, was rescued by a dolphin; Thetis, the Nereid, mother of Achilles; the Sirens, Ligea and Parthenope, whose tomb was adored at Naples. Milton fairly revels in allusions such as these, and his poetry is full of like passages. Warton gives several parallels from previous poets in the use of these myths and the epithets with which they are described. It may be noted that Drummond and Campion show, with Spenser before them and Browne after them, a like skill in the interweaving of classical allusion and proper names in their verse.

40 33. **Where grows the willow,** etc. Cf. *The Faithful Shepherdess*, iii. 1, where the river god speaks thus:

> I am this fountain's god: below,
> My waters to a river grow,
> And twixt two banks with osiers set,
> That only prosper in the wet,
> Through the meadows do they glide.

40 34. **My sliding chariot,** etc. This idea of Sabrina's chariot seems suggested by Drayton's *Polyolbion*, *Song*, v. 1, ed. Hooper, I, 129:

> Now Sabrine, as a queen, miraculously fair,
> Is absolutely placed in her imperial chair
> Of crystal richly wrought, that gloriously did shine.

Cf. the two passages at length.

40 35. **Azurn.** Italian *azzurrino*, suggests Todd. Cf. *cedarn* below, 42 15.

40 36. **Turkis.** Turquoise.

40 39. **Printless feet.** Cf. *Tempest*, v. 1. 34: "And ye that on the sands with printless feet do chase the ebbing Neptune" (Warton).

41 49. **Enchanter vile.** Cf. *Faery Queen*, iii. 12. 31 (Todd).

41 53. **Thus I sprinkle.** Cf. with this removal of the charm various like passages in *The Faithful Shepherdess*, collected and quoted by Warton.

41 63. **Amphitrite's bower.** Drayton uses the same expression, *Polyolbion*, *Song*, xxviii.

41 64. **Daughter of Locrine.** Cf. above, p. 39. The old genealogy derives the descent of Brute or Brutus, father of Locrine, from Æneas and Anchises.

41 66. **Brimmèd.** Rising to the brim or margin. Cf Lucretius, ii. 362: "Fluminaque illa queunt, *summis labentia ripis*."

41 75. **Beryl . . . golden ore . . . groves of myrrh and cinnamon.** The fanciful beauty of these charges invoked to bless an English stream is in the best vein of that poetical mythology which is one of the charms of the poetry of Michael Drayton.

42 1. **To the ocean now I fly,** etc. These four lines are in the very rhythm and rhyme of the first four in Ariel's song in the *Tempest*, v. 1:

> Where the bee sucks, there lurk I (Masson).

42 4. **Broad fields of the sky.** Cf. Æneid, vi. 887: "Aëris in campis latis" (Warton).

42 7. **Hesperus, and his daughters.** It was in the garden of the Hesperides that the golden apples, given Juno as a marriage gift, were watched by the dragon Ladon.

42 15. **Cedarn.** Cf. the similar form *azurn*, 40 35, possibly both of them due to their Italian forms *azzurrino* and *cedrino*.

42 18. **Blow.** Cause to blow. Cf. *Shakespeare Grammar*, § 291.

42 19. **Flowers.** Dissyllabic. Cf. 88 11.

42 20. **Purfled.** Fringed, embroidered with colors or gold (Fr. *pourfiler*). Cf. *Faery Queen*, i. 2. 33: "Purfled with gold."

42 27. **Th' Assyrian queen.** Astarte, identified with Venus, as her lover, Thammuz, was identified with Adonis. Cf. *Paradise Lost*, i. 446, and *Ezekiel*, VIII, 12–14. See Masson's *Milton*, iii. 434, for an elaborate note on this passage in its relation to the entire poem of *Comus*.

43 42. **Corners of the moon.** Cf. *Macbeth*, iii. 5. 23 (Warton).

43 46. **Sphery chime.** Cf. *Arcades*, 63–73, and Masson's note thereon, III, 392.

43. **Thomas Carew** is described as a somewhat indolent student while at Oxford, "roving after hounds and hawks," later in the diplomatic service, and finally, on attracting the notice of Charles I, sewer (i.e., cupbearer) in ordinary and gentleman of the privy chamber to that monarch. Carew's intimate literary friends were Suckling and Davenant. The text of Carew is from the reprint of the ed. of 1640, Edinburgh, 1824, collated with Hazlitt's unsatisfactory ed. of 1870.

43. **The Marigold.** This poem is referable to the *Wyburd MS.*, written about 1634 (Hazlitt's *Carew*, p. xv) and there given this title. In the ed. of 1640 it appears with the title *Boldness in Love*.

44. **Thomas Randolph,** after an honorable career as a student pensioner at Trinity, Cambridge, went up to London and was adopted one of the "sons of Ben." Randolph died young, more reputed for his promise than for actual achievement. Anthony Stafford, to whom this poem is addressed, was a notable prose writer in his day. His most important book was *Stafford's Heavenly Dog, or the Life and Death of the Cynic Diogenes*, 1615. *Stafford's Niobe, or his Age of Tears*, 1611, and *Stafford's Niobe dissolved into a Nilus* were earlier works, both of them "a general invective against vice and a laudation of virtue." See Collier's *Rarest Books in the English Language*, IV, 90, for a further account of Stafford's work. I take the text of Randolph's poems from the original quarto, Oxford, 1638.

44 4. **Charge'ble.** Expensive and burdensome.

44 16. **Puisne of the Inns-of-Court.** A junior student in the law

courts, a freshman. Cf. Cowley, *A Poetical Revenge*, *Sylva*, ed. Grosart, p. 26: "A semi-gentleman of the Inns of Court."

45 23. **No finger lose.** An allusion to the poet's loss of a finger in a fray. See his *Epigram*, ed. Hazlitt, p. 553.

45 32. **Hyde Park,** originally a game preserve, became a fashionable promenade in the reign of Charles II. See Shirley's play *Hyde Park*.

45 36. **The beauties,** etc. The Cheap, now Cheapside, was the principal retail street of old London. *Lombard Street* contained the financial wealth of the city and the homes of some of the most substantial citizens.

46 76. **Barkley's health.** Possibly capable of indentification with Sir John Berkley, Governor of Exeter, to whom Herrick addresses spirited lines, ed. Grosart, II, 250.

46 78. **Phrygian melody.** The text sufficiently suggests the contrast between the wild and orgiastic music of Phrygia and the sombre and dignified Doric.

47 20. **Leave.** Cease. Cf. Drayton, "To his Coy Mistress," *Elizabethan Lyrics*, p. 196.

48. **The Arcadian Princess,** a prose romance, "was translated," says Mr. Bullen, "from the Italian of Mariano Silesio, a Florentine, who died in 1368."

48. **Themista's reproof.** This piling up of similitudes is a device common to a large group of verses of this time. Among the earliest is the poem beginning "Like to the falling of a star," attributed to Beaumont, for which see *Elizabethan Lyrics*, p. 170. The lines of the text are scarcely more than a mock lyric, and yet some of the similitudes are so apt and the whole thing is so characteristic that I should hesitate to omit it.

48 11. **Mopping.** Doating; a mop was a fool.

48 14. **Minion.** Darling.

49. **Poems, 1645.** There are three editions of Waller's poems bearing this date: (1) that "printed for Thomas Walkley" and entitled *The Works of Edmond Waller*, denounced in the advertisement which appears in both (2) and (3) as an "adulterate copy, surreptitiously and illegally imprinted to the derogation of the author and the abuse of the buyer"; (2) that printed for H. Moseley by I. N.; and (3) that printed for the same publisher by T. W. Mr. G. Thorn Drury, the most recent editor of Waller, states that (1) is "full of misprints," and that (3) consists "of the sheets of (1) bound up with a fresh title and the addition of the last seven poems contained in (3)." He is further of the opinion that none of these editions "had the countenance of the author"

(Drury's Waller, p. 277). In 1664 appeared the poet's own authoritative edition. Waller's popularity had by this time become very great.

49. **Lady Lucy Sidney** was a younger sister of the more famous Lady Dorothea, Waller's Saccharissa. The title is found in the first ed. of 1645. I assign the probable composition of this and the following two poems to 1635, when the Lady Dorothea was some eighteen years of age. Fenton's date, 1632, is too early.

49 8. **May know too soon.** This is Fenton's reading; Drury reads *so soon.*

49 13. **Hope waits upon the flowery prime.** Cf. Cicero, *De Senectute*, 70.

50. **Saccharissa and Amoret.** Saccharissa was Lady Dorothea Sidney, eldest daughter of the Earl of Leicester and grand niece to Sir Philip Sidney. Amoret has been identified by the diligence of Fenton as Lady Sophia Murray. Waller is generally supposed to have begun the stately courtship of his Saccharissa about the year 1632. Drury places this later, "towards the end of the year 1635." The episode was at an end in July, 1639, when Lady Sidney became Lady Spencer. The poems that connect the names of Waller and Saccharissa are very few in number, and more has been made of them than seems at all warranted by the circumstances. The genuineness of the poet's passion does not concern us; his verses warrant the assumption that the matter was not very serious. See Drury, *Poems of Waller*, *Introduction*, and Mr. Gosse's *From Shakespeare to Pope* on this subject.

50 8. **Neither.** Ed. of 1645 reads *neither's*.

50 10. **Still beguilèd.** Ever beguiled. Cf. 5 9, 33 12.

50 15. **Decline.** Avoid.

52 39. **Amoret as sweet.** Drury punctuates: "Amoret! as sweet," etc. "Amoret['s] as sweet," etc., may be conjectured as possibly the right reading. Professor Kittredge suggests: "Amoret is sweet," etc., the ordinary ellipsis of *as*.

53. **Francis Quarles.** "This voluminous saint," as Campbell calls him, was successively cupbearer to the queen of Bohemia, chronologer to the city of London, and secretary in Ireland to Archbishop Usher. Despite his diffuseness, extravagant hunting of conceit, and inequality, Quarles is not unvisited at moments by the fancy of a true poet, and there is an ingenuousness and fervor about him that goes far to account for his all but unexampled contemporary popularity. Quarles wrote much prose besides his extensive verse, all of which Dr. Grosart has reprinted in his edition in the *Chertsey Worthies' Library*, 1881.

53. **Emblems** is a series of five books of quasi-allegorical devotional

poems, in which a scriptural text is taken as the subject — or at least the point of departure. A fitting quotation from some one of the saints or fathers of the church follows, and a short epigram concludes. This work is modelled, if not largely borrowed, from Herman Hugo's *Pia Desideria Emblematibus, Elegiis et Affectibus SS. Patrum Illustrata*, Antwerp, 1624, and illustrated by extraordinary allegorical cuts, also of Dutch origin. This poem is the third of the fifth book. The text is from *Canticles*, II, 16.

53. **O whither shall I fly?** *Job*, XIV, 13. From the third book of *Emblems*, No. XII.

53 12. **Clip.** Move swiftly, a favorite word with Quarles. Cf. *Emblems*, v. 13, 17, and 34.

53 13. **Entertain.** Harbor.

54 31. **Ingenuous** is Grosart's reading; other editions read ingenious.

55 1. **Ev'n like two little bank-dividing brooks.** Cf. two very diverse uses of the same figure of a stream in Cartwright's poem, *Love but One*, below, p. 97, and Jean Ingelow's verses entitled *Divided.*

55 5. **Conjoin . . . mine.** A perfect rhyme in Quarles' time and long after. Cf. *coin* and *mine*, below, vv. 17, 18; and see the same rhyme in Carew, below, 71 27.

55 18. **The world's but theirs,** etc. Note that this line alone of those concluding each stanza fails of the required Alexandrine length. The verse of Quarles, like that of Wither, shows not infrequent evidence of a fatal facility. Professor Kittredge suggests regarding *theirs* as dissyllabic and inserting *best* before *beloved's* in conformity with the other concluding lines.

55 19. **Thespian ladies.** From Thespiæ, the native town of Phryne, where was preserved the celebrated statue of Eros by Praxiteles.

56. **George Sandys** was much admired in his own day for his devotional poetry, although few of his verses were more than translations, such as the *Psalms of David*, *A Paraphrase of the Book of Job*, *Ecclesiastes.* Son of an archbishop, Sandys received the best education which Oxford, the court, and foreign travel could give. Of his travels, which were very extensive, he published an account upon his return in 1615, and the book enjoyed a great popularity. While in the colony of Virginia, 1623, as the Company's treasurer, he translated Ovid's *Metamorphoses.* Sandys was a personal friend of Charles I and highly esteemed by that king. He was held in great respect by the critics of the days of Dryden and Pope.

56. **Deo Optimo Maximo.** This poem concludes the volume of Sandys' poems published in 1641, and displays his versification at its best.

56 4. **Steadfast centre of the world.** Sandys had evidently not accepted the Copernican system; Bacon never did. Cf. v. 9, below, and Waller's figure, above, 6 12.

57 26. **Successive.** Uninterrupted.

58 54. **Panchæa.** District in the neighborhood of Mecca, mentioned with a reference to Ovid, *Meta*. i. 10, in the *Travels*, fourth ed., 1670, p. 97. Sandys does not seem to have been nearer to Mecca than Cairo.

58 55. **New found-out world.** Virginia. See note on Sandys, above.

58 62. **Judah's hill.** The third book of the *Travels* is devoted to his journeyings in the Holy Land, including his visit to the Temple of Christ's sepulchre. The allusions of the succeeding lines are not traceable in the *Travels*, which are written very impersonally.

59 83. **Pirates.** A very real peril in 1610.

59. **Abraham Cowley.** A poet in print at fifteen, Cowley witnessed the third edition of his *Poetical Blossoms* before he had been a year at college. Ejected from Cambridge for his royalist leanings, after a short stay at Oxford he entered the service of Queen Henrietta Maria, retiring with her to Paris on the surrender of the king. There it was that he found his college intimate, Crashaw, in penury and sent him with a royal introduction to Rome. Cowley, whose life was cleanly, religious, and somewhat austere, was neglected by Charles at the Restoration, but was repaid at his death by a royal *bon mot*. If Cowley's poetry was soon eclipsed by a new, dominant mode, and his loyalty interpreted largely a matter of sentiment, his honesty, his unaffected love of literature, and his genuine scholarship deserve a respectful remembrance.

59. **A Vote.** An ardent wish, a vow. This is the title of this poem in *Sylva*, an early volume of Cowley's verse. The stanzas here given are only the last three, which the author himself selected for quotation in his *Several Discourses by way of Essays in Verse and Prose*, 1661. I have given the later readings, which improve the text in two or three small particulars. Cowley says: "The beginning of it is boyish, but of this which I here set down (if a very little were corrected) I should hardly now be much ashamed" (*Several Discourses*, ed. 1680, p. 143).

59 5. **Unknown.** *Sylva* version reads *ignote*.

59 7. **Have.** *Sylva*, *hug*.

59 15. **And pleasures yield.** And my garden should yield pleasures which Horace might envy.

59 17. **Thus would I double,** etc. "You may see by it," says Cowley, "I was even then acquainted with the poets, for the conclusion

is taken out of Horace." Cf. *Several Discourses*, p. 144. Indeed, the whole tone of these delightful essays is that of a gracious Epicureanism. Again and again does Cowley return to the pleasant theme, paraphrasing Horace or Claudian's *Old Man of Verona*.

60 6. **Track.** *Tract* is the reading of *Sylva*, ed. Grosart; *tract* and *track* were commonly confused.

60 7. **Fond.** Foolish.

60 15. **Horse.** Pack-horse.

61. **Sir John Suckling** inherited wealth and high social position when but eighteen years of age. He soon plunged into the gayest and wildest of lives, and became no less famous for his verses and his wit than notorious for his lavish extravagance, inveterate gaming, and dissolute life. Suckling was not conspicuous for his bravery either in the field against the Scotch or in private life. A loyalist by right of his birth, he was accused of scheming to save Strafford, and fled the realm, cutting the thread of an ill-spent life by his own hand in Paris when less than thirty-five years old. As a writer of *vers de société*, delightful, daring and cynical, perfectly well-bred, and at times of the highest artistic merit, Suckling at his best was unexcelled in his age. See Lord de Tabley's fine poem, "On a Portrait of Sir John Suckling" (*Poems Dramatic and Lyrical*, 1893), in which Suckling is perversely, though poetically, glorified as the ideal soldier and gentleman, as well as the typical poet of an age which Lord de Tabley appears to believe was far better than ours.

61. **Aglaura** was acted at Blackfriars. Suckling bestowed eight or ten new suits on the players upon the occasion, an unheard-of liberality.

61. **Why so pale.** This is the very perfection of the bantering, satirical lyric, in which the age of Charles excelled. Cf. Cotton's poem, *Advice*.

In a school edition of "The Cavalier Poets," a prudent American Bowdler has expunged the last line of this poem, lest the infant mind be polluted by the wicked freedom of old Sir John's Muse.

61. **True Love.** This poem exhibits the direct influence of Donne. Cf. *Love's Growth*:

I scarce believe my love to be so pure
As I had thought it was,
Because it doth endure
Vicissitude and season as the grass;
Methinks I lied all winter when I swore,
My love was infinite, if spring make it more.

62 1. **Ah Ben.** Herrick left Cambridge in 1620; he went to Dean Prior in 1629. In this interval, and perhaps before, he must have enjoyed the convivial circle of Jonson and have taken him for his master. Cf. with the spirit of this poem, *A Lyric to Mirth*, *To live merrily, and to trust to good verses*, *An Ode to Sir Clipseby Crew*, etc., *Selections from Herrick*, by Professor Hale, Athenæum Press Series, pp. 19, 31, and 92, whose assignment of date I follow.

62 5. **The Sun, the Dog, the Triple Tun.** Names of London taverns of the day. The Sun was in Fish Street Hill and continued noted up to the time of Pepys; the Dog was in the vicinity of Whitehall and Westminster Hall, and much frequented by the Tribe of Ben; the Three Tuns was in Guildhall Yard, and was famous later as the tavern at which General Monk lodged in 1660 (*London Past and Present*, *s.v.*).

63 3. **Candies the grass.** Cf. Drayton's *Quest of Cinthia*, Bullen's *Selections*, 1883, p. 109:

> Since when those frosts that winter brings
> Which candies every green.

Cf. also Browne's *Britannia's Pastorals*, I, p. 4 (Fry).

63 6. **A sacred birth to the dead swallow.** *Sacred* is the reading of the reprint of the edition of 1640, Edinburgh, 1824, and of the two other editions which I have consulted. It may be suspected that Carew wrote *a second birth* in allusion to the popular superstition concerning the hibernation of swallows, by which they are supposed to hang in caves or lie in clinging masses, plunged in water under the ice to revive with the return of spring or by means of artificial heat. See Timbs' *Popular Errors Explained* and *Notes and Queries*, Series I, XII, 512, and Series III, VI, 539, 403.

64 24. **June in her eyes, in her heart January.** Cf. with this fine conceit Greene's lines in *Perimedes the Blacksmith*, ed. Grosart, VII, 90:

> Fair is my love for April in her face,
> Her lovely breasts September claims his part,
> And lordly July in her eyes takes place,
> But cold December dwelleth in her heart.

Another version is found in Morley's *First Book of Madrigals*, 1594. Oliphant suggests an Italian origin.

64. **Persuasions to Love.** This poem is addressed to A. L. in the original. Mr. Saintsbury declares that it is "an unwearying delight" to read it. See the rest of his appreciative comment on Carew (*Elizabethan Literature*, p. 361).

64 2. **Fresh as April.** MS. reads "Fair as Helen, fresh as May" (Hazlitt).

65 39. **Abron.** A variant of auburn.

65 49. **To your friend.** For, or as, your friend. See *Shakespeare Grammar*, § 189.

65 51. **Still.** Ever. Cf. 5 9, 33 12, 50 10.

66 63. **Pined.** Wasted away. Cf. Fletcher's *The Sea Voyage*, ii. 2:

> I left in yonder desert
> A virgin almost pined.

66 80. **Do reason.** Act reasonably.

67 13. **The Assyrian king.** Nebuchadnezzar, *Daniel*, III, 5, 6.

68 1. **Quick.** Living.

69 6. **Fortress.** Cf. this and the third stanza below with Suckling's verses, *The Siege*, below, p. 108.

70. **Celia Singing.** Cf. with this *Song*, Campion's *Of Corinna's Singing* and Marvell's *The Fair Singer*, below, p. 157.

70 1. **Fair copy.** Cf. an imitation of this poem in *Holburn-Drollery*, 1673, p. 25.

71 20. **The stamp of kings imparts no more.** Cf. Burns:

> The rank is but the guinea's stamp,
> A man 's a man for a' that.

I notice that Mr. Richard Le Gallienne, following a correspondent of *Notes and Queries*, Series II, VII, 184, mentions this parallel in his appreciative little review of Carew (*Retrospective Reviews*, II, 80).

73. **Epitaph.** Carew wrote several epitaphs of much grace, especially the three on the Lady Mary Villiers. I have preferred this on Lady Mary, daughter of Sir Thomas Wentworth, as more characteristic, if fuller of conceits.

73 6. **A cherubin.** Cf. 30 5.

74 3. **Beauty's orient deep.** This is the reading of the reprint of 1640, the word being spelled *beautie's*. The apostrophe was, of course, not in the original, and might be placed so as to read *beauties'*. Mr. Saintsbury reads *For in your beauties, orient deep.*

74 11. **Dividing.** Performing music, especially with divisions or variations.

74 18. **Phœnix.** The allusions to this famous myth throughout the literature of this and the previous century are legion. The story seems to have been introduced into the literatures of Western Europe in the *Elegia de Phœnice*, a poem of the third century, usually attributed to

Lactantius. Lactantius had as his chief source the version of the legend by Manilius, which is now lost, but was extant in the fourteenth century. See in later literature *The Phœnix and the Turtle*, 1601; Browne's *Song of the Sirens;* and Herrick's *Nuptial Song to Sir Clipseby Crew.*

75. **Murdering Beauty.** This poem appears also in *Wit's Recreations.*

75 6. **Murderers.** Cannon loaded with scattering missiles, and so called from their infliction of superfluous death.

75. **Delight in Disorder** and the poem immediately following are assigned to the earlier part of Herrick's vicarage at Dean Prior. In 1640 he was probably in London, arranging for the publication of his poems, for in that year there is a stationer's register of *The Several Poems written by Master Robert Herrick.* The book does not appear to have come to press.

75 1. **A sweet disorder,** etc. Cf. *Upon Julia's Clothes* and *Upon Julia's Ribband*, Herrick, ed. Hale, pp. 112 and 20. See also Jonson's *Simplex Munditiis*, Herrick's probable original, and the dainty verses beginning: "My love in her attire doth show her wit," in Davison's *Poetical Rhapsody* (*Elizabethan Lyrics*, pp. 151 and 127).

75 2. **Wantonness.** Sportiveness.

75 4. **Distraction.** Confusion. Cf. 37 20.

75 5. **Erring.** In its original signification, wandering.

75 12. **Civility.** Good breeding.

75 13. **Do more bewitch me,** etc. Cf. Jonson:

> Such sweet neglect more taketh me
> Than all th' adulteries of art;

and Herrick's own charming lines:

> Whenas in silks my Julia goes,
> Then, then, methinks, how sweetly flows,
> That liquefaction of her clothes.
>
> Next, when I cast mine eyes, and see
> That brave vibration each way free;
> Oh, how that glittering taketh me!

76. **To the Virgins.** This song was early set to music by Lawes and enjoyed great popularity. It appears in an early ed. of *Wit's Recreations.*

77 5. **Teemed.** Poured out.

78 2. **Protestant.** Queried *protester* by Dr. Grosart. To which Professor Hale adds: "*His Protestation to Perilla* gives us the probable meaning. He will live to assert his devotion to her."

79. **To Meadows.** Cf. Vaughan's *The Hidden Flower*, below, p. 147.

79 6. **Wicker arks.** Baskets.

79 8. **Richer.** More golden in color.

79 10. **In a round.** Dancing. Cf. the poet's *The Country Life:* "Tripping the homely country round."

79 20. **Estates.** Conditions.

81 15. **Brave.** Cf. 34 5.

81 6. **My Prue.** Prudence Baldwin, immortalized for her fidelity by her master in this and in other verses:

> These summer birds did with thy master stay
> The times of warmth, but then they flew away,
> Leaving their poet, being now grown old,
> Expos'd to all the coming winter's cold.
> But thou, kind Prue, did'st with my fates abide
> As well the winter's as the summer's tide;
> For which thy love, live with thy master here,
> Not one, but all the seasons of the year.

81 10. **Creaking.** Cackling. Harrison says of geese: "It is ridiculous to see how they will peep under the doors, and never leave off *creaking* and gaggling, etc. (*Elizabethan England*, ed. Camelot, p. 163).

82 24. **Miching.** Skulking.

82 26. **Tracy.** Herrick's dog, of which he writes:

> Now thou art dead, no eye shall ever see,
> For shape and service, spaniel like to thee.

83 7. **Ward.** Protect.

83 22. **Unfled.** Undamaged by mould. A Shropshire word, according to Halliwell.

83 28. **Pulse.** Peas or beans.

84 31. **The worts, the purslane.** *Wort* is an old generic term for vegetable; *purslane* was formerly used in salads and for garnishing.

84 39. **Wassail bowls.** The wassail bowl was compounded of spiced ale and drunk amongst friends and neighbors on New Year's Eve in good fellowship and for the drowning of former animosity. The custom continued long in the greatest popularity. See Brand's *Popular Antiquities*, ed. 1813, I, 1.

84 42. **Soils.** Manures, makes fruitful.

85. **Nox Nocti,** etc. Cf. *Psalms*, XIX. "The heavens declare the glory of God; and the firmament sheweth his handiwork." This verse forms the text of the whole poem.

85 3. **So rich with jewels hung,** etc. Cf. *Romeo and Juliet*, i. v. 47:

> It seems she hangs upon the cheek of Night
> Like a rich jewel in an Ethiop's ear.

85 5. **My soul her wings.** Cf. *Isaiah*, XL, 31.

85 8. **In the large volume of the skies.** Cf. Drummond's "fair volume of the world" in the sonnet entitled *The Book of the World*, *Elizabethan Lyrics*, p. 205, and note thereon.

85 9. **For the bright firmament.** Cf. *Psalm*, XIX, 1.

86 25. **That from the farthest north.** Cf. *Jeremiah*, I, 14, 15, *et passim*, and *Daniel*, XI, 13–15.

86. **Cleodora** was performed at Whitehall before the king and queen by the Earl of Pembroke's own servants, the scenes and costumes being very rich and curious.

87. **The Imposture.** I assign this play, with Mr. Fleay, *Biographical Chronicle of the English Drama*, II, 246, to 1640, because of the line of the Prologue: "He has been stranger long to the English scene." Shirley returned permanently from Ireland between February and June, 1640.

88 11. **Flowers.** Dissyllabic.

88 16. **Owe.** Own. Cf. *Midsummer Night's Dream*, ii. 2. 79.

88 5. **Each shade,** etc. As the sun rises the shadows of the earth, here identified with earthly things, become short, and our attention is turned to the radiance of heaven. If we wait until "the star of peace" sets, we must lose our way in earthly shadow.

89. **The Contention of Ajax and Ulysses.** This masque "was represented by young men of quality at a private entertainment."

89 1. **The glories of our blood.** This one song should preserve Shirley immortal.

90. **His Winding-Sheet.** I follow Professor Hale in placing this poem before 1641, in which year the Star Chamber alluded to was abolished. Professor Hale calls this "of all Herrick's more serious pieces, the chief," and notes the remarkable absence in it of "any Christian thought on immortality."

90 19. Cf. *Job*, III, 18, 19.

90 29. **The Court of Requests** was also abolished in 1641.

91 47. **The Platonic Year** is that wherein everything shall return to its original state, the year in which the cycles of the seven planets are fulfilled on the same day. Cf. Plato, *Timæus*, cap. 33 (Hale).

91. **George Wither.** As to this fertile and worthy pamphleteer in verse and prose, see *Elizabethan Lyrics*, p. 281. Although Wither's

devotional verse began with *The Hymns and Songs of the Church*, 1623, his best work of the kind is to be found in the three parts of *Haleluiah*. Wither's simplicity of diction and freedom from adornment seem better suited to the subject of the poem in the text than to some of his more ambitious efforts. No one who knows *The Shepherd's Hunting* and *Fair Virtue* can for a moment deny the poet in Wither. To him there was a greater mistress than art; but instead of enlisting art in the service of religion, he felt that her ornaments and gauds were to be discarded as among the deceitful appearances which lure men from the straight and narrow way. Though kindly, Wither is thus in his devotional poetry always didactic.

91. **A Rocking Hymn.** The text is from the reprint of the *Spenser Society*, 1879. The following quaint note precedes the verses: "Nurses usually sing their children asleep and, through want of pertinent matter, they oft make use of unprofitable (if not worse) songs. This was therefore prepared that it might help acquaint them and their nurse-children with the loving care and kindness of their Heavenly Father."

94. **William Cartwright** was one of the "sons of Ben," a writer of plays in his youth while at Oxford, a priest in orders after 1638. His works, posthumously published, are preceded by more than fifty pages of commendatory verse amongst the writers of which are James Howell, Sherburne, Jasper Mayne, and Alexander Brome. Ben Jonson is reported in the preface to have said, "my son, Cartwright, writes like a man." Cartwright exhibited great promise in his poetry, and not inconsiderable achievement in his dramas. It is not easy to select many poems which are entirely good from Cartwright, though many separate stanzas or lesser passages display unusual merit. The text is from the first edition, as indicated; 1641 is the latest date assigned to any poem in the volume. These erotic songs were doubtless written several years earlier.

94 5. **Sense.** Cf. 36 2.

94 7. **Art we see.** Note the omission of *that* and cf. *Shakespeare Grammar*, § 281.

96. **A Valediction.** Few poems could better show the influence of Donne's subtle intellectual refinements than this and the previous one. Cartwright at his best, as here, seems to me to preserve also much of Donne's sincerity.

96 12. **Nor would those** (the showers) **fall nor these** (the sunbeams) **shine forth to me.**

96 15. **Parting view.** My eyes as I part with you.

96 17. **Snatch and keep.** Take eagerly to myself and preserve in memory.

96 19. **Fancy.** Imagination.

97 1. **See these two little brooks.** Cf. one of the best of Quarles' *Emblems*, v. 3, above, p. 55, and Jean Ingelow's *Divided*, in which the idea is fully expanded.

97 13. **Presents.** Represents.

98. **The Sad Lover.** I do not succeed in finding this poem elsewhere. The original edd. of *Wit's Recreations* are not accessible to me. From the reprint of Park, 1817, it appears that the section entitled "Fancies and Fantastics," in which this poem and the following are found, was not in the first ed. of 1640. I may state that even the enumeration of edd. in the preface of this unsatisfactory book is incorrect.

98 6. **Straight.** Suddenly. Cf. 164 3.

98 17. **Epact.** The epact is "the excess of a solar over a lunar year or month." The figure is here applied to the difference between what seems to be the seasonable moment in which to court and what is really that seasonable moment. See the stanza above, where the lover longs for "some almanac," etc. Donne is the parent of the metaphysics and the physics of all such passages.

99. **Richard Crashaw** was a precocious student and poet while at Cambridge. In 1643 Crashaw (with five others, fellows of Peterhouse) lost his fellowship because he refused to take the oath of the Solemn League and Covenant. Entering the priesthood of the Roman Catholic Church he was recommended to Rome by Queen Henrietta, but died soon after as beneficiary or sub-canon of the Basilica church of Our Lady of Loreto.

99. **Wishes to his Supposed Mistress.** I have given the text of the Harleian MS. of this poem. The vastly inferior version in *Wit's Recreations* shows that the poem was well known in 1641. How much earlier it may have been written, or whether the revision came after that date, it is impossible to say.

99 2. **She.** The common use of the pronoun for the noun. Cf. 134 17, 182 10, and *Shakespeare Grammar*, § 224.

99 18. **Tire.** Attire, dress.

99 20. **Taffeta or tissue.** Taffeta was a fine, smooth silk fabric; tissue, a cloth interwoven with gold or silver.

99 20. **Can.** Cf. a like usage of this verb, 2 3.

100 25. **A face that 's best by its own beauty drest.** Cf. Herrick's *Delight in Disorder*, p. 75, and the note thereon.

100 30. **Ope.** Open.

100 33. **Writes what the reader sweetly ru'th.** "Depict that

beauty which makes the beholder suffer the sweet sorrow of love" (Kittredge).

100 36. **His.** Its. Formerly neuter as well as masculine. See *Shakespeare Grammar*, § 228, and cf. 99 17, above.

100 40. **Looks that.** I.e., looks that *oppress*, overpower the richest apparel which decks them, which clothe and dress up the barest costume.

100 43. **Eyes that displace . . . out-face . . . grace.** This is Grosart's reading on the authority of the Harleian MS.; Turnbull prints, with the version of *Wit's Recreations:*

> Eyes that displaces
> The neighbor diamond, and outfaces
> That sunshine by their own sweet graces.

101 57. **Long choosing a dart.** Long finding a weapon powerful enough to reach so well-controlled (well-tamed) a heart.

101 70. **Fond and flight.** Foolish and fleeting.

101 74. **Those** [that] **are shed.** Cf. 1 2, 4 6, 9 2, 18 5, 94 7.

102 88. **Sydneian showers of sweet discourse.** Explained by Mr. Palgrave: "Either in allusion to the conversations in the *Arcadia*, or to Sidney himself, as a model of gentleness in spirit and demeanor" (*Golden Treasury*, p. 357).

102 98. **Name.** Report, fame.

102 100. **Flattery,** etc. Painting and poetry may flatter her, but let her own virtue be her sole counsellor.

102 103. **Store of worth,** etc. I wish that she may have such an abundance of worth that she may not need many wishes for things not already in her possession.

103 118. **Enjoy.** This word was pronounced in Crashaw's day and long after so as to rhyme with the last syllable of *apply*. Cf. *coin* rhyming with *resign*, 71 25, and 114 5.

102 123. **Determine.** End them, resolve them into.

103. **The Merry Beggars.** The text of this song is from the reprint of Brome's plays by Pearson, 1873. It seems almost too good for Brome. In the same play a song is introduced which is undoubtedly Campion's.

104 16. **Remore us.** Delay us. Cf. remora, the creature fabled to delay ships by attaching itself to their bottoms.

104. **Lord Strafford's Meditations.** Occasional lyrics such as this, though not up to the standard of the highest literary art, have fre-

quently a genuineness and fervor of passion that brings them literally within Wordsworth's famous designation of poetry as "the spontaneous overflow of powerful emotion." A large and interesting collection of such applied poetry might be made from the literature of the sixteenth and seventeenth centuries. Cf. the pieces ascribed to Raleigh in Hannah's ed. of Raleigh and Wotton, the works of several of the poets contained in Dr. Grosart's *Fuller Worthies' Miscellanies*, and *Elizabethan Lyrics*, pp. 27, 94, 129, and 188.

105 33. **In Thetis' lap he lies.** In allusion to the deep security which one might enjoy in the depths of the sea.

106 41. **Did fly in Charles's wain.** *Charles's wain*, like the dipper, was a popular appellation applied to the cluster of seven stars in the constellation of Ursa Major. The play upon words by which Charles's (the King's) wain (wagon) is likened to the chariot of the Sun, and Stafford's "ambitious wings" to the audacious act of Phaethon in attempting to drive his father's fiery steeds, is as apt as it is obvious. Cf. the similar play upon words in *The Passionate Man's Pilgrimage*, where Christ, described as "the King's Attorney, . . . hath angels, but no fees." See also below, 106 63. These conceits seem not the result of cool ingenuity, but the genuine product of a fancy heightened by momentary excitement.

106 52. **Glorious seat.** Alike the exalted position of the star and of the statesman figured forth by it.

106 53. **Influence.** In the original astrological sense of the word: "The effect of the planets in determining the events of man's life."

107. **Fragmenta Aurea,** *a Collection of all the Incomparable Pieces written by Sir John Suckling*, was the title under which the poetry of Suckling was published posthumously. I have before me the third ed. 1658, and Langbaine mentions a later one of 1676, "to which are added several poems and other pieces, which were by his sister's permission allowed to be published."

108. **The Siege.** The figure which is elaborated in this poem has been frequently employed both before and later. In Mr. Arber's *English Garner* (I, pp. 74, 128, 460, and 651) will be found several parallels. Sedley's song in *Bellamira* beginning, "When first I made love to my Chloris," gives us another. See Bullen's *Musa Proterva*, p. 84. Cf. also the third stanza of Carew's *A Deposition in Love*, p. 69, above, and a paper, *Notes on Lyrical Poetry*, by the editor, *Modern Language Notes*, April, 1899.

109 13. **I brought down great cannon-oaths, and shot a thousand . . . to the town.** Thus imitated by Sedley:

Cannon-oaths I brought down
To batter the town.
. . . .
Billets-doux like small shot did ply her.

109 31. **Honor was there.** Notice the emphasis produced by the trochee in place of the iambus.

110 4. **Still.** Ever. Cf. 5 9, 33 12, 50 10, 65 51.

112. **Song.** Cf. Herrick, *To Œnone*, ed. Hale, p. 80.

112 15. **I 'm best resolved.** I have found a solution.

113. **When the assault,** etc. This is Milton's own heading, as appears in the Cambridge MS., the words "On his door when the city expected an assault" having been crossed out. This was in November, 1642, when the withdrawal of the Parliamentary forces under Essex to Warwick after the indecisive skirmish of Edgehill left the road to the capital open to the forces of Charles.

113 5. **He can requite thee.** Pattison cites several parallels, among them Shakespeare's *Sonnets*, lv, lxxxi; Drayton, *Idea*, *sonnet* vi.

113 5. **Charms.** Spells, magical effects.

113 10. **Emathian conqueror.** Alexander. So called from Emathia, a district of Macedonia, the original seat of the Macedonian monarchy.

113 10. **Bid spare,** etc. This story is told by Pliny, *Hist. Nat.*, vii. 29; Ælian, *Var. Hist.*, xiii. 7, and many others. Pattison suggests that Milton had it from the *Vita Pindari* of Thomas Magister.

113 13. **Sad Electra's poet.** Euripides. His tragedy *Electra* was produced during the period of the Sicilian expedition, 415–413 B.C. Euripides was a favorite author with Milton.

113 14. **To save the Athenian walls.** "On the taking of Athens by the Lacedæmonians, 404 B.C., the leaders of the combined Greek forces deliberated as to how the city should be dealt with. The Thebans proposed to raze it to the ground and to turn the site into a sheep walk. While the decision was in suspense, on one occasion the generals were at wine together, and it so happened a Phocian sang part of a chorus of the *Electra*, which begins:

Ἀγαμέμνονος ὦ κόρα, ἤλυθον κ.τ.λ. (*Electra*, 167).

Those present were so affected that they agreed it would be an unworthy act to destroy a city which had produced such noble poets" (Ælian, *Var. Hist.*, xiii. 7. Pattison).

113. **Steps to the Temple.** So entitled in relation to *The Temple*

of George Herbert. Cf. *The Preface, To the Reader:* "Reader, we style his sacred poems, *Steps to the Temple*, and aptly, for in the temple of God, under his wing he led his life in Saint Mary's Church near Saint Peter's College; there he lodged under Tertullian's roof of angels ; there he made his nest more gladly than David's swallow near the house of God, where like a primitive saint he offered more prayers in the night than others usually offer in the day : there he penned these poems, steps for happy souls to climb heaven by." These poems were then written before Crashaw's loss of his fellowship in 1643.

114 5. **Joy.** Cf. 103 118.

114 5. **To all our world . . . he slept.** Cf. *Shakespeare Grammar*, § 188 ; we still say : "Dead to the world."

114 21. **Thy day . . . did rise,** etc. A common figure in the erotic verse of the time. Cf. Carew, 70 16 ; Davenant, 184 12, and the note thereon.

115 38. **Starry.** Celestial ; a favorite word with Milton.

115 44. **Contest.** For the accent, cf. *Shakespeare Grammar*, § 490.

115 46. **Phœnix'.** Cf. 74 18.

115 48. **Embraves.** Makes beautiful.

116 60. **For well they now can spare their wing.** A typical conceit of the school to which Crashaw belongs.

116 78. **Welcome.** Though born neither to gold nor to silk, thou art born to more than the birthright of Cæsar.

116 80. **Two sister seas.** This stanza is one of those — too frequent in Crashaw — in which the stroke of wing fails, and the song falls earthward.

117 84–89. This stanza is omitted in the Paris edition of 1652. See Introduction to this volume, p. xxxi.

117 89. **Points.** Cf. 121 21, and Donne, *The Ecstasy:*

> Our eye-beams twisted and did thread
> Our eyes upon one double string.

117 92. **Slippery souls in smiling eyes.** Notice the alliteration and the correspondence of sound in *smiling* and *eyes*.

117 93. **Shepherds' homespun things.** This is the reading of Grosart.

117 93. **Homespun.** Cf. Shakespeare's conversion of this adjective into a noun, *Midsummer Night's Dream*, iii. 1. 79 : "hempen homespuns."

118 8. **Silver mate.** Cf. *silver doves* above, and *Psalms*, LXVIII, 13.

118 8. **Rise up, my love.** Cf. *Solomon's Song*, II, 10–14.

118 20. **Or quickly would, wert thou once here.** It is interesting to notice this classical thread — in allusion to the springing up of flowers about the footsteps of Spring — and the conceit, *except so much* [rain] *as we detain in needful tears*, etc., below, woven into the glowing fabric of the old Hebraic poetry.

120. "And those other of his pieces, intituled *The Delights of the Muses*, though of a more human mixture, are as sweet as they are innocent" (*To the Reader*, Crashaw, ed. 1646).

120 3. **Consults the conscious spheres.** A popular belief in astrology was still prevalent in Crashaw's day. The poets are full of such allusions as these, 91 47, 98 17, 106 52.

120 12. **Love's fortune-book.** The book of Love's fortune.

121 17. **Love's native hours were set.** However the horoscope of the natal hours of Love was arranged.

121 18. **Starry synod.** Assemblage of stars; the position of the planets with reference one to the other determined the particulars of the horoscope.

121 21. **Sharp rays, putting on points.** Her glances. Cf. Crashaw's use of the word *point*, above. Cf. 117 88.

121 25. **Aspects.** The aspect was "the relative position of the heavenly bodies as they appear to an observer on the earth's surface at a given time" (Murray). Here *aspects* is almost equivalent to *influences*.

121 25. **Twined,** etc. "United to give a combined influence which was extremely favorable." Cf. Donne, *The Ecstasy*, quoted above, 117 88.

121 33. **Influence.** Cf. 106 53.

121 36. **Black.** The color of evil. Cf. 128 16.

122 52. **Love shall live, although he die.** This subtly varied refrain finds its original in Donne. Cf. his *Lover's Infiniteness*, *Love's Infiniteness*, *The Will*, *The Prohibition*.

122. **Sonnet.** The lady to whom this sonnet is addressed is not known. Philips mentions a Miss Davis, whom Milton thought of marrying when deserted by his first wife; and Pattison quotes a suggestion "that the virtues celebrated in these lines were those which Milton would have sought for in a wife." Pattison continues of this sonnet: "Imagery here is the hackneyed biblical allusion; the thought commonplace; the language ordinary; yet it will hardly be denied that the effect is impressive. . . . It is due to the sense that here is a true utterance of a great soul."

122 2. **The broad way.** *Matthew*, VII, 13.

122 2. **And the green.** Because a green way is a pleasant one. Cf. *Il Penseroso*, 66; *L'Allegro*, 58, and Shelley's sonnet beginning: "Ye hasten to the dead."

122 5. **Ruth.** The perfect rhyme was not regarded as a blemish in Milton's day.

122 6. **Overween.** A favorite word with Milton, *Paradise Lost*, x. 878; *Paradise Regained*, i. 147, etc.

122 11. **Hope that reaps not shame.** *Romans*, V, 5.

122 12. **Feastful.** Cf. *Samson Agonistes*, 1741.

123. **To Phyllis.** This poem appears in *Wit's Recreations* and was set to music in Playford's *Select Airs and Dialogues*, 1659. I hesitate to assign a date to any of Waller's lyrics, although this may have been written as early as 1639, considering its position in the earlier editions of his poems. Waller was much given to repolishing and filing his verses that they might conform to the poetical standards which prevailed after the Restoration — standards the setting up of which he was especially emulous to have generally believed to have been of his devising.

123. **On a Girdle.** This poem appeared first in an appendix to the second ed. of 1645. It was probably written not long before that date.

124 5. **It was.** *Is* in the ed. of 1645, where the present tense is kept up through the poem.

124 11, 12. The ed. of 1645 reads:

> Give me but what this riband tied,
> Take all the sun goes round beside.

See also the Introduction, p. xxviii f.

124 9. **Thyrsis'.** "Thyrsis, a youth of the inspirèd train"; the name assumed by Waller in his poetical courtship of Saccharissa. See *The Story of Phœbus and Daphne Applied*, Drury's *Waller*, p. 52.

125 1. **Go, lovely rose.** This famous lyric, which it seems to me has been somewhat overrated, appears also in *Wit's Recreations*, followed by two other poems on the same subject — one of them Waller's, entitled (in his works) *The Bud;* the other Herrick's, entitled (in the *Hesperides*) *To the Rose, Song.* The first stanza runs:

> Go, happy rose, and interwove
> With other flowers bind my love.
> Tell her too, she must not be
> Longer peevish, longer free,
> That so long hath fettered me.

The resemblance is only superficial. In Mr. Drury's *Waller* will be found a number of other parallels. The fact that these poems of Herrick and Waller occur towards the end of *Wit's Recreations*, intermixed with verse of Sir Edward Sherburne, whose volume of poetry, *Salmacis, Lyrian, and Sylvia*, appeared first in 1651, makes it likely that all were collected into a late edition of *Wit's Recreations*, probably that of 1654.

125 7. **Graces spied.** Mr. Gosse (*From Shakespeare to Pope*, p. 60) finds these syllables "drag painfully on the tongue" and remembers "to have heard the greatest living authority on melodious numbers [Tennyson?] suggest that Waller must have written *graces eyed*." He adds: "The first edition of 1645, however, has, by an obvious misprint, *grace spy'd*." The reprint of *Wit's Recreations* reads *graces spy'd;* Fenton reads as in the text. If another conjecture may be made, may not Waller have written *grace espied?*

126 7. **Thetis' streams.** The ocean.

126. **Fie on Love.** I have preferred the longer and more finished version of this poem, which appears in Goffe's *Careless Shepherdess*, 1656. A shorter version is found in *Shirley's Poems*, 1646. I have no hesitation in assigning the lines to Shirley; they are much in his manner. Cf. note on *Love's Hue and Cry*, above, p. 6.

126. Henry Vaughan, the Silurist, so called by his contemporaries from his birth among the people of South Wales, entered Jesus College, Oxford, in 1638. Both Henry and his brother Thomas were zealous in the royal cause, although the poet does not seem to have borne arms. Vaughan had a glimpse of the last of the great age preceding. He knew Randolph and venerated Jonson, though he could hardly have met him personally. This contact with literary London inspired Vaughan's first work, *Poems, with the Tenth Satire of Juvenal Englished. Olor Iscanus*, a second book of secular poems and translations, appeared without the author's sanction in 1651.

127 19. **Sense.** Senses, perceptions. Cf. 36 2, 37 30, 94 5.

127 22. **Element.** Compose, make up their love. A favorite word of Donne's. Cf. his *Upon Parting from his Mistress, Elizabethan Lyrics*, 102 16.

127. **The Inconstant.** This poem was prompted by Donne's *Indifferent*, to which it is as inferior as the flippancy of persiflage is inferior to imaginative cynicism. There is a clever mock poem on the same topic, having Donne's title and Cowley's treatment, in Alexander Brome's *Works*, Chalmers's *English Poets*, VI, p. 645.

127 5. **Devil.** Monosyllabic here, as frequently. Cf. the Scotch deil.

127 6. **Legion.** Trisyllabic. Cf. 37 20, 75 4, 121 26.

128 13. **Proper.** Handsome.

128 16. **Black.** Cf. Shakespeare's *Sonnet*, cxlvii, where there is a play on the meaning of black as the color of evil. Cf. 121 36, 134 13.

128 30. **The man** [that] **loves.** Cf. 1 2, 4 6, 9 2, 94 9.

129. **Thomas Stanley,** remembered for his work in the history of philosophy, was also a poet in his youth, publishing several volumes, chiefly of translation, between 1647 and 1651. Stanley's poetical work seems to have belonged wholly to his college days. *Poems and Translations* is the first of Stanley's volumes of poetry. Much of this volume is reprinted with slight variation in the subsequent ones.

129. **The Tomb.** I prefer the shorter and apparently revised version of this poem which appeared in *Poems by T. S.*, 1651.

129 20. **As thine.** As thy sacrifice.

130. **The Relapse.** This poem is entitled simply *Song* in the ed. of 1647.

130 7. **Fall.** The reading of the ed. of 1651; the earlier ed. reads *name*.

131. **Richard Lovelace** is described in his youth, by Wood, as "being then accounted the most amiable and beautiful person that ever eye beheld, . . . of innate modesty, virtue, and courtly deportment." Lovelace was educated at Oxford and distinguished himself at court and in the field. He was twice imprisoned and ultimately wasted his entire fortune "in useless attempts to serve his sovereign." He died in poverty. There seems no particular reason for supposing that Lucasta (*lux casta*) was a real person, Lucy Sacheverell, as does Wood; or that Lovelace, after his loss of Lucasta, married Althea. Lovelace has been variously estimated as "a mere reckless *improvisatore*" and as "the most fastidious of the concettists." Many of his minor lyrics fall into utter unintelligibility and into a slovenliness of style not to be accounted for by mere corruptness of text.

131 1. **If to be absent.** Cf. the idea of absence not a separation but an etherealization of passion, in Donne's *Song* beginning: "Soul's joy, now I am gone," Davison's *Poetical Rhapsody*, *Ode*, ed. Bullen, I, 117; Shirley's *To his Mistress Confined*, ed. Dyce, VI, 409; Carew, *To my Mistress in Absence*, reprint of 1824, p. 27; all perhaps ultimately referable to the *Symposium* of Plato. The following stanza of Cartwright well sets forth the contemporary estimate of "Platonic love":

> Tell me no more of minds embracing minds,
> And hearts exchanged for hearts;
> That spirits' spirits meet as winds do winds
> And mix their subtlest parts;
> That two embodied essences may kiss, etc.

The song of the text was set by Lawes and appears in his *Airs and Dialogues*, 1653–1658.

132 10. **Blow-god.** Aeolus the wind god. Explained as Neptune by Mr. Palgrave, with the reading *blue-god.* The original reads *blew-god.*

132 18. **Greet as angels greet.** Cf. Donne's *The Ecstacy* and *Air and Angels*, and Carew's *To my Mistress in Absence.*

132 1. **Tell me not, sweet.** "Suckling's inconstancy and Lovelace's constancy," says Mr. Saintsbury, "may or may not be equally poetical. . . . The songs remain, and remain yet unsurpassed, as the most perfect celebrations, in one case of chivalrous devotion, in the other of the coxcomb side of gallantry, that literature contains or is likely to contain" (*Elizabethan Literature*, p. 376).

133 1. **Amarantha.** This song appears in Lawes' *Airs and Dialogues*, 1653, and likewise in Colgrave's *Wit's Interpreter*, 1655. I follow Lawes in presenting but two stanzas.

133 2. **Ah braid no more.** Lawes reads *Forbear to braid.*

133 4. **'T was last night,** etc. Cf. Donne's *Woman's Constancy:*

> Now thou hast loved me one whole day,
> Tomorrow, when thou leav'st, what wilt thou say?

and Suckling's *Constancy*, above, p. 111.

134 13. **Black.** Cf. 128 16.

134 15. **Un-plowed-up.** *Wit's Interpreter*, ed. 1662, reads *unbidden.*

134 17. **She.** Cf. 99 2 and 182 10.

134. **To Althea from Prison.** This famous song is set to music by John Wilson in his *Cheerful Airs or Ballads*, 1660.

134 5. **Tangled in her hair.** Cf. Peele's *David and Bethsabe*, i. 1, ed. Morley, p. 85, and *Lycidas*, 69.

134 7. **Gods.** The original reading. There is no authority for *birds*, the usual reading.

134 10. **Thames.** A familiar classicism. Cf. *Æneid*, i. 472:

> Priusquam
> Pabula gustassent Trojae Xanthumque bibissent.

135 17. **Like committed linnets.** The usual reading, *When linnet-like confinèd, I*, is a refinement of Bishop Percy, which I am surprised to find Mr. Saintsbury accepting without comment in his *Seventeenth Century Lyrics.* Cf. with this whole poem an imitation, sufficiently base, by Thomas Weaver, in his *Songs and Poems of Love and Drollery*, Beloe's *Anecdotes*, VI, 88.

135. **Thomas Forde,** the dramatist, not to be confused with the musician Thomas Ford or the more famous dramatist John Ford, is described as a "staunch and pious royalist." Forde wrote several moral pamphlets and emulated his friend's, James Howell's, *Familiar Letters* in his *Fænestra in Pectore*. *Love's Labyrinth* is a dramatization of Greene's *Menaphon*.

136. **To Perilla.** The grave beauty of this poem is beyond praise. Professor Hale writes thus in the Introduction to his ed. of Herrick, p. xxxvi: "To Herrick the two greatest things of life were Love and Death, — and his mind turned constantly to the thought of one or the other. And finding in his own religion no true satisfaction for his whole feeling, it would really seem as though he had sometimes fancied, half-seriously, half in sport, a strange cult of imaginary deities in the ritual of whose service, had it ever existed, he might have found a satisfaction which was given him nowhere else."

136 7. **First cast in salt.** These rites are imaginary and picturesque rather than founded upon actual folklore. See, however, Brand's *Popular Antiquities*, ed. 1813, II, 203, 484.

136 18. **Still in the cool and silent shades of sleep.** One of the most beautiful lines in our literature.

137. **His Poetry his Pillar.** Cf. with this *The Pillar of Fame*, the last poem of the *Hesperides*.

138. **Jasper Mayne,** Archdeacon of Chichester, and dramatist, wrote much occasional verse, some of which is to be found in *Jonsonus Virbius* and prefixed to the second folio ed. of Beaumont and Fletcher, 1679. Mayne gave up poetry in middle life. The lyric of the text is by far the best of his shorter poems.

140. Crashaw's volume *Carmen Deo Nostro* was published in Paris, with fine plates, said to be of the poet's own designing. See *An Epigram*, Turnbull's *Crashaw*, p. 145.

140. **James Graham,** Marquess of Montrose, for a time the great military stay of Charles in Scotland, was finally defeated and gave up his life in the royal cause a year after the execution of his royal master. "The great Marquess's verses," says Mr. Saintsbury, commenting upon the poem of the text, "are amateurish beyond all doubt, and the present piece is defaced by the political flings at 'synods' and 'committees.' But the root of the matter is in it" (*Seventeenth Century Lyrics*, p. 311). The few poems which Montrose has left — chief among them the well-known epitaph on Charles I — will be found in the Appendix to Napier's *Montrose and the Covenanters*, ed. 1838, II, 566 *et seq.* See also Hannah's *Courtly Poets*, p. 203.

142. **Phineas Fletcher,** the author of *The Purple Island*, was the son of Dr. Giles Fletcher, who wrote the sonnet sequence *Licia*. John Fletcher, the dramatist, was Phineas' first cousin, and Giles the younger, author of *Christ's Victory and Triumph*, his brother. The list of poetical Fletchers is completed with the name of Dr. Joseph Fletcher, who appears not to have been related to John and Phineas. The earlier lyrics of Phineas, some of great merit, fall before our period. See Dr. Grosart's ed. of Fletcher's work.

142 17. **Shades fill** into substance.

143 30. **He, he thy end.** It is a pity that so fine a poem should be blemished by an obscurity, apparently easily to be remedied.

143. **Silex Scintillans.** It is one of the strange vicissitudes that seem to rule even in literature, that Herbert, in his own age, as since, has enjoyed a wider popularity than either of his greater disciples, Crashaw and Vaughan. The titles of these poems are Vaughan's own.

143. **The Retreat.** This fine poem courts comparison with Wordsworth's great *Ode on Intimations of Immortality from Recollections of Early Childhood*, and our interest becomes only the greater when we learn on the authority of Archbishop Trench that "Wordsworth had a copy of *Silex Scintillans* and that it bore many marks of earnest use" (Grosart's *Vaughan*, II, lxiv).

143 1. **Happy those early days.** Cf. with this and the following lines these verses from *Corruption*, ed. Lyte, p. 86:

> Sure it was so. Man in those early days
>   Was not all stone and earth;
> He shined a little, and by those weak rays
>   Had some glimpse of his birth.
> He saw heaven o'er his head, and knew from whence
>   He came, condemnèd, hither,
> And, as first love draws strongest, so from hence
>   His mind sure progressed thither;

an even closer reminder of the great *Ode* (Grosart).

143 2. **Angel-infancy.** Infancy pure as angels.

144 26. **City of palm-trees.** Jericho, often so called. Cf. *II Chronicles*, XXVIII, 15.

144 17. **Ranges.** Wanderings.

145 1. **Since in a land,** etc. Since my lot is fallen in a land not ever barren, etc.

145. **The World.** This poem is followed by this quotation in the original. It seems fitting that more than the reference be given here:

"For all that is in the world, the lust of the flesh, and the lust of the eyes, and the pride of life, is not of the Father, but is of the world.

"And the world passeth away, and the lust thereof; but he that doeth the will of God abideth forever" (*I John*, II, 16, 17).

145 2. **Like a great ring.** Cf. with this sublime image Rossetti's conception of space, *The Blessed Damozel:*

> Beneath the tides of day and night
> With flame and darkness ridge
> The void;

and further on:

> She saw
> Time like a pulse shake fierce
> Through all the world (Grosart).

146 30. **As free.** As freely as he would have drunk had it not rained tears and blood.

146 31. **Fearful.** Timorous.

146 34. **Above.** In heaven.

147 38. **Downright.** Out in out.

147 40. **While others,** who had slipped into excess, said little less than the epicure.

147 43. **Think them brave.** The present here used to express the habit of thinking such trivial things beautiful and worth having.

147 44. **And** is almost antithetical here; and meanwhile Truth sate, etc.

147 1. **I walked the other day.** Cf. with this stanza Herrick's *To Meadows*, above, p. 79.

148 14. **Bower.** An inner or private room, hence a place of hiding or protection.

148 21. **Of us unseen.** Cf. *Shakespeare Grammar*, § 170.

148 23. **Strow.** Spread apart for the purpose of considering; here equal to ponder.

150. **Andrew Marvell,** son of the Master of Kingston-upon-Hull Grammar School, received a sound education, which he improved by foreign travel. He is said to have founded his lifelong friendship for Milton while at Rome. Nearly all the lyrical and lighter poems of Marvell belong, according to general opinion, to the years which he spent in travel and as tutor to the daughter of the famous parliamentary general, Lord Fairfax. It was early in 1652 that Marvell was recommended by Milton for the post of Assistant Latin Secretary; and although he did not obtain the appointment until later, he had evidently left his seclu-

sion for public life. Marvell's after career, as the daring and incorruptible satirist of Charles II and his dissolute life, does not concern us here. As a poet and as a man Marvell was worthy the friendship of Milton.

150 22. **Curious frame** [of flowers]. Cf. above, v. 7:

> The fragrant towers
> That once adorned our shepherdess's head.

150 24. **Set.** Arranged.

151. **Bermudas.** These islands were settled in the first quarter of the seventeenth century by settlers from England, who fled, like the Pilgrim Fathers, to escape the tyranny which led to the Rebellion.

151 23. **Apples.** Pineapples.

152. **Clorinda and Damon.** Despite superficial matters of style there is an unaffectedness and genuine appreciation of nature in Marvell's little pastoral lyrics that takes us back through the long line of sophistication to the pastorals of Greene, Breton, and Lodge. Nor does Marvell lose in this mode when compared with Dryden.

152 2. **Late.** Lately. Grosart places a comma after *late*.

152 5. **Aim.** "The use of the noun in sense of *intent* is common, and both are due to the (then) common practice of archery" (Dr. Nicholson in ed. Grosart, to whom I am indebted for several of the following notes).

152 8. **Vade.** Pass away, perish, a by-form of *fade*. Cf. Shakespeare's *Sonnets*, xiv. 10; *Richard II*, i. 2. 20.

153 14. **Concave shell.** Cave, hollow, out of which the fountain issues. Cf. Milton's "aery shell," *Song* from *Comus*, 39 2.

155 13. **Nest,** and hence make their home.

156 24. **Lightfoot.** Evidently a dog's name.

156 28. **Antedate.** Anticipate.

157. **The Fair Singer.** Dr. Grosart mentions what he calls "a grotesquely quaint anticipation" of this poem by one N. Hookes, 1653. The date makes it more probably an imitation. Four lines will suffice, and they are worth quoting for the truly original picture they present:

> Hark to the changes of the trembling air!
> What nightingales do play in consort there!
> See in the clouds the cherubs listen yon,
> Each angel with an otacousticon.

It may be glossed that an otacousticon is an ear trumpet.

159 29. **Quaint.** Nice; perhaps here, out of place.

159 40. **Slow-chapt.** Slowly devouring. "Cf. the substantive *chap*, the jaw, and also *chop*. The sense is: Let us devour Time in our joys, rather than by your coyness languish in his slow-devouring jaws" (Nicholson).

159. **T. C.** The name of the subject of this charming poem has not come down to us. Dr. Nicholson suggests, in a pencil note in Grosart's ed.: "Evidently some one born in a commanding position; but I can find no Cromwell nor Claypole to correspond." Mr. Palgrave remarks of the poem: "Delicate humor, delightfully united to thought at once simple and subtle. It is full of conceit and paradox, but these are imaginative, not as with most of our Seventeenth Century poets, intellectual only" (*Golden Treasury of English Lyrics*, p. 357).

159. **Prospect.** View, landscape.

159 4. **Aspect.** Look, perhaps involving the astrological meaning of the influence or effect of a planet upon men's fortunes.

160 22. **But more despise.** Only the more despise those that yield.

160 38. **Make th' example yours.** "Act in your case in accordance with the example which you set (in plucking the buds)" (Kittredge).

160 39. **Ere we see** [them], i.e., our hopes.

161 5. **Comets.** As to the portentous nature of comets in the vulgar estimation of the day, see *1 Henry IV*, i. 1. 10; *Julius Cæsar*, ii. 2. 30.

161 7. **Higher.** The reading of the ed. of 1681. Later editions read *other*.

161 9. **Officious.** Office-doing, dutiful.

161 1. **Survey.** Map, plot.

162 15. **Gaudy.** Here in both the modern sense of bright-colored and with the older meaning, joyful.

162 19. **Ought.** Ought to have done.

162 26. **Companions of my thoughts more green.** Cf. Marvell's beautiful poem *The Garden:*

> Annihilating all that 's made
> To a green thought in a green shade.

163. **Sir Edward Sherburne** held for many years a place in the office of ordnance. He endured many vicissitudes for his loyalty and his faith, losing at one time all his property and with it a valuable library of his own collecting. Sherburne was best known in his day as a translator and was intimate with Edward Philips, the nephew of Milton, who dedicated his *Theatrum Poetarum* to Sherburne and Sher-

burne's kinsman, Thomas Stanley. I find a graceful and agreeable strain in Sherburne's trifles, which seem not too much the echo of others. Sherburne has not been reprinted except in Chalmers, vol. VII. I take my text from the original ed. of 1651. Many of Sherburne's poems appear in the last two editions of *Wit's Recreations.*

164 3. **Straight.** Immediately. Cf. 98 6.

165 3. **Captived.** Captivated.

165 5. **Admire.** Wonder at.

166. **Sonnet XVI.** This sonnet was, like the one to General Fairfax, not included in the edition of Milton's poems, 1673, but appeared first as indicated in the title in the text. Philips made several changes which were necessary to the times. The Cambridge MS. has fortunately enabled subsequent editors to give the true version. In this MS. the poem bears the date May, 1652, and has also the additional heading "On the proposals of certain ministers at the Committee for Propagation of the Gospel.". This shows that the sonnet is not to be regarded as Milton's expression of general admiration for Cromwell but "as a special appeal invoked by certain circumstances." The committee of the Rump Parliament, alluded to above, had proposed "that the preachers should receive a public maintenance" (Pattison).

166. **Cromwell.** Cf. Milton's eulogistic review of the character and services of Cromwell, in the *Second Defense*, *Prose Works*, ed. Bohn, I, 282–291.

166 1. **Our chief of men.** "In respect of his personal qualities and thorough going liberality of opinion, and not merely as the foremost man in the Commonwealth" (Pattison).

166 1. **A cloud.** Cf. *Æneid*, x. 809.

166 5. **On the neck.** Cf. *Genesis*, XLIX, 8; *Joshua*, X, 24, etc., one of the Biblical phrases formally employed in the common speech of the day.

166 7. **Darwen.** A stream near Preston, where Cromwell defeated the Scotch, August, 1648. Dunbar, in which the Scotch were routed, was in September, 1650. Worcester, a year later, witnessed the complete defeat of Charles, who had invaded England to avenge his father's death.

166 10. **Peace hath her victories.** Pattison refers us to Ronsard, *Sonnets Divers*, v. 303, and Tennyson's *Ode on the Death of the Duke of Wellington:*

For one so true
There must be other, nobler work to do
Than when he fought at Waterloo.

166 11. **New foes.** For a discussion of the contemporary circumstances that seemed to Milton to justify these last lines, I must refer the student to Pattison's or Verity's ed. of *Milton's Sonnets.* That the vigor of this special application of the sonnet should have betrayed the poet, here alone, into a final couplet is but natural. In whatever light we may view this sonnet its conclusion offers an undoubted instance of the destruction of the universality of art by the infusion of a specific purpose.

167. **Cupid and Death, a Masque,** was acted before the ambassador of Portugal, March, 1653. The title of the song is Mr. Bullen's. This poem may be well compared with its companion in the same tone: "The glories of our blood and state." See above, p. 89.

167 1. **Avenge, O Lord.** This sonnet was called forth by the sufferings of the Vaudois, or Waldenses, against whom the Duke of Savoy sent an armed force, upon their refusal to conform to the Church, April, 1655. The excesses of this expedition filled the Protestant world with horror, and Cromwell himself declared that it "came near his heart as if his own nearest and dearest had been concerned." On the subject, see Pattison's *Life of Milton*, p. 126.

167 1. **Whose bones lie scattered.** Cf. *Tenure of Kings*, Milton's *Prose Works*, II, 19.

167 2. **On the Alpine mountains cold.** Cf. *Propertius*, i. 21. 9; and Fairfax' *Tasso*, xiii. 60, where the very words occur.

167 3. **Who kept thy truth.** Milton speaks later of the Vaudois as "those ancientest reformed churches of the Waldenses — if they rather continued not pure since the apostles" (*The Likeliest Means to Remove Hirelings out of the Church*, *Prose Works*, III, 16. Verity.).

167 4. **Worshipped stocks and stones.** In his tract on *True Religion*, 1659, Milton "lays down that the reason for excepting Popery from general toleration is solely because it is idolatrous" (*Prose Works*, II, 514).

168 7. **That rolled mother and infant.** This incident is related as a fact by Sir William Moreland, Cromwell's agent in Piedmont, in his account of the massacre published in 1658.

168 10. **Their martyred blood and ashes sow.** "Plures efficimur, quoties metimur a vobis; semen est sanguis Christianorum," Tertullian, *Apologia*, 50 (Pattison).

168 12. **The triple Tyrant.** The Pope, in allusion to his tiara surrounded with three crowns.

168 13. **Who.** Those who.

168 14. **Babylon** was Rome to the Puritans. Cf. the Babylon of the *Apocalypse*.

168. **On his Blindness.** This sonnet is usually, but conjecturally, assigned to the year 1655. Milton's eyesight had been long failing, and he became totally blind about March, 1652. His steady persistence in writing his *Defensio pro populo Anglicano contra Salmasium* hastened this calamity. Not the least merit of this noble sonnet is its freedom from the note of complaint and repining. Cf. with this a passage from a letter of Milton's to Philaras, quoted by Pattison (*Sonnets*, p. 205), and also *Paradise Lost*, vii. 27, and *Samson Agonistes*, 80.

168 3. **One talent.** Cf. *Matthew*, XXV, 14.

168 8. **Fondly.** Foolishly.

168 12. **Thousands** of angels. Cf. *Christian Doctrine*, i. 9, and *Paradise Lost*, iv. 677.

168 13. **Post.** Cf. *Julius Cæsar*, iii. 1. 287.

168 14. **Stand.** Cf. *Daniel*, VII, 10, and *Luke*, I, 19.

169 1. **They are all gone into the world of light.** These words recall Lamb's beautiful refrain, "All, all are gone, the old familiar faces." The two poems are, however, very different. The title is not in the original; Dr. Grosart's title is *Beyond the Veil.*

169 7. **Those faint beams . . . after the sun's remove.** Cf. *To Amoret*, above, p. 126, where there is a more elaborate picture of this moment after sundown.

169 10. **Trample.** Tread close upon, follow closely.

169 21. **He that hath found.** Had Vaughan always written as he wrote in this and the following exquisite stanza, he need not have yielded to any of his contemporaries.

169 25. **And yet, as angels in some brighter dreams.** Cf. Wordsworth's *Ode on the Intimations of Immortality:*

> There was a time when meadow, grove, and stream,
> The earth, and every common sight,
> To me did seem
> Apparelled in celestial light,
> The glory and the freshness of a dream.

170 35. **Resume.** Take back again.

170 38. **Perspective.** Accent on the first syllable, as in *All's Well*, v. 3. 48, and commonly.

170. **The Throne.** Cf. *Revelation*, XX, 11, Vaughan's own reference.

171. **Charles Cotton,** the friend of Izaak Walton, is described as a very accomplished man, travelled, and devoted to literary pursuits, angling, and horticulture. Cotton appears to have been something of

a *bon vivant*, the marriage of two fortunes and his own large patrimony not sufficing to keep him out of debt. He is best known by his treatise on fly-fishing, published in 1676 as a Second Part to Walton's *Complete Angler*. Coleridge said of Cotton's poetry: "There are not a few poems in that volume, replete with every excellence of thought, image and passion, which we expect or desire in the poetry of the milder muse; and yet so worded, that the reader sees no one reason either in the selection or the order of the words, why he might not have said the very same in an appropriate conversation, and can not conceive how indeed he could have expressed such thoughts otherwise, without loss or injury to the meaning" (*Biographia Literaria*, American ed., 1884, p. 436).

171. **Poems on Several Occasions, 1689.** The text is from this posthumous volume, which was very carelessly collected, some poems appearing twice. Chalmers reprinted much of this volume in his *English Poets*, 1810. Cotton has escaped even the editorial assiduity of Dr. Grosart, and remains, except for his continuation of Walton, little known.

171. **Ode.** Charles I surrendered in May, 1646, when Cotton was about sixteen years old. This song may have been written before the execution of the king three years later; it is more likely, however, that the final line refers to Charles II, then in exile.

171 1. **The day is set.** The day, which adorned the earth, is set (i.e., the sun has set, but also is set, seated, like a man, at table) to drink, etc.

171 8. **For.** Despite.

172 1. **Fair Isabel.** Cotton married Isabella, daughter of Sir Thomas Hutchinson of Owthorp, in 1656. I place this poem shortly prior to that event.

173. **Miscellanies.** Many of the poems of this division of Cowley's own folio of 1656 were written far earlier, especially the poems previously published under the titles *Sylva* and *Poetical Blossoms*. Neither of the poems which follow appeared, as far as I can ascertain, before 1656.

176 74. **Matchavil.** A shortening and corruption of Machiavel, an anglicized form of Macchiavelli, for generations regarded as the type of the arch-schemer.

176 78. **Holinshed or Stow.** The well-known English chroniclers.

176. **Anacréontique.** This is a sufficiently original version of the six lines, Εἰς τὸ δεῖν πίνειν, ascribed to Anacreon, to deserve a place here. Cf. Cotton's less successful paraphrase, *Poems*, ed. 1689, p. 217.

177. **Henry King,** bishop of Chichester, was the friend of Sandys, James Howell, Izaak Walton, and Jonson. His elegy on the last is one of the best pieces of the memorial volume *Jonsonus Virbius*. There is nothing to determine the probable date of the writing of the little poem of the text, as King seems to have amused himself with poetry throughout his life. His elegies on Gustavus Adolphus and on Donne appeared as early as 1633. King's poetry, while often excellent, is very unequal. It has been much confused with the writings of Jonson, Beaumont, Corbet, and others.

178. **Henry Harrington.** Of this Harrington I can find no word.

178. **On his Deceased Wife.** This was Milton's second wife, Catarine Woodcock, whom he married Nov. 12, 1656. She died in childbirth, February, 1658, soon followed by her child. "Milton's private life, for eighteen years now," says Professor Masson, "had certainly not been a happy one; but this death of his second wife seems to have been remembered by him ever afterwards with deep and peculiar sorrow. She had been to him during the short fifteen months of this union, all that he had thought saint-like and womanly, very sympathetic with himself, and maintaining such peace and order in his household as had not been there till she entered it" (*Life of Milton*, V, 382). Hallam refers by way of parallel to a sonnet by Bernadino Rota, beginning: "In lieto e pien di riverenza aspetto" (Pattison).

178 2. **Alcestis** died for her husband, but was brought back to the world by Hercules, *Jove's great son*. Cf. *Alcestis*, 1136. Euripides was a favorite author of Milton's.

178 5, 6. In allusion to the Mosaic ceremonies for purification after childbirth, *Leviticus*, XII.

178 8. **Full sight of her.** Milton was already blind at the time of his second marriage.

178 10. **Her face was veiled,** as was the face of Alcestis at first, when Hercules brought her back to her husband's presence (Verity).

178 14. **Night.** His blindness. Cf. *Paradise Lost*, viii. 478.

179. **Thomas Flatman,** the miniature painter, was a disciple of Cowley. This poem, *For Thoughts*, is the strongest piece of his work. It is reprinted by Mr. Bullen in his *Musa Proterva*. A fortunate chance which has brought into the possession of the library of the University of Pennsylvania a manuscript of several poems and songs of Flatman enables me to give the precise date. The version of this MS. differs in some particulars from Mr. Bullen's text, in almost every instance for the better. I have followed the MS., which is headed "Miscellanies by Tho: Flatman," and collated it with the third ed. of

1682, which presents a generally inferior text, though it may have had the revision of the author.

179 11. **The stupefying wine.** The hemlock of the ancients.

179 13. **Trembling.** Bullen reads *shivering*, with the ed. of 1682.

179 17. **Magic.** Ed. of 1682 reads *enchantments.*

179 19. **Awful.** Ed. of 1682 omits this word.

179 21. **Brother and uncle to the stars and sun.** Zeus, probably. The cosmogony of Flatman seems somewhat mixed. The phrase, however, is a fine one.

179 22. **Toys.** Bullen reads *joys*, an evident misprint.

179 27. **My thoughts can eas'ly lay.** Bullen and ed. of 1682 read *My thoughts, my thoughts can lay.*

180 30. **Th' eleven orbs.** According to a theory of the old astronomy there were nine crystalline spheres or heavens, each revolving within the other and ranging from the sphere of the moon, which was nearest the earth, to the *primum mobile*, the most remote. Some authors made out twelve heavens, adding to this last and the spheres of the seven planets the *nonum cœlum* and the *decimum cœlum*, immediately within the *primum mobile*, and making the *cœlum empyræum* the outermost sphere of all. *Through all the eleven orbs* would then mean to the furthest limit of the heavens, as thought would pass through eleven orbs to reach the twelfth.

180 30. **Shove a way.** Campbell, who includes this poem in his *British Poets*, reads *away*, with the ed. of 1682.

180 31. **My thoughts.** Ed. of 1682 reads *these, too.*

180 39. **Huge.** Ed. of 1682 reads *rare;* **glisters,** in the next line, *glimmers.*

180 42. **There can I dwell** [gaze] **and 'live** [glut] **mine eyes.** The words in brackets indicate the readings of ed. of 1682.

180 51. **Non-addresses.** Apparently here equal to *prohibition of intercourse.*

181. **A Wish.** This is the title given this poem in the MS. mentioned above. It is there dated Sept. 10, 1659. The previous poem bears date May 13 in the same year. *A Wish* is described as "set by Captain S. Taylor."

181 2. **Heads.** Ed. of 1682 reads *head.*

181 16. **Whence the sun darts.** Ed. of 1682 reads *whence Phœbus darts.*

181 19. **Ever.** Ed. of 1682 reads *never.*

182. **Alexander Brome** is described as "an attorney of London in the Civil Wars." He was the author of some plays published before

the Restoration, and appears, from verses prefixed to his *Poems*, to have been more or less intimate with Charles Cotton and Izaak Walton. He begins a witty preface *To the Reader* by attributing his collection of his poems to laziness and a long vacation, "the one inclining me to do nothing else, and the other affording me nothing else to do." I take my text from the third edition, 1668. Brome's erotic verse is neither musical nor very original. His most characteristic productions are his *Cavalier Songs*, which have abundance of rough vigor, if little poetry, in them.

182 10. **A she.** Cf. 99 2.

182 11. **The only argument.** Cf. Wither's immortal "Shall I, wasting in despair" (*Elizabethan Lyrics*, p. 168).

182 18. **Stain,** i.e., by comparison. Cf. Lyly's *Song of Daphne* in *Midas*: "My Daphne's beauty stains all faces."

182 19. **Shadows.** This is the reading of the ed. of 1668 and of Chalmers. Mr. Saintsbury, *Seventeenth Century Lyrics*, reads *shadow*.

183. **Sir William Davenant** was godson of Shakespeare, poet laureate preceding Dryden, dramatist, and author of the epic *Gondibert*. His work is not without merit, but rarely rises above mediocrity. I cannot find anything beyond these two little poems in Davenant's bulky folio to serve my purpose.

184 1. **The lark now leaves his wat'ry nest.** Cf. *Venus and Adonis*, 853:

> Lo, here the gentle lark, weary of rest,
> From his moist cabinet mounts up on high.

184 12. **Draw your curtains, and begin the dawn.** A common sentiment of the poets. Cf. Crashaw, 114 21, Carew, 70 16, and Herrick, *Upon Electra*:

> When out of bed my love doth spring
> 'T is but as day a-kindling;
> But when she 's up and fully drest
> 'T is then broad day throughout the east.

184. **Katherine Philips,** whose maiden name was Fowler, gathered about her at her home in Cardigan, and on her visits to London, "a society of friendship, the members of which were distinguished [after the manner of the romances of the day] by various fanciful names." Thus her husband was known as Antenor, she herself as Orinda, to which her admirers affixed the adjective "matchless." Her earliest work appeared in 1651, prefixed to the volumes of poems of Henry Vaughan

and William Cartwright. Most of her verses were published after her death; they are largely devoted to friendship. We may agree with Mr. G. Thorn Drury, the writer of the article on this excellent lady in the *Dictionary of National Biography*, that "Orinda's fame as a poet [was] always considerably in excess of her merits."

185. **Sir William Killegrew** was elder brother of the dramatists Henry and Thomas. He wrote several plays, all of them acted after the Restoration. His later work was chiefly devotional.

186. **Sir George Etheridge** was the author of three comedies and much reputed for his wit. He was employed abroad as envoy to Hamburg and minister to Ratisbon, in which latter place he died.

186. **Song.** This song was lengthened into a broadside ballad. Cf. *Roxburghe Ballads*, XVI, 133–135 (Bullen).

186 10. **His** is Mr. Bullen's reading for *this* of the original.

187. **The Indian Queen** was published as "written by the Honorable Sir Robert Howard," the brother-in-law of Dryden. Dryden not only touched up the whole play, but wrote large portions of it. The songs are in his manner.

187 7. **Zempoalla** is the usurping Indian queen.

187 8. **On her dismal vision wait.** After these words the queen impatiently interrupts the incantation, which then continues.

187 9. **Toad . . . adders'.** Cf. Middleton's *The Witch*, v. 2:

> The juice of toad, the oil of adder,
> Those will make the younker madder.

187 14. **Clifts.** Dryden uses this form of the word "cliff" elsewhere, *Translation of Persius*, vi. 17.

187 24. **Use.** Are accustomed to.

188. **"The Indian Emperor,"** says Scott, "is the first of Dryden's plays which exhibited, in a marked degree, the peculiarity of his style, and drew upon him the attention of the world."

188 5. **Does.** Later ed. reads *would*.

188 13. **Fall, fall, fall.** Cf. Jonson's lyric in *Cynthia's Revels*, i. 2:

> Like melting snow upon some craggy hill,
> Drop, drop, drop, drop.

188. **Sir Charles Sedley** led the usual dissipated life of his age. He is thus distinguished as a wit from his two great rivals by Bishop Burnet: "Sedley had a more sudden and copious wit, which furnished a perpetual run of discourse; but he was not so correct as Lord Dorset,

nor so sparkling as Lord Rochester" (*History of His Own Time*, I, 372). Sedley appears to have become somewhat less frivolous in later life, and took sides against the Stuarts at the Revolution. I read from the collected ed. of Sedley's *Works*, 1778.

188. **The Mulberry Garden** is described by Ward as "partly founded on Molière's *L'École des Maris*." The title of this lyric is given in the play a few lines above the poem. Cf. a very different treatment of a similar theme by Marvell, *The Picture of Little T. C. in a Prospect of Flowers*, p. 159, above.

190 7. **I only care.** I care alone. Cf. 199 6.

191 22. **Joy.** *Bliss* in some editions, with a change of the fourth line of the stanza to "No less inhuman is." This version concludes with an additional stanza, which is no gain to the poem.

191 6. **Knotted.** Knotting was a kind of fancywork similar to lace making. See Ashton's *Social Life in the Reign of Queen Anne*, I, 17.

192 1. **Phyllis, men say.** There is an amplification of the last stanza of this song in most editions of Sedley. This destroys the unity of the poem, as the addition is distinctly inferior.

193. **Tyrannic Love** is one of the most characteristic of the heroic plays of Dryden; *An Evening's Love*, largely a translation from various sources, is a very vivacious comedy.

194. **You Charmed Me.** The simplicity, directness, and choice diction of this little song show the master hand of a strong poet.

194. **John Wilmot, Earl of Rochester,** is thus tersely described by Walpole: "A man whom the Muses were fond to inspire and ashamed to avow; and [who] practised, without the least reserve, that secret which can make verses more read for their defects than their merits" (*Noble Authors*, II, 43). Rochester died at thirty-two a ruined debauchee. The text is from the ed. of 1680.

195 8. **That tears,** etc. In later editions: "That tears my fixèd heart from love."

195 11. **Where love,** etc. A later reading is: "Where love, and peace, and honor flow."

196. **Upon Drinking in a Bowl.** A spirited paraphrase of the song ascribed to Anacreon, Εἰς ποτήριον ἀργυροῦν. Rochester has delightfully enlarged upon the Greek: "Deepen the cup as much as you can (ὅσον δύνῃ βάθυνον)," to suggest "vast toasts on the delicious lake, like ships."

196 11. **Maestrick** was captured by the French under Louis XIV and Vauban in July, 1673. The English were his allies in this war.

Evelyn, in his *Diary* under date of August 21, 1674, describes an out-of-door tableau at Winsor, in the meadow, showing the Siege of Maestricht. I do not identify the allusion to Yarmouth leaguer.

196 15. **Sir Sidrophel** is the name of the astrologer in the Second Part of *Hudibras*, Canto iii, the argument to which begins thus:

> The Knight, with various doubts possest,
> To win the Lady goes in quest
> Of Sidrophel the Rosycrucian,
> To know the Dest'nies' resolution.

William Lilly, a famous almanac maker of the day, was Butler's original. Ten years later the satirist applied the name to a member of the Royal Society who was pleased to doubt Butler's authorship of *Hudibras*.

197 8. **Will still love on.** This phrase and the corresponding phrase of the next stanza is repeated in the original, probably owing to the demands of some popular melody to which it was set.

197 13. **His smart.** *His* is a later reading; the ed. of 1680 reads *this*.

198 2. **Things, may melt.** Things that may melt. Cf. 1 2.

199 6. **Are only free.** Alone are free. Cf. 190 7.

200. **Aphara, Aphra** or **Afra Behn,** whose maiden name was Johnson, was the first woman in England to make authorship a profession. She wrote a great deal and succeeded as a dramatist, a writer of stories and other prose. Despite the fact that she "trod the boards loosely," in the manner of her age, some of the works of Mrs. Behn are not without merit. This is especially true of her story *Oroonoko*, a book which exhibits many sentiments which forebode Rousseau, and courts, from its subject, a comparison with *Uncle Tom's Cabin*.

200. **Abdelazer,** a tragedy, is a *rifacimento* of Marlowe's *Lust's Dominion*. The text is from *Plays Written by the Late Ingenious Mrs. Behn*, 1724. This poem appears also in *The Loyal Garland*, ed. 1686, and elsewhere.

201. **Troilus and Cressida** is one of Dryden's several quarryings in the works of Shakespeare and Milton. The anapæstic movement of this little lyric is worthy of note. Cf. Rochester's *Song* (*Poems*, ed. 1680, p. 43):

> To this moment a rebel, I throw down my arms;

and, far earlier, Davenant's irregular *Wake all the dead*, Saintsbury's *Seventeenth Century Lyrics*, p. 113.

201. Horace Walpole says of Dorset: "He was the finest gentle-

man of the voluptuous court of Charles II, and in the gloomy one of King William. He had as much wit as his first master, or his contemporaries, Buckingham and Rochester, without the royal want of feeling, the duke's want of principles, or the earl's want of thought" (*Noble Authors*, II, 96). The lyrics of Dorset are found only in collections and miscellanies. While it is impossible accurately to determine the time of the writing of his poems, the range of his activity as an author certainly extends from soon after the Restoration to the death of Charles. There is a piece addressed to Dorinda, who has been identified with Catherine Sedley, Countess of Dorchester, bearing date 1680. His most famous poem, the *Song, Written at Sea*, bears date 1665.

202 7. **Blackguard boy.** Linkboy.

202 1. **Phyllis, for shame.** This song, so far as I can ascertain, did not appear in print until 1700, in the collection *Works of Celebrated Authors of whose Writings there are but Small Remains.*

203. **The Spanish Friar** was what was known as a Protestant play. This was not the only instance in which Dryden diverted his genius into the paths of applied drama.

204. **The Duke of Guise,** a play of palpable political import, was the joint work of Dryden and Nathaniel Lee. This song is certainly Dryden's. In Scott's edition, as revised by Saintsbury, the original music is given.

204 9. **Cordial.** Anything which invigorates; used elsewhere by Dryden in this general sense. Cf. "Charms to my sight and cordials to my mind."

205. **John Norris,** rector of Bemerton, was a student of Platonism, a disciple of Malebranche, and a voluminous author. His poems have been collected and published by Dr. Grosart in his *Fuller Worthies' Miscellanies. The Hymn to Darkness* is Norris' best poem, and that is improved by Mr. Palgrave's judicious curtailing, a process which the plan of this book will not permit. See the *Golden Treasury of English Lyrics*, p. 128, where the poem is described as "a lyric of a strange, fanciful, yet solemn beauty; Cowley's style intensified by the mysticism of Henry More."

205 9. **This monument.** The world, explains Mr. Palgrave.

207. **The Morning Quatrains.** This poem, with its companions, *Noon Quatrains*, *Evening*, and *Night*, has a charming naturalness in description not common in the poetry of Cotton's contemporaries.

208 21. **Xanthus and Æthon,** the horses of the sun.

208 36. **Humanity** in the Latin sense of kindliness towards others, civility.

208 44. **Imprime.** Here evidently an early song. Prime was the first canonical hour of prayer. I have not found this word elsewhere.

209 49. **Repairs.** The original reads *prepares*.

209 55. **Purlieus.** Here in the more original sense of the borders of the wood.

209 65. **Slick.** Sleek.

210. **Rondeau.** Cotton is interesting for his practice of the rondeau, a French form not imitated in English literature, at least by a poet of respectable rank, from Wyatt to Cotton or (with the solitary exception of the examples of that group of political satirists who are responsible for the *Rolliad*, 1784, and its successors) from Cotton to the general revival of interest in French forms a few years since. Cotton translated many books from the French, with the literature of which country he was much at home. It is not easy to select from Cotton, because of what Mr. Saintsbury has justly called "his curious blend of thoroughly poetical conception with imperfect poetical execution." Moreover, not a few of the poems of Cotton, which rank highest poetically, are unquotable to-day. I could scarcely venture to include all the poems for which Mr. Saintsbury finds a place in his *Seventeenth Century Lyrics*, and have thus been compelled to omit one of the most "quaint and pleasing."

211 16. **Rove.** To shoot at rovers was to shoot at an irregular or uncertain mark. "Love is conceived as shooting at random, careless whom he hits."

214 14. **That.** That which.

214. **The Lover's Watch,** *or the Art of making Love, being Rules for Courtship for Every Hour in the Day and Night*, so runs the comprehensive title of this tract of mingled verse and prose. The text of this little song is from the ed. of 1699.

215. **O Love that Stronger art than Wine.** Mr. Bullen raises the question, "Did Mrs. Behn write these fine verses?" and he cites the fact that the poem was printed in the same year, 1687, in Henry Playford's fourth book of *The Theater of Music*, with these words at the end of the song: "These words by Mr. Ousley" (*Musa Proterva*, p. 11).

215 11. **Learns a clown.** This verb was commonly used transitively in the seventeenth century and earlier. Cf. *Tempest*, i. 2. 365.

215 13. **Free.** Liberal.

215 19. **Finest.** Refinest.

216. **Of the Last Verses.** There is a transcript of these verses by a son of the poet, headed: "The last verses my dear father made" (Drury).

216. **Saint Cecilia.** The patron saint of musicians, martyred in the reign of Septimius Severus. In 1680 a musical society was formed in London for the annual commemoration of St. Cecilia's day. "An ode, written for the occasion, was set to music by the most able professor, and rehearsed before the society and their stewards upon the 22d November, the day dedicated to the patroness." Dryden's ode for the year 1687 was set to music "by Draghi, an eminent Italian composer." Further account of this ode, which has been perhaps unduly eclipsed by the more vivid qualities of *Alexander's Feast*, will be found in the Scott-Saintsbury ed. of *Dryden*, XI, 169.

217 15. **Diapason.** A chord including all notes. Cf. *The Faery Queen*, ii. 9. 22, Dryden's avowed source.

217 17. **Jubal struck the chorded shell.** There is apparently here some confusion between Biblical and classical story.

218 52. **Her organ.** St. Cecilia is said to have invented the organ.

218 63. **Untune the sky.** Mr. Saintsbury remarks: "I do not understand 'untune.'" Is not Dryden's meaning the following: Concord is conceived as the power which has created the world in its perfection from the ground note to the last, thus completing the diapason. Correspondingly the untuning of the spheres, with the return to the discord of chaos, is conceived as taking place when the trumpet blast of the resurrection shall be heard announcing that "the dead shall live, the living die." Professor Kittredge suggests: "The untuning of the spheres is the same as the destruction of the world — the spheres cease to be tuneful because they cease to exist."

219. **King Arthur** was an opera, the music (which was much admired) by the celebrated Dr. Purcell. See Burney's *History of Music*, III, 492.

219. **No, No, Poor Suffering Heart.** The music of this song is to be found in D'Urfey's *Pills to Purge Melancholy*. Mr. Saintsbury remarks upon it: "The verse [of *Cleomenes*] is often exquisite, and the song *No, No, Poor Suffering Heart* . . . is in itself a triumphant refutation of those who deny passion and tenderness in poetry to Dryden; but for a few turns of phrase, the best name of the Jacobean age might have signed it" (Scott's *Dryden*, VIII, 212).

220. The *Miscellanies* of Dryden were collections of poetry by various writers, sometimes of pieces which had already appeared elsewhere. The *First Miscellany* was published in 1684, the *Second* in the next year. It is interesting to notice that some of the most notable writers of the next age made their *début* in this irregular periodical. Dryden contributed to the *Fourth Miscellany* in 1694.

221. **Matthew Prior,** for years an able and useful diplomatist, held many offices of political importance under William and Anne, the most important being that of minister plenepotentiary to the Court of France. Some still profess to admire his epic *Solomon*, others find it unreadable. Prior's occasional verse is nearly the best of his age; his shorter lyrical poems have earned for him, not altogether undeservedly, the title, the English Horatian.

221. **Poems,** etc. The ed. of 1709 seems to have been the first genuine publication of Prior's poems. There had been an unauthorized edition bearing a similar title in 1707. I am not able to say which of my selections first appeared therein.

221. **A Song.** I assign this song to about the year 1693, as it immediately precedes the *Hymn to Dr. Purcell*, which is dated 1693–1694. The arrangement of the collected editions of Prior seems roughly chronological.

222. **Love Triumphant** was Dryden's last drama. It was not a success.

222 27. **In only thee.** In thee alone. Cf. 190 7, 8.

223 1. **The merchant, to secure his treasure.** This "ode" precedes the famous *Ode on the Taking of Namour*, which bears date 1695.

223 4. **Chloe.** Some old gossip as to Prior's Chloe will be found in Rimbault, *Fly Leaves*, p. 6.

224 11. **Fantastic.** Capricious.

225. **George Granville** was a dramatist and late disciple of Waller, by whom he was praised. Owing to his espousal of the cause of James, he lived in literary retirement during the reign of William, emerging into public life with the accession of Queen Anne. Myra was the Countess of Newburgh. "As he wrote verses to her ladyship," says Dr. Johnson gruffly, "before he was twenty, he may be forgiven if he regarded the face more than the mind." Pope dedicated *Windsor Forest* to Lord Lansdowne. Cf. verses 291–298.

225. **William Congreve** started life with a divided ambition — to become a literary man and to be "the first gentleman of his age," as an old phrase puts it. He achieved a substantial success in both, giving up the former for the latter about the year 1700. Congreve's literary reputation rests upon his sparkling dramas. In his lyrics, which are very few, he combines much of the grace of the earlier age with the precision of the age to come.

226. **The Secular Masque** was an entertainment to commemorate what the author was pleased to consider the beginning of a new cen-

tury; it was really the beginning of the hundredth year. The original music Malone believes to have been by Purcell. It was later set by Dr. Boyce and revived at Drury Lane, 1749. At both performances the Masque was a success, the *Hunting Song* was long especially popular.

226 4. **Wexing.** Waxing.

227 5. **Course.** Chase.

INDEX OF AUTHORS AND EDITORS.

Names printed in Roman letters denote authors; those in italics, editors; the dates following are those of birth, earliest authorship, and death. When the editor is unknown, MS. or other source is given. Original titles are printed in Roman; those assigned by others than the author, in italics; first lines are put in quotation marks.